PRACTICAL TRANSFORMATIONS AND TRANSFORMATIONAL PRACTICES: GLOBALIZATION, POSTMODERNISM, AND EARLY CHILDHOOD EDUCATION

ADVANCES IN EARLY EDUCATION AND DAY CARE

Series Editor: Stuart Reifel

Recent Volumes:

Volume 8:	Theory and Practice in Early Childhood Teaching Edited by Judith A. Chafel and Stuart Reifel
Volume 9:	Family Policy and Practice in Early Child Care Edited by C. Dunst and M. Wolery
Volume 10:	Foundations, Adult Dynamics, Teacher Education and Play Edited by Stuart Reifel
Volume 11:	Early Education and Care, and Reconceptualizing Play Edited by Stuart Reifel
Volume 12:	Bridging the Gap Between Theory, Research and Practice: The Role of Child Development Laboratory Programs in Early Childhood Education Edited by Brent A. McBride and Nancy E. Barbour
Volume 13:	Social Contexts of Early Education, and Reconceptualizing Play (II) Edited by Stuart Reifel and Mac H. Brown

ADVANCES IN EARLY EDUCATION AND DAY CARE VOLUME 14

PRACTICAL TRANSFORMATIONS AND TRANSFORMATIONAL PRACTICES: GLOBALIZATION, POSTMODERNISM, AND EARLY CHILDHOOD EDUCATION

EDITED BY

SHARON RYAN

Rutgers, The State University of New Jersey, USA

SUSAN GRIESHABER

Queensland University of Technology, Australia

2005

ELSEVIER
JAI

Amsterdam – Boston – Heidelberg – London – New York – Oxford
Paris – San Diego – San Francisco – Singapore – Sydney – Tokyo

ELSEVIER B.V.	ELSEVIER Inc.	ELSEVIER Ltd	ELSEVIER Ltd
Radarweg 29	525 B Street, Suite 1900	The Boulevard, Langford	84 Theobalds Road
P.O. Box 211	San Diego	Lane, Kidlington	London
1000 AE Amsterdam	CA 92101-4495	Oxford OX5 1GB	WC1X 8RR
The Netherlands	USA	UK	UK

© 2005 Elsevier Ltd. All rights reserved.

This work is protected under copyright by Elsevier Ltd, and the following terms and conditions apply to its use:

Photocopying
Single photocopies of single chapters may be made for personal use as allowed by national copyright laws. Permission of the Publisher and payment of a fee is required for all other photocopying, including multiple or systematic copying, copying for advertising or promotional purposes, resale, and all forms of document delivery. Special rates are available for educational institutions that wish to make photocopies for non-profit educational classroom use.

Permissions may be sought directly from Elsevier's Rights Department in Oxford, UK: phone (+44) 1865 843830, fax (+44) 1865 853333, e-mail: permissions@elsevier.com. Requests may also be completed on-line via the Elsevier homepage (http://www.elsevier.com/locate/permissions).

In the USA, users may clear permissions and make payments through the Copyright Clearance Center, Inc., 222 Rosewood Drive, Danvers, MA 01923, USA; phone: (+1) (978) 7508400, fax: (+1) (978) 7504744, and in the UK through the Copyright Licensing Agency Rapid Clearance Service (CLARCS), 90 Tottenham Court Road, London W1P 0LP, UK; phone: (+44) 20 7631 5555; fax: (+44) 20 7631 5500. Other countries may have a local reprographic rights agency for payments.

Derivative Works
Tables of contents may be reproduced for internal circulation, but permission of the Publisher is required for external resale or distribution of such material. Permission of the Publisher is required for all other derivative works, including compilations and translations.

Electronic Storage or Usage
Permission of the Publisher is required to store or use electronically any material contained in this work, including any chapter or part of a chapter.

Except as outlined above, no part of this work may be reproduced, stored in a retrieval system or transmitted in any form or by any means, electronic, mechanical, photocopying, recording or otherwise, without prior written permission of the Publisher.

Address permissions requests to: Elsevier's Rights Department, at the fax and e-mail addresses noted above.

Notice
No responsibility is assumed by the Publisher for any injury and/or damage to persons or property as a matter of products liability, negligence or otherwise, or from any use or operation of any methods, products, instructions or ideas contained in the material herein. Because of rapid advances in the medical sciences, in particular, independent verification of diagnoses and drug dosages should be made.

First edition 2005

British Library Cataloguing in Publication Data
A catalogue record is available from the British Library.

ISBN: 0-7623-1238-6
ISSN: 0270-4021 (Series)

∞ The paper used in this publication meets the requirements of ANSI/NISO Z39.48-1992 (Permanence of Paper).
Printed in The Netherlands.

Working together to grow
libraries in developing countries

www.elsevier.com | www.bookaid.org | www.sabre.org

ELSEVIER   BOOK AID International   Sabre Foundation

CONTENTS

LIST OF CONTRIBUTORS ... ix

ACKNOWLEDGMENTS ... xi

INTRODUCTION
Stuart Reifel ... xiii

PART I:
EARLY CHILDHOOD EDUCATION, GLOBALIZATION, AND POSTMODERNITY

TRANSFORMING IDEAS AND PRACTICES
Susan Grieshaber and Sharon Ryan ... 3

VOICES AT THE TABLE: AN ANALYSIS OF COLLABORATION IN THE POLICY PROCESS FOR A LOCAL PRESCHOOL INITIATIVE
Lucinda G. Heimer ... 19

PART II:
DIVERSITY AND DIFFERENCE IN EARLY CHILDHOOD CLASSROOMS

(DE) CENTERING THE KINDERGARTEN PROTOTYPE IN THE CHILD-CENTERED CLASSROOM
Elizabeth Graue ... 39

TEACHING NOTES
Felicity McArdle   *59*

THE AMORPHOUS PRETEND PLAY CURRICULUM: THEORIZING EMBODIED SYNTHETIC MULTICULTURAL PROPS
Richard Johnson   *93*

IMPLEMENTING *TE WHÀRIKI* AS POSTMODERNIST PRACTICE: A PERSPECTIVE FROM AOTEAROA/ NEW ZEALAND
Jenny Ritchie   *109*

PART III:
TEACHER EDUCATION AND PROFESSIONAL DEVELOPMENT

POSTCOLONIAL THEORY AND THE PRACTICE OF TEACHER EDUCATION
Radhika Viruru   *139*

BECOMING EARLY CHILDHOOD TEACHERS: LINKING ACTION RESEARCH AND POSTMODERN THEORY IN A LANGUAGE AND LITERACY COURSE
Celia Genishi, Shin-ying Huang and Tamara Glupczynski   *161*

PUTTING POSTMODERN THEORIES INTO PRACTICE IN EARLY CHILDHOOD TEACHER EDUCATION
Jennifer Sumsion   *193*

CHALLENGING THE CULTURE OF EXPERTISE: MOVING BEYOND TRAINING THE ALWAYS, ALREADY FAILING EARLY CHILDHOOD EDUCATOR
Sue Novinger, Leigh O'Brien and Lou Sweigman   *217*

IMPROVISATION: POSTMODERN PLAY FOR EARLY CHILDHOOD TEACHERS
Carrie Lobman 243

LIST OF CONTRIBUTORS

Celia Genishi	Department of Curriculum and Teaching, Teachers College, Columbia University, NY, USA
Tamara Glupczynski	Teachers College, Columbia University, New York, NY, USA
Elizabeth Graue	Department of Curriculum and Instruction, School of Education, University of Wisconsin, Madison, WI, USA
Susan Grieshaber	School of Early Childhood, Queensland University of Technology, Qld, Australia
Lucinda G. Heimer	University of Wisconsin, Madison, WI, USA
Shin-ying Huang	Teachers College, Columbia University, New York, NY, USA
Richard Johnson	Institute for Teacher Education, University of Hawaii at Manoa, Honolulu, HI, USA
Carrie Lobman	Graduate School of Education, Rutgers – The State University of New Jersey, New Brunswick, NJ, USA
Felicity McArdle	School of Early Childhood, Queensland University of Technology, Qld, Australia
Sue Novinger	Department of Education and Human Development, State University of New York, Brockport, NY, USA

Leigh O'Brien	Department of Early Childhood, Elementary, and Literacy Education, Montclair State University, Montclair, NJ, USA
Jenny Ritchie	Department of Professional Studies in Education, School of Education, University of Waikato, Hamilton, New Zealand
Sharon Ryan	Graduate School of Education, Rutgers – The State University of New Jersey, New Brunswick, NJ, USA
Jennifer Sumsion	Institute of Early Childhood, Australian Centre for Educational Studies, Macquarie University, Australia
Lou Sweigman	Department of Education and Human Development, State University of New York, Brockport, NY, USA
Radhika Viruru	Department of Teaching, Learning and Culture, Texas A&M University, TX, USA

ACKNOWLEDGMENTS

We thank sincerely the following people, who reviewed chapters for this edited collection. The reviewing process is often a thankless and invisible task, but we want to recognize the professionalism of these reviewers, as well as their insight into the manuscripts with which they engaged.

Debra Ackerman	National Institute of Early Education Research, Rutgers University, USA
Susan Adler	University of Illinois at Urbana Champagne, USA
Jo Ailwood	Queensland University of Technology, Brisbane, Australia
Judith Bernhard	Ryerson University, Toronto, Canada
Cary Buzzelli	Indiana University, USA
Barbara Comber	University of South Australia
Mary Curran	Rutgers, The State University of New Jersey, USA
Sue Dockett	University of Western Sydney, Australia
Karen Dooley	Queensland University of Technology, Brisbane, Australia
Alma Fleet	Institute of Early Childhood, Macquarie University, Sydney, Australia
Susan Golbeck	Rutgers, The State University of New Jersey, USA
Tara Goldstein	OISE, University of Toronto, Canada
J. Amos Hatch	University of Tennessee, USA
Alison Jones	University of Auckland, New Zealand

Liz Jones	Manchester Metropolitan University, UK
Elvira Katic	Rutgers, The State University of New Jersey, USA
Janice Kroeger	Kent State University, USA
Mary McMullen	Indiana University, USA
Peter Moss	Institute of Education, University of London, UK
Muriel Rand	New Jersey City University, USA
Kerry Robinson	University of Western Sydney, Australia
Joe Tobin	Arizona State University, USA
Karen Van Der Ven	University of Pittsburgh, USA

INTRODUCTION

Volume 14 of the *Advances in Early Education and Day Care* provides Sharon Ryan and Susan Grieshaber the opportunity to present current scholarship about early childhood education and care that reflects postmodern perspectives. This series has consistently intended to serve the field by providing multidisciplinary and interdisciplinary perspectives. Early childhood practices have drawn on ideas from child development, curriculum studies, social work, nursing, sociology, anthropology, and other fields that inform us about children, their care, and the settings in which we implement our programs, an effort that should by its nature require diverse perspectives. *Advances in Early Education and Day Care* has always attempted to respect the necessary diversity of perspectives that can inform the field, and to support work that may not fit in a tidy disciplinary nook.

This volume is dedicated in its entirety to postmodern perspectives that have appeared only on occasion in earlier *Advances* publications. Grieshaber and Ryan have gathered scholarship from around the world to illustrate the significance of, as they say in Chapter 1, "endeavors to problematize the complexities and challenges facing the field and the ways in which moves are being made in everyday classroom practice, policy, teacher education, and professional development to build a knowledge base that is grounded in empirical data and that reflects the diversity characteristic of a globalized society." If one begins with the assumption that a globalized society has multiple meanings for education, and that local contexts present complexities where those multiple meanings play out, then the doors for new scholarship from various points of view are opened. Ryan and Grieshaber are dedicated to showing the ways that empirical analyses that emerge from these assumptions can be part of transformation of the field. Part I of this volume (Early Childhood Education, Globalization, and Postmodernity) introduces and elaborates these ideas, with "Transforming Ideas and Practices" by Grieshaber and Ryan and "Voices at the Table: An Analysis of the Policy Process of a Local Initiative" by Lucinda Heimer.

Part II of the volume (Diversity and Difference in Early Childhood Classrooms) takes what seem like familiar topics in the field child-centeredness, difference/diversity, play, and cultural curriculum) and shows the many ways that particular settings can "trouble" our understandings. While dealing with more or less familiar phenomena, Elizabeth Graue, Felicity McArdle, Richard Johnson, and Jenny Ritchie provide a palette of new dimensions that seem necessary for understanding practice. The merits of their perspectives contribute to earlier work and calls for new knowledge related to practice that appeared in earlier *Advances* volumes (e.g., Campbell, MacNaughton, Page, & Rolfe, 2004; Cannella & Bailey, 1999; Williams, 1996; Lubeck, Jessup, & Jewkes, 2001; McBride & Grieshaber, 2001; Reifel, 1999; Reifel & Brown, 2001, 2004). This section brings detailed life to these matters. Notions of "the child," "diversity," "play," and "culture" can no longer be easily defined.

In Part III (Teacher Education and Professional Development) connects these matters to teacher preparation and development. Viruru, Genishi et al., Sumsion, Novinger et al., and Lobman bring us data and thinking about how early childhood teachers can become practitioners in the global society. As Grieshaber and Ryan tell us in Chapter 1, "A small group of teacher educators have been experimenting with introducing different kinds of knowledge to their students with the intent of helping them to consider the ways in which their agency and that of the children they teach is simultaneously constrained and enabled by various assumptions about best practice in the early years." We can now see what forms that knowledge might take, and the power struggles that teachers and teacher educators encounter as they deal with it. Again, these matters have been presented in earlier Advances (e.g., Chafel & Reifel, 1996; Ackerman, 2004), but now we have a collection of voices that make their argument even stronger.

Arguments supporting reconceptualizations of early childhood education have appeared for some time (e.g., Kessler & Swadener, 1992; Mallory & New, 1994; Grieshaber & Cannella, 2001). What we have not had is an effort, like Ryan and Grieshaber have created here, where the call for empirical work has been heeded. The ideas about postmodern reconceptualization of early education that have been proposed elsewhere have here been made concrete. This volume collects empirical work and demonstrates why this work is important and some of the ways research can be done. My gratitude to Sharon Ryan and Susan Grieshaber is profound. An important step can now be built on.

REFERENCES

Ackerman, D. J. (2004). Between a rock and a hard place: Teachers' experiences I meeting the *Abbott* mandate. In: S. Reifel & M. H. Brown (Eds), *Social contexts of early education, and reconceptualizing play(II). Advances in early education and day care*, (Vol. 13, pp. 93–136). Oxford: JAI/Elsevier Science.

Campbell, S., MacNaughton, G., Page, J., & Rolfe, S. (2004). Beyond quality, advancing social justice and equity: Interdisciplinary explorations of working for equity and social justice in early childhood education. In: S. Reifel & M. H. Brown (Eds), *Social contexts of early education, and reconceptualizing play(II). Advances in early education and day care*, (Vol. 13, pp. 55–91). Oxford: JAI/Elsevier Science.

Cannella, G. S., & Bailey, C. (1999). Postmodern research in early childhood education. In: S. Reifel (Ed.), *Foundations, adult dynamics, teacher education and play. Advances in early education and day care*, (Vol. 10, pp. 3–39). Stamford, CT: JAI Press.

Chafel, J. A., & Reifel, S. (1996). Theory and practice in early childhood teaching: Themes and advances. In: J. A. Chafel & S. Reifel (Eds), *Advances in early education and day care: Theory and practice in early childhood teaching*, (Vol. 8, pp. 263–294). Greenwich, CT: JAI Press.

Grieshaber, S., & Cannella, G. (Eds) (2001). *Embracing identities in early childhood education: Diversity and possibilities*. New York: Teachers College Press.

Kessler, S., & Swadener, B. (Eds) (1992). *Reconceptualizing the early childhood curriculum: Beginning the dialogue*. New York: Teachers College Press.

Lubeck, S., Jessup, P. A., & Jewkes, A. M. (2001). Globalization and its discontents: Early childhood education in a new world order. In: S. Reifel & M. H. Brown (Eds), *Early education and care, and reconceptualizing play. Advances in early education and day care*, (Vol. 11, pp. 3–57). Oxford: JAI/Elsevier Science.

Mallory, B., & New, R. (Eds) (1994). *Diversity and developmentally appropriate practices: Challenges for early childhood education*. New York: Teachers College Press.

McBride, N., & Grieshaber, S. (2001). Professional caring as mothering. In: S. Reifel & M. H. Brown (Eds), *Early education and care, and reconceptualizing play. Advances in early education and day care*, (Vol. 11, pp. 169–201). Oxford: JAI/Elsevier Science.

Reifel, S. (1999). Play research and the early childhood profession. In: S. Reifel (Ed.), *Foundations, adult dynamics, teacher education and play. Advances in early education and day care*, (Vol. 10, pp. 201–212). Stamford, CT: JAI Press.

Reifel, S., & Brown, M. H. (2001). *Early education and care, and reconceptualizing play. Advances in early education and day care*, Vol. 11. Oxford: JAI/Elsevier Science.

Reifel, S., & Brown, M. H. (2004). *Social contexts of early education, and reconceptualizing play(II). Advances in early education and day care*, Vol. 13. Oxford: JAI/Elsevier Science.

PART I:
EARLY CHILDHOOD EDUCATION, GLOBALIZATION, AND POSTMODERNITY

TRANSFORMING IDEAS AND PRACTICES

Susan Grieshaber and Sharon Ryan

INTRODUCTION

Most of the chapters in this book depict local attempts to transform practices in early childhood education. They represent endeavors to problematize the complexities and challenges facing the field and the ways in which moves are being made in everyday classroom practice, policy, teacher education, and professional development to build a knowledge base that is grounded in empirical data and that reflects the diversity characteristic of a globalized society.

Globalization has brought economic, political, and cultural changes that have affected all dimensions of education, including the early years. Economically, workplace organization has changed, as have consumption patterns and the flow of trade, so that workers and goods cross national boundaries (Burbules & Torres, 2000, p. 14). In terms of politics, globalization has meant that the nation state has less autonomy, particularly in regard to matters of educational policy (Apple, 2001). Culturally, there is a tension between "more standardization and cultural homogeneity...and more fragmentation" (Burbules & Torres, 2000, p. 14). In the U.S., for example, education has been shaped predominantly by neoliberal approaches to globalization (Apple, 2001), which are characterized by an agenda of standardization that "privileges, if not directly imposes, particular policies for evaluation, financing, assessment, standards, teacher training, curriculum, instruction, and testing" (Burbules & Torres, 2000, p. 15).

Because neoliberal approaches have concentrated on the agenda of standardization, arguments about fragmentation and diversity brought about by globalization have been subsumed to the extent that engaging pedagogically with different cultures, languages, and backgrounds has been forced to take a back seat and remains problematic. According to Kalantzis, Cope, and Harvey (2003), traditional curricula

> ... strove to excise diversity through selective inclusion, [and] more recent curricula have focused on the celebration of difference. This celebration, however, is a superficial one. Progressivist curricula, delivered through constructivist pedagogies, may unwittingly entrench marginalisation by their failure to engage explicitly with the realities of different lifeworlds. These popular contemporary approaches are underpinned by powerful yet hidden cultural assumptions, by which assimilation to a defined mainstream is tacitly encouraged. (p. 25)

Analyses of the celebration of difference in early childhood education have exposed the limits of this approach (Derman-Sparks, 1989; McLean, 1990), which manifests itself in tokenistic displays of cultural artifacts, food, and dress in educational settings. The complication for early childhood education is that progressivist curricula have been the mainstay of early childhood education for some time. Explicit teaching is not a feature of progressivist curricula, and because of this there is some doubt that early childhood practitioners would "engage explicitly with the realities of different lifeworlds", unless of course, they were from those different lifeworlds themselves. This cannot be left to chance alone.

Both traditional and progressivist curricula, however, are unable to provide effective means for the management of difference, let alone teach proactively about it. The way in which marginalization occurs and is entrenched in the education system has been described powerfully by Goldstein (in Darder, 2002; Goldstein, 2002):

> I knew through my personal experiences as a student, teacher, female, and working class Chicano from a non-traditional family, that young students, like older students, were also silenced and coerced into blind obedience...Many were weeded out in a process so insidious that even the most well-intentioned teachers did not (and do not) recognize their pivotal role in this economic and social maintenance of the status quo. (p. 178)

We have known for some time that the rhetoric of curriculum and policy documents is not enough (Ladson-Billings, 1994; Nieto, 2004). Failure to comprehend the implications of actions that play out subsequently in the social and economic arena reinforces that diversity is still mostly about the celebration of difference.

Although curriculum that celebrates difference provides only a superficial recognition of the value of diversity, it is a place to begin. Reaching the next level is somewhat daunting and while the gamut of the task has been made explicit (Kalantzis et al., 2003), realizing it is no easy task. For Kalantzis et al., transformative curriculum and pedagogy pave the way to greater engagement with diversity: it involves "learning-as-transformation – the journey into new and unfamiliar places that transforms the learner" (Kalantzis et al., 2003, p. 31). To Luke (2004), this means a focus on pedagogy and a

> ... reenvisioning of a transcultural and cosmopolitan teacher: a teacher with the capacity to shunt between the local and the global, to explicate and engage with the broad flows of knowledge and information, technologies and populations, artefacts and practices that characterise the present historical moment. What is needed is a new community of teachers that could and would work, communicate, and exchange physically and virtually across national and regional boundaries with each other, with educational researchers, teacher educators, curriculum developers, and, indeed, senior educational bureaucrats. (pp. 1438–1439)

As progressive and traditional teaching approaches are not enough, this new kind of early childhood teacher requires a different set of knowledges and curricular approaches. The critiques of child development (Bloch, 1992; Burman, 1994; Cannella, 1997) and developmentally appropriate practice (Hatch et al., 2000; Lubeck, 1998a, b; Mallory & New, 1994) point out the difference between curricula based on psychological theories and those that attend to factors such as race, ethnicity, and socio-economic issues, placing greater demands on the field to respond to the characteristics of a globalized world. In other words, the "social facts of mobile and heterogeneous, multilingual, and multicultural populations are calling into question conventional models of child development and their normative models of childcare, schooling, and early education" (Luke & Grieshaber, 2004, p. 8).

Spodek (1977) and Silin (1987) have both challenged the knowledge base on which early childhood curriculum is founded, condemning the total reliance on psychological criteria for making educational decisions and emphasizing that educational goals have political and moral concerns as their origins, thus making psychological theories unable to inform questions of what to teach. Over 20 years ago, Spodek and Saracho (1982) and more recently Silin (1995), called for the creation of a highly developed specialist early childhood research base that focuses on "theoretical and conceptual work within the field" (Silin, 1995, p. 107).

There is no doubt that the economic, political, social, and cultural characteristics of society have changed considerably since Spodek (1977) made his appeal for an early childhood knowledge base that moved beyond sole reliance on psychological theories. Along with calls for the creation of a specialist research base came a proposal from Goffin (1989) for the field to shift from research about the effects of early childhood programs, to a new research agenda that concentrated on the complexities of teaching and the significance of the role of the teacher. Peters (1993) also noted that teachers and what they do has not been a feature of research and this omission is echoed by Genishi, Ryan, Ochsner, and Yarnall (2001) who have argued that for most of the 20th century, research in early childhood education focused on learning and the development of young children, and "not the practices of teachers" (p. 1179).

These calls for a different kind of knowledge base for the teaching of young children have not gone unheeded. A number of scholars have been drawing on alternative and mostly critical and postmodern theories over the past 15 years (Cannella, 1997; Grieshaber & Cannella, 2001; Kessler & Swadener, 1992; Silin, 1995; Tobin, 1997), to rethink early education in response to the social, economic, and political changes catalyzed by globalization. However, some seem to prefer to insulate the field from the changing circumstances of everyday life by resisting moves to introduce information and communication technologies into early childhood curricula (Alliance for Childhood, 2002; see Clements, 1999), by banning superhero play (Hampton, 2002; Boyd, 2002), and by being reluctant to move beyond the shelter of developmentalism (e.g., Charlesworth, 1998). Others hark after what they perceive childhood has lost in this globalized world and cling to notions that position children as innocent, vulnerable, and naïve (see Cannella, 2002; Foley, Roche, & Tucker, 2001; Wyness, 2000). These resistances persist in part, because there is a lack of empirical data available that illustrate transformative approaches to dealing with diversity in early childhood education. Perhaps this is because "Critique is ... the easy bit" (Luke, 2003, p. 95) and the hard part is not so much finding those pockets of innovation that challenge the status quo, but making these ideas available to others.

The chapters in this volume are an effort to communicate some of the ongoing work that is occurring in early childhood settings, schools, and universities that is aimed at improving, and ultimately transforming practice. The authors consider some of the complexities and challenges of working with young children and their families, with community agencies, and government departments, of working in teacher preparation programs and with early childhood practitioners in professional development courses.

Although these chapters play their own part in contributing to the developing knowledge base of early childhood education, they do so on their own terms and in ways that confront traditional approaches to early childhood education. We consider that this dissensus is beneficial for the field as it adds to the theoretical and practical options available, sustains ongoing debate and discussion, and endorses the notion that there are "no scripts" to follow in these changed and changing times.

There are omissions from the texts in this volume in the sense that gaps in knowledge remain. Plugging them all seems a somewhat pointless endeavor, given the rate of change in the knowledge society. What we do need is more examples of those who are on the edge, that is, playing around with innovative ideas in their practice and developing unique approaches to the diverse educational circumstances that confront early childhood educators. The chapters that follow are efforts that respond to an array of issues that have been intensified or created by globalization. For the most part, they draw on empirical data to explore the relationship between globalization, postmodernism, and transformation.

POSTMODERNISM, GLOBALIZATION, AND TRANSFORMATION

Postmodernism is generally associated with a critique of science but its tenets (if it can be said to have any) remain the subject of much debate within and among postmodernists themselves, as well as among critics of postmodernism. This debate extends to this book, where readers are encouraged to engage in their own judgments of what postmodernism is, and how the following chapters slip and slide around being categorized as "practicing postmodernism." The debate has been ongoing between us as editors, with contributors to this volume, as well as being raised by some of the reviewers of the chapters in this book. Nevertheless, for Spiro (1996), the postmodernist critique of science

> consists of two interrelated arguments, epistemological and ideological. Both are based on subjectivity. First, because of the subjectivity of the human object, anthropology, according to the epistemological argument, cannot be a science; and in any event the subjectivity of the human subject precludes the possibility of science discovering objective truth. Second, since its much-vaunted objectivity is an illusion, science, according to the ideological argument, subverts the interests of dominant social groups (males, whites, Westerners), thereby subverting those of oppressed groups (females, ethnics, third-world peoples). (p. 759)

There is a large quantity of literature that stems from the postmodern critique of science and discusses positions, theorists, and critiques of postmodernism (which are not reiterated here).

Instead, we focus on the everyday practices that are described in the various chapters and their potential to transform early childhood education; practices that are associated specifically with oppressed groups. And this brings us to the point of the relationship between globalization and postmodernism:

> Postmodernity concentrates on the tensions of difference and similarity erupting from processes of globalization: the accelerating circulation of people, the increasingly dense and frequent cross-cultural interactions, and the unavoidable intersections of local and global knowledge. (Bishop, 1996, p. 993)

Many of the tensions that postmodernism elaborates stem from power relationships and the ways these relationships are enacted in everyday life. For early childhood education, this involves being marginalized because the field is associated primarily with women and children, and therefore positioned less powerfully. For those subjugated in society by virtue of race, ethnicity, class, ability, and so on, marginalization within early childhood education aggravates the situation even more. In exploring the "tensions of difference and similarity that erupt from processes of globalization", the chapters in this volume speak to relationships of power, and some to facets of domination in classrooms for children and adults in a range of contexts.

This discussion opens with Lucinda Heimer's chapter, *Voices at the Table: An Analysis of the Policy Process for a Local Preschool Initiative*. Investigating the preschool policy formulation process in one mid-western town in the United States, Heimer shows how the calls for collaboration in preschool policies disguise the ways in which the agency of participants is tied to social and economic circumstances. While the collaboration involved a range of participants from district, Head Start, community child care directors, and the city office for childcare, Heimer data show that the question of who speaks for teachers, children, and families, and how these opinions are translated into the policy process are attached firmly to those who are positioned via networks and institutions to have more authority. Heimer exposed the myths involved in the constructs of "collaboration" and "voice" attached to the project, concluding that collaboration is not possible without constant interrupting of the institutional forces at work that simultaneously empower some over others in policy initiatives. Moving from the policy table to the classroom, the next set of chapters explore new ways of thinking about and responding to diversity and difference in curriculum and pedagogy.

RESPONDING TO DIVERSITY AND DIFFERENCE

Dealing with diversity and difference in today's classrooms is just one component of teachers' work but is made more complex because of the intersection of educational, market and historical factors. For example, Luke (2004) described the flow on effect of policies such as *No Child Left Behind* as the commodification of textbook products because such policies have "translated educational practice into a form of commodity fetishism. That is, it [they] predicate[s] the efficacy of educational policy, the practice of teaching, and particular versions of student outcomes on product use" (p. 1434). As Luke sees it, part of the problem stems from the way in which teachers are connected both historically and in the present to the "regularities of industrial, modernist capital" (p. 1440). These regularities are the circumstances in which teachers are inscribed; they are positioned as commodity fetishists in a "model of performativity that...thereby implicates them in the production and reproduction of what appear to be increasingly outdated forms of human capital in the face of new economic, social and cultural dynamics" (pp. 1440–1441). Even though early childhood teachers might not acknowledge the macro economic, political and social factors that play out in everyday classroom contexts, they are not immune from these consequences of globalization. They tend to struggle with the more obvious, immediate and material effects of standardized testing, increased accountability measures and the like, and are more attuned to the everyday realities of having to deal with the expectations that children for whom English is an additional language complete standardized testing successfully. But Luke's point is that what happens outside the classroom necessarily impinges on what gets done inside. He advocates rebuilding the "symbolic capital of teachers and teaching", and reckons that it "requires an engagement with and redefinition of new material and economic conditions" (p. 1441). We turn now to early childhood education, to some who have contemplated what is going on both inside and outside classrooms from the vantage point of different material and economic conditions, to consider the intersections of curriculum, pedagogy, diversity and difference.

In considering the limits of traditional developmental approaches to early childhood education through investigating children who were identified as "different" by having readiness risks, Beth Graue (Chapter 3: (*De*) *Centering the Kindergarten Prototype in the Child-centered Classroom*) critiques one of the "truths" of early childhood education, the notion of child centeredness. There is no doubt that child centeredness is an enduring and fixed entity in early childhood education. In fact, it could be said that it is a revered concept.

However, Graue manages to turn it on its head and show the restrictions implicit in this construct for a sample of 14 children in a variety of settings across two school districts. The marking of these children as "different" seemed to have the effect of making them imperceptible to teachers, thus isolating the children from sustained interaction and engagement with the very professionals who were charged with remedying their "at risk" status. This pedagogical segregation sanctions maturational approaches, but at the same time makes a mockery of the reasons children were spending an additional year in a preschool setting or a second year in kindergarten.

Concentrating on her practice as a teacher of first grade children in Australia, Felicity McArdle (Chapter 4: *Teaching Notes*), delivers an enchanting array of stories that illustrate how sensitive children are to difference and their acute awareness of the intersection of difference and impropriety: "Children notice it, they remark on it, they fear it, they correct it, they worry about it, they seem to be forever vigilant when it comes to difference and transgression" (p. 63). McArdle's analysis invokes multiple readings of taken-for-granted practices that go with the territory of attending school. The accepted school rules and rituals are sources of mystification and estrangement that work to distance these first time school attendants and mark them as unknowing, until their bodies and minds have learnt and come to know their "place" in the regime of things. Disrupting these discourses of difference and how they do their work is McArdle's aim, but she has a bigger picture in mind as these cases are used to argue that instances of difference cannot be treated as "add-ons" to traditional early childhood curricula and must be used to teach children to engage critically with difference. The point is that the complexity of daily classroom life provides many pedagogical opportunities for teachers to do this with children.

Resources have always been considered essential in early childhood programs and over the years have evolved from the materials used by Froebel and Montessori to recent examples of what could be termed a "chicken and egg" interplay of market forces and perceived curriculum demands that are a legacy of globalization. What has resulted is a plethora of resources that enable teachers to deal with particular aspects of our globalized world, including representations of racial and ethnic difference through use of props such as "The Asian family" and "The Native American family" dolls, puzzles, and other play materials. Rich Johnson (Chapter 5, *The Amorphous Pretend Play Curriculum: Theorizing Embodied Synthetic Multicultural Props*) examines these appealing and "multicultural" artifacts of visual culture to trouble the way in which early childhood educators accept unproblematically the normative representations they embody. Quite apart from questions about the pedagogical limitations of tourist-oriented curriculum associated with the use of these play materials, Johnson makes a case that they symbolize the "classic child(ren) of early childhood education – that romantic, natural child, the unthreatened, enlightened being" (p. 106). These static images of visual culture play a significant part in perpetuating the status quo, because their very existence seems to excuse any necessity to teach explicitly about difference and diversity, that is, about other lifeworlds.

For many teachers, teacher educators and facilitators of professional development programs for early childhood practitioners, enacting a bicultural early childhood curriculum comes with a complex set of challenges and struggles. In New Zealand, the bicultural curriculum *Te Whàriki*, affirms the importance of the indigenous people and involves the provision of corresponding Màori language and content alongside "western" knowledges in all dimensions of early childhood curriculum. In Chapter 6, *Implementing Te Whàriki as Postmodernist Practice: A Perspective from Aotearoa/New Zealand*, Jenny Ritchie contemplates some of the bicultural requirements of *Te Whàriki* and how those in the field are dealing with decentering the "mainstream" curriculum and repositioning themselves "alongside Màori whànau (families) and Màori colleagues who remain the repositories of Màori knowledge" (p. 111). Ritchie uses extracts from participant transcripts to depict how power relations work at the local level, privileging particular practices in everyday routines and creating tension in places where several ethnic groups are present. Besides revealing the potential of *Te Whàriki* to transform practices, Ritchie details the way in which *Te Whàriki* is a "work-in-progress" alternative to the accepted and normalized version of early childhood curriculum that endorsed the cultural knowledge of the dominant group in New Zealand.

These chapters in the first section of the book consider aspects of curriculum and pedagogy as they are enacted in early childhood classrooms. The next section shifts the focus to teacher preparation and professional development programs, retaining the emphasis on power relationships, and agency.

EARLY CHILDHOOD TEACHER EDUCATION AND PROFESSIONAL DEVELOPMENT

Even though national policy documents (Bowman, Donovan, & Burns, 2001; Hyson, 2003) require the addition of content that addresses working with children and families from diverse linguistic and cultural backgrounds, recent research has found that 2- and 4-year early childhood pre-service teacher education courses in the U.S.A. provide little course work about educating children from such backgrounds (Early & Winton, 2001). The dominance of child development theory in teacher education has meant that many teachers are not necessarily prepared to work with children from backgrounds dissimilar to their own (Ryan & Ackerman, 2004). A small group of teacher educators have been experimenting with introducing different kinds of knowledge to their students with the intent of helping them to consider the ways in which their agency and that of the children they teach is simultaneously constrained and enabled by various assumptions about best practice in the early years.

One perspective that is advantageous when engaging with issues of power and agency is postcolonial theory. In Chapter 7, *Postcolonial Theory and the Practice of Teacher Education*, Radhika Viruru brings together these two highly contested domains. She argues that there are similarities between the two and that both can benefit from each other. Working through examples drawn from her classes as a teacher educator, Viruru employs postcolonial theory to interrogate some of the "basics", binaries, and stereotypes that litter the field of teacher education. Students discuss these issues as they relate to their own lives, including the taunts they are subjected to as a result of the "easy" major that they have selected (teaching). Being positioned as an easy major may serve as an introduction to the marginalization of the field, and for Viruru, is one of the ways of pairing postcolonial theory and teacher education to engage students in critical analyses of macro and micro issues of diversity and difference.

How pre-service students grappled with issues of race, class, gender, and life experience in a Language and Literacy course was the topic of an action research project undertaken by Celia Genishi, Shin-ying Huang, and Tamara Glupczynski (Chapter 8, *Becoming Early Childhood Teachers: Linking Action Research and Postmodern Theory in a Language and Literacy Course*). As instructors and researchers of the course, Genishi et al. drew on the institution's National Council for the Accreditation of Teacher Education (NCATE) conceptual framework to analyse two written assessment tasks submitted by students in the course. They were interested in knowing to what extent the students demonstrated "an understanding of issues of race, class, gender, language and ability" (p. 174); how the teacher education students were being prepared to "act sensitively and effectively with students whose life experiences are most often very unlike their own" (p. 174); and "To what extent did we and the students in this course construct 'counter narratives,' little stories that talked back to grand narratives, whether local or national?" (p. 187). Although this self study sought to link research and theory in the context of a teacher education course, it is ultimately about improving teaching and learning, and prefaced on a revisioned understanding of diversity and difference. The counternarratives created by the students, instructors, and researchers reinforced the multiplicity of positions, responses, and layers of meaning that are necessarily caught up in the complexities of teaching and learning for both adults and children.

In the final chapter that deals exclusively with teacher education, Jennifer Sumsion (Chapter 9, *Putting Postmodern Theories into Practice in Early Childhood Education*) gives three examples of her own "continual rereading and rewriting of ourselves and our practices" (p. 202). Like Genishi et al., this involved changing assessment practices, as well as the practicum component of the course. Further, as project leader charged with redressing the level of generic skills acquired by graduates from her department of the university (this was construed as a competitive weakness by university management), Sumsion tells how she worked with students and other teacher educators to produce an outcome that resisted dominant instrumentalist discourses. Aimed ultimately at transformation through being able to remove oneself from entrenched practices and standpoints to conceive anew, Sumsion argues for reflexivity, imagining, and hope, not only for teacher education, but also as constructs for a transformed society.

Kinsler and Gamble (2001) have made the point that the vast majority of professional development for teachers leads to no significant change in classroom practices, and Fullan and Stiegelbauer (1991) has shown that "one off" sessions and sequential workshops are ineffective without appropriate follow up support. These and other limits of traditional approaches to professional development are well known (Knight, 2002). Consistent with recent moves toward adopting alternative approaches to professional development (e.g., Burbank & Kauchak, 2003; Groundwater-Smith, Mockler, & Normanhurst, 2002; Knight, 2002), Sue Novinger, Leigh O'Brien, and Lou Sweigman (Chapter 10, *Challenging the Culture of Expertise: Moving Beyond Training the Always, Already Failing Early Childhood Educator*) scrutinize their own positions as "experts training novices". That is, they dissect their positions as teacher educators and providers of professional development programs for pre-and in-service teachers. Novinger et al. analyse discourses of expertise to expose their own experiences of struggle, disquiet, and uncertainty associated with the culture of expertise and in the process take apart the power relationships and agency involved in their daily work. The powerful stories in this chapter illustrate the multiple and changing positions of those who engage in professional development. Their efforts are directed toward a participatory and inclusive model where power and knowledge relationships are re-negotiated and continually reassessed.

Interested in improving teachers' interactions with children, Carrie Lobman (Chapter 11, *Improvisation: Postmodern Play for Early Childhood Teachers*) takes the unique view of teachers as improvisers and relates details of a research project that involved seven early childhood practitioners as they worked through ways of creating new performances in their lives. The ultimate aim was for participants to understand a different way of relating to children that is not prefaced on or by developmental pathways. Drawing on Vygotsky's work, Lobman argues that although Vygotsky's work has been used in early childhood education to "import 'culture'" (p. 251), this addition has made little difference to traditional conceptions of child development as a series of linear stages. However, the key is Vygotsky's activity theory, which for Lobman, has the potential to transform daily practice through techniques such as teaching early childhood practitioners how to use improvisation. The "in the moment" notions of improvisation sit comfortably with theories of the postmodern, and the introduction of a lesser known aspect of Vygotsky's work as a postmodern possibility is food for thought.

TRANSFORMATION AND TRANSFORMATIVE PRACTICES

Although the effects of globalization are experienced in a similar fashion to those in other areas of education, in early childhood education, there is little recognition of these effects beyond debates about the negative impact of testing and that conservative quick fixes and market-oriented reforms are not the answer. At the same time, many in our field remain committed to a developmental perspective, which while progressive in comparison to traditional or more "direct" forms of instruction, is nonetheless a standardized curriculum approach. Uniform approaches, however, are no longer adequate if teachers are to be able to respond individually to the range of experiences and understandings that children bring with them into early childhood programs.

The chapters contained in this volume offer some insight into the transformation of daily practices that can and will contribute to the revisioning of teaching and pedagogy that is called for in a global and postmodern world. Most of these accounts locate transformation at the local level, initiated by teachers, supported by teachers, and focused on specific classroom issues. That is, teachers are being exhorted to "push the boundaries of the social fields of teaching" in new ways (Luke, 2004, p. 1441). However, given the marginalization of early childhood education, and the diversity of formal education and professional experiences of the workforce, teachers will also need to be supported in their endeavors to transform practice and for these endeavors to be heard and seen by others. Luke (2004) argues that one way we might harness this support is through the creation of teacher "intercultural capital" (p. 1441) that would:

> ...constitute the kinds of embodied skills, competences, and knowledges that are requisite for modeling for students an agentive engagement in flows across cultures, geographies and sites. (p. 1441)

While the chapters in this book serve as models of this "agentive engagement" in a number of geographical locations, they will remain nothing more than isolated examples unless readers take up their challenge and continue with this transformative work. To do otherwise is to risk remaining mired in outdated ideas and practices that can only result in the perpetuation of educational inequities and missed opportunities to actually create spaces for change and improvement in the lives of young children.

REFERENCES

Alliance for Childhood. (2002). Fool's gold: A critical look at computers and childhood. In: K. M. Paciorek (Ed.), *Taking sides: Clashing views on controversial issues in early childhood education* (pp. 39–41). Guilford, CA: McGraw-Hill/Dushkin.

Apple, M. W. (2001). *Educating the "right" way: Markets, standards, god and inequality.* New York: RoutledgeFalmer.

Bishop, R. (1996). Postmodernism. In: D. Levinson & M. Ember (Eds), *Encyclopedia of cultural anthropology* (Vol. 3, pp. 993–998). New York: Henry Holt.

Bloch, M. (1992). Critical perspectives in the historical relationship between child development and early childhood education research. In: S. A. Kessler & B. B. Swadener (Eds), *Reconceptualizing the early childhood curriculum: Beginning the dialogue* (pp. 3–20). New York: Teachers College Press.

Bowman, B. T., Donovan, M. S., & Burns, M. S. (Eds) (2001). *Eager to learn: Educating preschoolers.* Washington, DC: National Academy Press.

Boyd, B. J. (2002). Teacher response to superhero play: To ban or not to ban? In: K. M. Paciorek (Ed.), *Taking sides: Clashing views on controversial issues in early childhood education* (pp. 96–103). Guilford, CA: McGraw-Hill/Dushkin.

Burbank, M. D., & Kauchak, D. (2003). An alternative model for professional development: Investigations into effective collaboration. *Teaching and Teacher Education, 19,* 499–514.

Burbules, N. C., & Torres, C. A. (2000). Globalization and education: An introduction. In: N. C. Burbules & C. A. Torres (Eds), *Globalization and education: Critical perspectives* (pp. 1–26). New York: Routledge.
Burman, E. (1994). *Deconstructing developmental psychology*. London: Routledge.
Cannella, G. S. (1997). *Deconstructing early childhood education: Social justice and revolution*. New York: Peter Lang.
Cannella, G. S. (2002). Global perspectives, cultural studies and the construction of a postmodern childhood. In: G. S. Cannella & J. K. Kincheloe (Eds), *Kidworld: Childhood studies, global perspectives, and education* (pp. 3–18). New York: Peter Lang.
Charlesworth, R. (1998). Developmentally appropriate practice is for everyone. *Childhood Education, 74*(5), 274–282.
Clements, D. H. (1999). The future of educational computing research: The case of computer programming. *Information Technology in Childhood Education Annual, 1,* 147–179.
Darder, A. (2002). *Reinventing Paulo Freire: A peadagogy of love*. Boulder, CO: Westview Press.
Derman-Sparks, L. & the Anti-Bias Task Force. (1989). *The anti-bias curriculum*. Washington DC: National Association for the Education of Young Children.
Early, D. M., & Winton, P. J. (2001). Preparing the workforce: Early childhood teacher preparation at 2-and 4-year institutions of higher education. *Early Childhood Research Quarterly, 16,* 285–306.
Fullan, M. G., & Stiegelbauer, S. (1991). *The new meaning of educational change* (2nd ed.). London: Cassell.
Foley, P., Roche, J., & Tucker, S. (2001). Foreword: Children in society: Contemporary theory, policy and practice. In: P. Foley, J. Roche & S. Tucker (Eds), *Children in society: Contemporary theory, policy and practice* (pp. 1–6). Basingstoke: Palgrave.
Genishi, C., Ryan, S., Ochsner, M., & Yarnall, M. (2001). Teaching in early childhood education: Understanding practices through research and theory. In: V. Richardson (Ed.), *Handbook of research on teaching,* (4th ed) (pp. 1175–1210). Washington, DC: American Educational Research Association.
Goffin, S. G. (1989). Developing a research agenda for early childhood education: What can be learned from research on teaching? *Early Childhood Research Quarterly, 4,* 187–204.
Goldstein, C. (2002). Teaching hope to children in special education. In: A. Darder (Ed.), *Reinventing Paulo Friere: A pedagogy of love*. Boulder, CO: Westview Press.
Grieshaber, S., & Cannella, G. S. (Eds) (2001). *Embracing identities in early childhood education: Diversity and possibilities*. New York: Teachers College Press.
Groundwater-Smith, S., Mockler, N., & Normanhurst, L. (2002). *Building knowledge, building professionalism: The coalition of knowledge building schools and teacher professionalism.* Paper presented to the Australian Association for Research Education Annual Conference. The University of Queensland, Brisbane, Queensland.
Hatch, A., Bowman, B., Jor'dan, J. R., Morgan, C. L., Hart, C., Soto, L. D., Lubeck, S., & Hyson, M. (2000). Developmentally appropriate practice: Continuing the dialogue. *Contemporary Issues in Early Childhood, 3*(3), 439–457.
Hampton, M. (2002). Limiting superhero play in classrooms: A philosophy statement. In: K. M. Paciorek (Ed.), *Taking sides: Clashing views on controversial issues in early childhood education* (pp. 86–95). Guilford, CA: McGraw-Hill/Dushkin.
Hyson, M. (Ed.) (2003). *Preparing early childhood professionals: NAEYC's standards for programs*. Washington, DC: NAEYC.

Kalantzis, M., with Cope, B., & Harvey, A. (2003). Toward diversity in education. In: S. Dinham (Ed.), *Transforming education: Engaging with complexity and diversity* (pp. 25–37). Canberra: Australian College of Education.
Kessler, S. A., & Swadener, B. B. (Eds) (1992). *Reconceptualizing the early childhood curriculum: Beginning the dialogue.* New York: Teachers College Press.
Kinsler, K., & Gamble, M. (2001). *Reforming schools.* London: Continuum.
Knight, P. (2002). A systemic approach to professional development: Learning as practice. *Teaching and Teacher Education, 18*, 229–241.
Ladson-Billings, G. (1994). *The dreamkeepers: Successful teachers of African American children.* San Francisco: Jossey-Bass.
Lubeck, S. (1998a). Is developmentally appropriate practice for everyone? *Childhood Education, 74*(5), 283–292.
Lubeck, S. (1998b). Is DAP for everyone? A response. *Childhood Education, 74*(5), 299–301.
Luke, A. (2003). After the marketplace: Evidence, social science and educational research. *The Australian Educational Researcher, 30*(2), 87–107.
Luke, A. (2004). Teaching after the market: From commodity to cosmopolitanism. *Teachers College Record, 106*(7), 1422–1443.
Luke, A., & Grieshaber, S. (2004). New adventures in the politics of literacy: An introduction. *Journal of Early Childhood Literacy, 4*(1), 5–9.
Mallory, B., & New, R. (Eds) (1994). *Diversity and developmentally appropriate practices: Challenges for early childhood education.* New York: Teachers College Press.
McLean, S. V. (1990). Early childhood teachers in multicultural settings. *The Educational Forum, 54*(2), 197–204.
Nieto, S. (2004). *Affirming diversity: The sociopolitical context of multicultural education* (4th ed.). Boston: Pearson Education.
Peters, D. (1993). Trends in demographic and behavioural research on teaching in early childhood settings. In: B. Spodek (Ed.), *Handbook of research on the education of young children* (pp. 493–505). New York: Macmillan.
Ryan, S., & Ackerman, D. (2004). *Creating a qualified workforce part I: Getting qualified: A report on the efforts of preschool teachers in New Jersey's abbott districts to improve their qualifications.* New Brunswick, NJ: National Institute for Early Education Research.
Silin, J. G. (1987). The early educator's knowledge base: A reconsideration. In: L. G. Katz (Ed.), *Current topics in early childhood education* (pp. 17–31). Norwood, NJ: Ablex.
Silin, J. G. (1995). *Sex death and the education of children: Our passion for ignorance in the age of aids.* New York: Teachers College Press.
Spiro, M. E. (1996). Postmodernist anthropology, subjectivity, and science: A modernist critique. *Comparative Studies in Society and History, 48*(4), 759–780.
Spodek, B. (1977). What constitutes worthwhile educational experiences for young children? In: B. Spodek (Ed.), *Teaching practices: Reexamining assumptions* (pp. 5–20). Washington, DC: National Association for the Education of Young Children.
Spodek, B., & Saracho, O. (1982). The preparation and certification of early childhood personnel. In: B. Spodek (Ed.), *Handbook of research in early childhood education* (pp. 399–425). New York: Free Press.
Tobin, J. (Ed.) (1997). *Making a place for pleasure in early childhood education.* New Haven: Yale University Press.
Wyness, M. G. (2000). *Contesting childhood.* London and New York: Falmer.

VOICES AT THE TABLE: AN ANALYSIS OF COLLABORATION IN THE POLICY PROCESS FOR A LOCAL PRESCHOOL INITIATIVE

Lucinda G. Heimer

ABSTRACT

This chapter tells the story of the Early Childhood Collaborative (ECC), a committee set up to formulate a plan for the delivery of universal preschool education for 4-year-olds in a medium sized Midwestern city in the United States. As I explore the policymaking interactions of this collaborative, the issue of who was included, the capital needed for inclusion, and the power related to social networks and how that shapes collaboration are illuminated. It is argued that in order to bring diverse voices to the table, alternate ways of creating space for participants in policy formulation need to be considered. It is in these spaces that it might be possible to create and present counter narratives to dominant views of how early childhood education should be enacted.

"From the beginning, invite everyone." Arborville Department of Public Instruction (2003)

Collaboration is usually defined as a coming together of interested individuals to work on a common project of some kind. With the continuing expansion of publicly funded preschool programs, collaboration is being touted as a method to ensure that high-quality preschool programs are implemented successfully in local settings. Collaboration in this sense refers to the bringing together of various program types (Head Start, public schools, child care) that have for the most part operated alongside, rather than with one another (Barnett, 1995). Research evidence (Barnett, 1995; Bredekamp, Knuth, Kunesh, & Shulman, 1992; Lubeck, 2001; Reynolds, Wang, & Walberg, 2003) indicates that if the expansion of preschool programs is to harness the benefits associated with high quality model programs then fragmented systems have to be simplified requiring communication and participation of all stakeholders within a community. The bulk of the early education policy research supporting this emphasis on collaboration is generated in a positivist paradigm suggesting that there are specific answers that address disparate situations for all children. In this chapter, I use the case of one early childhood collaboration to illustrate how the "success" of a policy depends upon, how the policy is read and interpreted, and who has access to the policy at different stages of its formulation (Ball, 1994).

WHAT IS POLICY?

Policy is not simply a text to read but is also a process. Within every context at which the policy is used, it is interpreted, recreated, and altered in specific ways. According to Stephen Ball (1994), policy is both a process and an outcome. There are multiple ways that policy is defined, used, and positioned in social settings. He articulates two versions of policy: policy as text and policy as discourse. These versions are "implicit in each other" (Ball, 1994, p. 15).

For Ball, a policy text is read and interpreted and as such is never "clear or closed or complete. (It is) the product of compromises at various stages" of policy development, negotiation, and interpretation (Ball, 1994, p. 16). "Policies *are* [italics in the original] textual interventions into practice" (Ball, 1994, p. 18). Practice is determined by a reading and interpretation of the policy. For example, teachers read and implement (or do not) a particular curriculum policy, while at the same time they negotiate how policy poses problems that must be resolved in context. In other words, policy does not determine practice, but it does limit the options available and the possible outcomes.

Discourse is seen "as practices that systematically form the objects of which they speak. Discourses are not about objects; they do not identify objects, they constitute them and in the practice of doing so conceal their own invention" (Foucault as cited in Ball, 1994, p. 21). There is a dynamic of power relationships (most often hidden) at work that constructs certain meanings around a policy and how it is interpreted and enacted. Discourses also determine individual access to the process in terms of power and capital. That is, even when individuals are invited to collaborate in the process of formulating early childhood policies, some, because of their position and status, have more say than others. The discourses at work in a policy setting determine who is included, who gets to speak, and whose voice is heard.

My research focuses on the Early Childhood Collaborative (ECC) a policy formulation committee who were involved in exploring a universal public education program for 4-year-old children (commonly known as 4 K) in a medium-sized Midwestern city (Arborville) in the United States. In 2001, I was invited to participate in the initiative as a preschool director in Arborville. Over the course of 2 years, my role in the process changed as I left my position in the field to return to school and become a doctoral student, and consequently a researcher. In my time in graduate school, I had the luxury of sitting back and rethinking how theory impacts practice. In doing so, I realized that early childhood policy is more complex than a text to follow. Upon closer inspection, I realized there were multiple layers of power and relationships that create discourses of authority. Although, I wanted to believe that my activist nature and my desire for social justice in early education would prevail, I began to feel defeated by the suggestion that power is changing and truth (in this case collaboration) is a constructed concept (Foucault, 1984). Yet, as I consider the experience of the last few years, I wonder if this story might help others think of new ways of disrupting the traditional notions of policy making in early childhood.

THE EARLY CHILDHOOD COLLABORATIVE

The ECC is located in Arborville, a medium-sized Mid-western city in the United States. Arboville is seen as a family-friendly city having received several awards that include the *Child Magazine* sixth best city for families, and recognition by *Ladies Home Journal* as the best small city for women to live in (Arborville website, 2003 fact sheets). Not only does Arborville enjoy national prestige as a supportive environment for women, children, and families, but in 2002, the Arborville School District (ASD) was the only district in the country to have National Schools of Excellence at all levels (elementary, middle, and high) (Arborville website, 2003 fact sheets).

Given this reputation, the news that the public kindergarten for 4-year-old children "at risk" (generally understood to mean lower SES and/or special needs) was ending came as a surprise to most of the local early childhood community. In March 2001, a letter from the Mayor and City Schools Superintendent was sent to center directors, family childcare providers, and parents of children who were currently enrolled in the public school program for 4-year-olds. The reason given for canceling the program of 30 years was that the district, in operating the program for a targeted population, was no longer in compliance with the universal access provision according to the State Constitution (Arborville School District Website, 2003).

While six districts within the state had already started community-based approaches to 4-year-old public schooling programs in the same (2000 – 2001) academic year, Arborville was offering public preschool primarily through Head Start (Barnett, Robin, Hustedt, & Schulman, 2003), a federal program that serves lower income families. As the State Constitution required that public education should be universally available, the district administration had to create a new form of public preschool program if it were to offer public schooling for four-year-olds at all. To get the process started, the Arborville School District Administration hired two part-time consultants to begin exploring the needs of the community. This was the birth of the ECC.

Policy formulation involves key policy writers (defined as "legitimate actors") seeking to address the information needs of the policy at hand (Nakamura & Smallwood, as cited in Rist, 1998, p. 406). The universal policy-formulation process in Arborville was enacted through collaboration among representatives of the school district, Head Start, the city office for childcare,[1] and community child care centers. Joe Miller (Arborville School District Consultant) set the tone of this process early on at one of the first early childhood community workshop:

> Welcome everyone to the first gathering of individuals interested in creating new possibilities for our 4-year-old children in Arborville. We are glad to have you join us for this journey we are embarking on. We are hoping to challenge ourselves as a group to consider a total paradigm shift to help us maintain the "big picture" as we work together. We would like to begin by going around the circle today and introducing ourselves. Please state your name, your position in the community and why you are here.

Participants were recruited through community meetings like the one above. As time passed, a core group of interested community members began to meet and plan a collaborative effort (Head Start, city child care offices, the school district, and the local university) to meet the educational needs of 4-year-olds in Arborville using existing programs as well as newly created partnerships.

The vision of the ECC generated by this group was succinct, "ECC is a comprehensive high quality early learning system that meets the developmental needs of all young children in the Arborville area" (Board Meeting Packet, 2002). Basically, four different service options were created to better meet the needs of families. These options included: (1) offering half-day preschool in at least one public school classroom, with wrap around care available through local child care services, (2) offering half-day preschool in local community child care programs staffed by teachers recruited by the ASD, (3) ASD contract with community-based child care programs to provide half-day preschool and these programs recruit certified teachers to teach preschool, and (4) community-based and accredited family child care programs with certified teachers providing in-home preschool (see Table 1). With all of these options, the ASD was to provide special education services and other support services (e.g. transportation) as needed. Using these options and working as partners, the ECC hoped to avoid decimating existing quality childcare programs, while at the same time ensuring that families already enrolled in child care programs could potentially remain with their provider.

Thus, after meeting and working together for 21 months (March 2001 until December 2002), the ECC had created policy that identified several options to enable four-year-olds in Arborville to participate in preschool programs. This policy formulation process also resulted in defining the various components of this new preschool system including the participants, funding sources, curriculum, staffing, and support services that would be needed within each option.

The preschool proposal of the ECC was presented at the ASD school board meeting in December 2002. Given other pressing financial demands for the school board, the preschool proposal was tabled. In addition, the school board raised concerns regarding the composition of the ECC committee and asked the ECC to develop a plan for non-accredited centers and family day care providers, and to find ways to ensure that the perspectives of all ethnic groups of Arborville were gathered. The final comment of the e-mail written by Sally Clinger (chair of the ECC) included this sentence:

> As stated earlier and confirmed at the BOE (board) meeting, our group needs to represent the diverse population of Arborville ... and we don't. It is critical to have multiple voices at the table, because each of us, as we have learned, sees the world through our

Table 1. Early Childhood Collaborative 4-Year-Old Service Delivery Options.

Option I Public School Staff/School Site	Option II Public School Staff/Community Site	Option III Contracted Services/Community Site	Option IV Contracted Services/Family Child Care Home Site
Option IA: One classroom • AM and PM classes (2.5 h each, school year) provided by district staff • Children will be enrolled based on living in school combined attendance area or parents work in attendance area, or other reasons • Children are not enrolled in an early education and care program for any other part of the day	• AM and PM classes (2.5 h each, school year) • Pubic school teacher works within existing part-day or full-day community early childhood site • Site may or may not be city/nationally accredited, but must be working on accreditation	• Community sites (center based programs, Head Start, Family Child Care, part-day preschool programs) will have their own 4-year degreed/DPI licensed teacher • Sites would need to hold NAEYC/City of Arborville accreditation, meet Head Start performance standards • Funds could be contracted on a per child basis, so sites could serve any number of eligible 4-year-olds	• Community Family sites will have their own 4-year degreed teacher • Sites would need to hold City of Arborville accreditation, and/or hold NAFCC accreditation • Funds could be contracted on a per child basis, so sites could serve any number of eligible 4-year-olds

Option IB: Two or more district classrooms
- Same criteria as above except that extended education and care programming provided by non-district staff contracted with accredited non-district early learning centers on school site

- ECC staff will be supported in working toward DPI licensure
- Minimum of 437 h of "instruction" time provided for each child-site would have flexibility in scheduling within the school year

- The contracted per child funding could be used by the site administrator chooses (i.e., enhanced salaries for staff, operational expenses, etc.)
- Minimum of 437 h of 'instruction' time provided for each child-site would have flexibility in scheduling

- The contracted per child funding could be used by the site in whatever way the site provider chooses (i.e., enhanced salaries for staff, operational expenses, etc.)
- Minimum of 437 h of 'instruction' time provided for each child-site would have flexibility in scheduling

Option IC: One Classroom and child care community site
- AM and PM classes (2.5 h each, school year) provided by district staff. Children enrolled based on: Living in school combined attendance area, childcare in combined attendance area, parents work in combined attendance area, other. Extended education and care programming provided by an accredited community agency (center-based or family home child care off site)

- Site could serve children from outside of ASD but only ASD children would be funded
- ASD support services would follow the children
- Collaboration team comprised of all partners to create appropriate match of teacher to center

- Site could provide the program for children in a multiaged group, and serve children from outside of ASD getting funding only for the ASD 4-year-old children
- ASD support services would follow the children
- Collaborative team comprised of all partners

- Site could provide the program for children in a multiaged group and serve children from outside of ASD, getting funding only for the 4-year-old ASD children
- ASD support services would follow the children
- Collaborative team comprised of all partners

own operating lens. I encourage you to make contacts with your networks, so that our community is well represented in this important, collaborative initiative.

Although, the primary reason for putting this preschool initiative on hold was financial paradoxically, concerns were raised regarding the work of the ECC because the collaborative itself was not deemed to be representative of the community of child care providers and families of Arborville. In the next section, I use postmodern concepts to theorize why the collaboration of the ECC was not effective in creating a policy that spoke to, and for all, community members.

VOICES AT THE TABLE

Over the course of 2 years, I observed and participated in the ECC. My role in the collaboration began as one of the early childhood educators on the ECC and then shifted to also being a researcher when I returned to the university to pursue my doctorate. To describe how the collaborative came together to enact new early childhood policy, I collected data via interviews, field notes, and textual analysis of meeting minutes. The analysis presented here concentrates on two aspects of collaboration: meeting attendance and meeting structure. Each of these topics provides a unique lens to consider the ECC project from beginning to end. The first area of focus digs more deeply into the issue of attendance, and who gets to have a voice in collaborations by considering capital and access. Meeting structure, which includes workshops, meetings, and public forums, is also examined in terms of participation and efficiency to highlight how participation does not necessarily guarantee collaboration.

Participation on the ECC

Ball suggests that policy "discourse is about what can be said, and thought, and also about who can speak, when, where, and with what authority" (Ball, 1994, p. 21). According to Ball, the power in discourse is in the authority it gains through key actors and their social relationships in the policy process. Individuals continue to have impact on the policy through their presence or absence and their adherence or defiance in each stage of the process. Who facilitated the meetings, who was invited to the meetings, and who got to speak all provide insights into the power relationships at work in the ECC.

After the Mayor's letter in the spring of 2001, a follow-up letter was sent to invite directors ("early childhood community members") to a summer

(2001) workshop. How this initial mailing list was constructed and who constructed it raises issues of access and presence. A local non-profit clearinghouse in conjunction with the ASD consultants generated the letter. Facilities included on the list were city accredited (a regulatory process unique to Arborville) or registered with a support organization for family childcare providers. Once the ECC was underway, the question of who to contact was referred to as the "mailing list", the "council list", or the "team list". The ECC Contact Persons/Mailing list was comprised of 297 recipients that included 151 day care/preschool community members (teachers, staff, and directors), 84 agency members (non-profit clearinghouse, Dobson County Parent Council, State Council for Children and Families), 42 parents (as indicated by no agency/school affiliation), and 20 ASD Personnel.

The names that later appear as participants and committee members in the ECC represent the same population that has been involved on other related community committees (Literacy Campaign, etc.). For example, one of the initial consultants on the project also worked for Head Start and eventually wrote in collaboration with the Department of Public Instruction (DPI) and university representatives for the state economic summit in support of early childhood. She also worked with DPI on projects regarding teacher licensure. In addition, three of the five key agency administrators had already worked on at least two other community committees together. Although it makes sense that interests overlap, the point is that the networks were fairly well established and involvement on projects was based on prior experience on similar projects or recommendations of colleagues. The same "movers and shakers" were involved in this process that were involved in most other initiatives for children. The initial invitations were based on broad affiliation with early childhood education in the community. This suggests that district employees must have been familiar with either the individual or the agency to ensure an invitation.

Although just over half of the participants were individuals working in community childcare programs, only those in accredited centers were invited to the table. This meant that families of children attending non-accredited child care services whether they were center or home based had little representation on the ECC. At the October 2001 meeting, the minutes note that there was some discussion regarding the failure to connect with non-accredited centers and lack of access to communities who might benefit the most from universal access. However, it appears that this concern while officially documented was not placed at a position of importance as it appears that no outreach occurred with persons or groups that never made the list.

Belonging to some kind of early childhood networks played a large part in getting an invitation. These networks provided social capital (Bourdieu, 1984) as the power needed to access the ECC was only available to those belonging to these networks (accredited early childhood centers and recognized agencies).

Attendance Requirements

A telephone call during the second year of the ECC:

Carol	Yeah, hi can you hang on just a sec....kids keep it down...Josh please wait to pour your milk until I can help. Sorry, anyway where is this meeting tomorrow? The research park? Where the heck is that? Is it on a bus line? If not I just can't make it. It is – great. Okay, so I guess I'll see you tomorrow night.
Researcher	It's at 7:30a.m.
Carol	What?! It's at 7:30 in the **morning**? There is **no** way I can make that – who would watch the kids? I can't just take off! This is crazy... not only did I just hear about this thing yesterday through the grapevine but it is next to impossible for me to make it. It seems to me like they just don't want "my type" (family day provider) there. I know it's not your fault...but this whole idea of including the "community" seems bogus to me. Don't call yourself a collaboration if some of us who really care can't even participate.

An invitation was not necessarily a guarantee that individuals would be able to voice their perspectives and participate fully in the ECC. As this conversation indicates, in order to participate at meetings, one must be available during days, have child care available, have time to give to the project, speak English, as well as transportation to and from meetings. While the meetings were located in a variety of sites (accredited childcare centers, Head Start, sponsoring agencies, etc.), little attention was given to the resources needed to enable individuals like Carol to attend meetings. At the same time, some areas of town were not included as potential sites for meetings of the ECC. There were no southside centers represented in the collaboration other than Head Start yet, services and individuals in this area of Arborville served the highest proportion of low-income families. Given these conditions, the ECC was comprised predominantly of white middle class women working in early childhood agencies who were provided with release time from work to attend (I, too, fit in this classification). Analysis of meeting attendance indicates that a little over a year after the inception of the ECC, the majority (77%) of the participants were no longer child care and providers of early childhood services, but administrative agency members and district employees.

As mentioned previously, in order to get invited to the table and participate in the ECC, one had to have a certain amount of symbolic capital (social, economic, and cultural resources) or at least perceived capital (Bourdieu, 1977). This capital was obtained by either belonging to an officially recognized agency or network concerned with early childhood education or working in a service deemed to be of a higher quality than others (e.g. accredited centers versus non-accredited programs, center-based versus family home care). Individuals with symbolic capital therefore have more power and authority than others and therefore tend to protect what they have. This capital enabled those involved in the ECC to use what Bourdieu (1984) calls symbolic violence. Symbolic violence is a way of creating "relations of personal dependence" (veiled either as gift or debt) without using overt economic or physical violence (Bourdieu & Wacquant, 1992). In this situation, the notion of collaboration was used to disguise the invisible ways recognized and validated early childhood agencies and individuals exercised power (invitation lists, district staff as facilitators) to protect their own interests. While the use of a community collaboration implies inclusion, the agencies and individuals with more authority used their capital to initially prevent non-accredited centers, family day care providers, and families in lower income communities to be actively recruited and involved in policy formulation. This limited the participants comprising the ECC and "symbolically silenced" a large and diverse group of collaborators. Yet, this group of non-participants was the population that would most likely benefit from universal preschool. Given the invisible ways power was operating in the ECC, one has to ask whether even if these marginalized groups were included at the policy table, could their voices be heard?

The Form and Structure of ECC Meetings and Forums

At a community forum created to inform the public regarding the work of the ECC, November 2002:

Community member   I have a question, why haven't parents of young children been involved from the start?

Chairperson   That is a great question but we are out of time, I am sorry. I want to be respectful of people's personal time and we said we would wrap up promptly at 8. Thanks so much for coming.

In addition to who was invited and allowed to participate in the ECC, the structure of the collaboration changed over time as evidenced in alterations to the meeting purpose and structure, room organization, and leadership. As exemplified in this conversation, the meeting structure changed from a rather open and "organic" process to a highly structured and formal setting marked by strict time keeping (see Table 2).

Initial forums in 2001, although guided were open ended and ambiguous. Framed as a journey, the purposes of these forums were to share information about the creation of a new universal preschool program and to seek the input of community members. The room arrangement invited this participation as tables and chairs were arranged in small clusters to facilitate conversation and discussion of the issues. A year later, the purposes of the forum had not changed drastically. However, while the organizers still sought to build consensus and to share information about preschool policy, the room was not arranged to invite participation. Under new leadership, the public forum in August 2002 highlighted a power point presentation sharing facts about child care centers, the district, and numbers of children to be served. To be sure, there was some time allowed for questions, but the room was set up in a lecture style so that participation and discussion among all individuals present was curtailed.

Finally, at the actual ASD Board meeting in 2002, the Board views the process and the presentation literally from the center of the room while perceivably holding the power to support or veto. Although, the process is marketed as democratic in nature with time set aside for public input, it quickly becomes obvious that phone calls have been made to individual board members by concerned residents to better ensure their voice is heard through a position of perceived power. This supports the notion that there have been community members willing to be involved, that have been missed at some point who have now recognized the opportunity to get involved through the elected officials at the table.

The shift from a more abstract get together to efficient meetings is not necessarily contradictory to collaboration, but many times efficiency trumped voice. As the form and structure of the meetings changed, individual power was even less likely as voices were constrained to specific

Table 2. Meeting Structure.

	Workshop Summer 2001	Forum Fall 2002	Board Meeting Dec. 2002
Agenda	Open ended framed as a "Journey"	No printed agenda – power point presentation	ECC not formally on agenda for the board rather the presentation falls under "other"
Room design	United Way Small groups around tables	Table at front for power point Chairs in rows	The Board sits at the center in a circle – "guests" sit at the back of the room or along the wall
Presentation	Interactive small group and large group sharing	Presentation – 1.5 h, 30 min allowed for questions	Set agenda – board members determine amount of time given to the topic- formal presentation by ECC district staff member
Public sharing: Why or why not? Outcome	Encouraged as a necessary part of the process. Frustrated, public not clear what the purpose was but felt involved	Public expected to share but not given much time. Cards with questions from public read by facilitators rather than sharing verbally. Frustrated public for feeling stifled or controlled and expected to accept the ideas	Public allowed to speak if filled out speaker card. Time allotted to speak before the ECC presentation. Controlled sharing frustration re: timing for the sharing
Purpose	Consensus building, information sharing	Consensus building, information sharing	Request for support from political entity that controls access to resources

time frames within an agenda often determined by outside agencies particularly the ASD rather than members of the ECC.

Foucault (1980) suggests that there is a false sense of power in governance structures such as board meetings or public forums. For Foucault, power does not reside in a person, group, movement, or artifact but instead, it circulates through social relations.

> Power is employed and exercised through a net-like organization. And not only do individuals circulate between its threads; they are always in the position of simultaneously undergoing and exercising this power. They are not only its inert or consenting target; they are always also the elements of its articulation. In other words, individuals are the vehicles of power, not its points of application. (Foucault 1980, p. 98)

Therefore, the issue of who gets to be at the table and participate in the collaborative is the wrong question. Rather by recognizing policy as both text and discourse the issue becomes not so much the power of voice, but rather the power relations attached to the voice.

For the ECC, the authority for policy implementation resided with the ASD and its Board of Education. It was the Board that tabled the policy claiming an inadequacy of resources only to announce three months later the creation of a new partnership with the Wilson Center (a university research group), and Head Start to implement a pilot preschool program at Greentree Elementary School beginning September 2003 (Erickson, 2003). Despite the creation of the ECC, and efforts made to include diverse voices of the community, the ECC policy process began with the ASD Board. As one Head Start administrator said:

> ...we (the ECC group) are not in charge so you can't be completely collaborative. But there's been a lot of collaboration in setting up the model and trying to figure out how they'll (district and child care providers) work together ... it's a collaboration as much as it can be when you have a single decision maker (ASD) but you know that, that's still not bad... Yeah the only true collaboration would be everybody puts in a portion and there is a consensus building and that's pretty much utopia.

IMPLICATIONS

In many ways, the policy emphasis on collaboration as a means of ensuring the implementation of high-quality systems of preschool education seems like a sensible goal. After all, it makes good sense for families to be able to locate and access preschool in their local communities, knowing that it will be of high quality and similar to other programs regardless of auspice. As any top-down policy initiative requires the buy-in and input of stakeholders if it is to be successfully adopted, it also seems very logical to involve community members in the policy formulation process.

Antonio Novoa writes that collaboration fits into what he calls "planetspeak" or "banalities universally accepted as truth that have no known origin and do not need to be questioned" (Franklin, Popkewitz, & Bloch, 2003, pp. 3–4). However, in the ECC, what started as an attempt to be collaborative and include voices at the policy table became a series of meetings, in which key agencies exercised increasingly more authority thus marginalizing many stakeholders. Despite the promise of collaboration, early childhood policies will not be responsive to the communities they serve without some reconsideration of how collaboration is defined and enacted. Using my experiences with the ECC, I would like to suggest two actions with this aim in mind.

First, individuals need capital to be able to access and participate with some authority in policy discourses. In order to ensure broader participation in early childhood policy initiatives, every effort must be made by those who already have access to networks and authority because of our positions to enable community members to participate in policy formulation. One simple way that might enable broader participation is to hold meetings across the community, at a variety of times and places, as well as providing childcare so that parents can attend. Similarly, invitations need to go out to services and individuals who are usually not accessible via typical networks. This may mean canvassing the neighborhood and building a potential mailing list from the ground up, but such efforts will ensure broader participation at the beginning of an initiative.

Once broader participation has been achieved, it is also necessary to consider ways of providing social capital to those often excluded from the policy table (parents, non-accredited programs, for-profit child care) so that their perspectives are included in the decision-making process. This is a much larger task that is fraught with complexity given the differing discourses and power relations that shape policymaking. One possible way this social capital might be accrued is through the creation of counter narratives to dominant understandings of what it means to be able to speak for early childhood (Ryan & Grieshaber, 2003). Discourses only have power because individuals speak and write them into existence, therefore, one way these counter narratives might gain credence is through the building of alliances. The ECC, for example, helped to motivate child care teachers and agencies to band together and through this grouping increased the power they had in the policymaking process.

Finally, if these counter narratives are to have continued presence and force in the field, then it is crucial that those of us working in early childhood document our efforts. Much of the work on early childhood policy is written from an academic or economic perspective. Research evidence is used to bolster economic arguments for the benefits of an early education. While we want policy attention on early childhood education, we also need to be able to show that policies cannot exist without taking into account the particularities of context and the multiple perspectives of the community. In this way, it might be possible to disrupt current policies that seek to limit the participation of parents, teachers, and others to impose a "one size fits all" approach to systemizing preschool. One example of this kind of documentation is Silin and Lippman's (2003), in which teachers, staff developers, and administrators working in an urban setting write about their experiences in a policy collaboration process.

In conclusion, collaboration is currently touted as a key component for successful early childhood education programs. However, if early childhood policy is to be responsive to the communities in which it is enacted, then collaboration must be redefined as a policy goal. Instead of bringing together communities in the pretense of eliciting their perspectives, efforts must be made to develop the social capital of marginalized groups and document local efforts to make change. While there is no utopian or "right way" to create preschool policy, by acknowledging the politics of the process, it may be possible to develop programs that meet the needs of those they serve.

NOTE

1. The Office for Child Care exists within the Office of City Outreach, a city department. One responsibility of this office is to offer credentialing for child care programs that operate within city limits.

REFERENCES

Arborville Department of Public Instruction (DPI) website. (2003, February) *Community approaches to serving four year old children in (this state)*. Retrieved from the web November 28, 2003, from http://www.dpi.state.(this state's abbreviation) .us/dpi/dlcl/bbfcsp/ec4yrpag.html. Address is confidential due to use of pseudonyms.

Arborville School District Website, (n.d.). Retrieved from the web November 28, 2003, from http://www.arborville.k12.(this state).us/parents.htm

Arborville Website, (n.d.). *Arborville: Built on the quality connection between great living and great business*. Retrieved from the web November 28, 2003, from http://www.cityof (arborville).com/econdev/2003fct.pdf.

Ball, S. J. (1994). *Education reform: A critical and post-structural approach*. Philadelphia: Open University Press.

Barnett, S. (1995). Long-term outcomes of early childhood programs on cognitive and school outcomes. *The Future of Children, 5*(3), 25–50.

Barnett, S. W., Robin, K. B., Hustedt, J. T., & Schulman, K. L. (2003). *The state of preschool. 2003 state preschool yearbook*. New Brunswick, New Jersey: Rutgers University, The National Institute for Early Education Research.

Board meeting packet, December 9, 2002, Arborville school district.

Bourdieu, P. (1977). *Outline of a theory of practice*. New York: Cambridge University Press.

Bourdieu, P. (1984). *Distinction: The social critque of the judgement of taste*. Cambridge: Harvard University Press.

Bourdieu, P., & Wacquant, L. (1992). *An invitation to reflexive sociology*. Chicago: University Press.

Bredekamp, S., Knuth, R. A., Kunesh, L. G., & Shulman, D. D. (1992). *What does research say about early childhood education?* Oakbrook: North Central Regional Educational Laboratory. Retrieved on June 8, 2003, from http://www.ncrel.org/sdrs/areas/stw_esys/Serly_ch.htm.

Erickson, D. (2003, March 21) (Arborville) school district delays plan of offering 4-year-old's kindergarten. Chronicle (pseudonym used for local paper). P. C1.

Foucault, M. (1980). In: C. Gordon, (Trans. and Ed.), *Power/knowledge. Select interviews and other writings by Michel Foucault, 1972–1977*. New York: Pantheon.

Foucault, M. (1984). *The Foucault reader*. (P. Rabinow, Ed.) New York: Pantheon Books.

Franklin, B. M., Popkewitz, T. S., & Bloch, M. N. (2003). *Educational partnerships and the state: The paradoxes of governing schools, children and families*. New York: Palgrave Macmillan.

Lubeck, S. (2001). *Early childhood education and care in cross – national perspective: Introduction*. Phi Delta Kappan, *83*(3), 213–215.

Reynolds, A. J., Wang, M. C., & Walberg, H. J. (Eds) (2003). *Early childhood programs for a new century*. Washington, DC: CWLA Press.

Rist, R. (1998). Influencing the policy process with qualitative research. In: N. Denzin & Y. Lincoln (Eds), *Collecting and interpreting qualitative materials*. London: Sage Publications.

Ryan, S., & Grieshaber, S. (2003). Early childhood in the spotlight: Critically appraising the current policy interest in educating young children. Paper presentation at the 11th Interdisciplinary Conference on Reconceptualizing Early Childhood Education, Tempe, AZ.

Silin, J. G., & Lippman, C. (2003). *Putting the children first: The changing face of Newark's public schools*. New York: Teachers College Press.

PART II:
DIVERSITY AND DIFFERENCE IN EARLY CHILDHOOD CLASSROOMS

(DE) CENTERING THE KINDERGARTEN PROTOTYPE IN THE CHILD-CENTERED CLASSROOM

Elizabeth Graue

ABSTRACT

On the basis of data from a project that examined the school experiences of children who were seen to have readiness risks, this chapter examines the child in the child-centered classroom and how this child shaped by our notions of development. Across the classrooms observed, the teachers seemed to teach to a kindergarten prototype, a generic child who had the social, physical, and academic maturity and did not have much pedagogical support. The data are then read through three conceptualizations of development (postmodern deconstruction, developmental realism, and cultural developmentalism). I argue that I use these conceptualizations almost simultaneously in my work and that a hybrid reading highlights the invisibility of individual children in child-centered classrooms.

A foundational idea in western early childhood practice is the notion of child-centered curriculum. According to this idea, our practice is linked to children – their needs, interests, and challenges. If our practice is child centered, it is more likely to be developmentally appropriate, because it reflects our understanding of developmental patterning and needs. Child centeredness and developmental practice are so closely linked that they are often interchangeable in discussions of teaching and learning. They are linked because discursively the field has positioned educators/caregivers/teachers in relation to children and their development, with expectations that pedagogy is responsive to or centered on the child. But who is the child in a child-centered classroom? And how is this child shaped by our notions of development? In this chapter, I explore these questions through a study of classroom practice. On the basis of data from a project that examined the school experiences of children who were seen to have readiness risks, I carefully analyzed classroom practice and its intended audience. I attempt to locate the child who is the center of the curriculum, contrasting approaches that fit broadly under the umbrella of child centeredness. Attempting to understand how the educational settings constructed the child as ready (or not), I analyze the instructional practices in a variety of early childhood settings.

In this analysis, I draw on the notion of a kindergarten prototype (Graue, Kroeger, & Brown, 2003). The construction and operation of the kindergarten prototype in the classrooms studied is made visible by drawing on postmodern perspectives such as deconstruction (Burman, 1994). Following Burman (1994), deconstruction is used as critique to "bring[ing] under scrutiny, the coherent moral–political themes that developmental psychology elaborates" (p. 1). In this case, it is the themes that are present in the classrooms studied that are brought under scrutiny. Deconstruction enables a reading of the historically created child that shapes developmental and social views, causing all practices in local and meta communities to converge in the production of a static, knowable, and unchanging version of the child. In this chapter, I respond to the following research questions, drawing on notions of developmental realism, cultural developmentalism, and the tool of deconstruction:

- Who is the focus in a child-centered classroom?
- How do teachers enact notions of development through their practice?

Asking the first question retains a developmental emphasis but at the same time it shifts the agenda from the developmental and taken-for-granted assumption that the child *is* the center of a child-centered classroom and that teachers enact responsive and child-centered curricula. It opens spaces for multiple readings of data that range from developmental to deconstructionist perspectives. Likewise, the second question enables multiple readings of teachers' daily practice, including if and how they enact a developmental curriculum. It also has the potential to make visible other day-to-day activities that are not evident when a developmental perspective is the sole frame of reference used.

RESEARCH METHODS

I designed this study to understand the experiences of children who are typically seen to have readiness risks. It focused on experiences of redshirts (children eligible for kindergarten who are spending an additional year in a preschool setting), agemates (the youngest children in the kindergarten cohort who attend school in the first year of eligibility), and retainees (children who are spending a second year in kindergarten). I examined the nature of the instruction to explore the links among notions of readiness and pedagogy and their enactment in practice.

I solicited parents who were delaying their child's kindergarten entrance through letters to local daycare centers, preschools, and pediatricians. From a pool of 20 parents I selected five to represent the typical gender breakdown of redshirts (predominantly boys), a range of care settings (family child care, center care), and geographic locations within a Midwestern metropolitan area. Each redshirt's future elementary school was identified and agemates and retainees were chosen. This school-focused approach came out with the assumption that meanings of readiness are socially negotiated in local communities (Graue, 1993).

The sample was primarily white and middle class, in line with folk wisdom and research that redshirting is a practice of the relatively affluent (Shepard, 1990; Shepard, Graue, & Catto, 1989; Zill, Loomis, & West, 1997). The retainees in the sample were less economically privileged. Within the sample of 14 children (see Table 1), we worked in eight distinct schools/centers, across two school districts, in public and parochial elementary schools, family day care, part-time nursery school, and full-time day care in a university setting.

Graduate research assistants[1] conducted two-hour observations in each educational setting across the span of the academic year (with an average of eight observations per child), watching the focal child, his/her interactions, and the nature of the educational activities. These observations were scheduled across the instructional day to portray the breadth of child experience. The researchers worked as participant observers who supervised small

Table 1. Project Participants.

Redshirt	Agemate	Retainee
Susan White female, 9/1/94 Home day care Jenny – home day care provider Joe – Computers	Cindy White female, 7/27/94 St. Thomas Elementary – Jane Babbs Rene – Pediatrician, Bob – Lawyer	Paula White female, 5/6/93 Frank Elementary (1st K attendance at St. Thomas) Lacy Newberry Lilly – unemployed printer Ken – dental repair technician
Jacob White male, 7/1/94 Oliver Heights Nursery School Andrea – stay home mom (library science) Carl – University Professor/scientist	Richard White male, 7/15/94 Oliver Heights Elementary – Valerie S Miriam – Stay home mom (computer design) Joe – University researcher	
Ford White male, 8/21/94 Oliver Heights Nursery School – Sarah Overton Amy – teacher Paul – Video Tape operator sports	Larry White male, 8/25/94 Elm Grove Elementary – Wendy Connor Jane – Part-time accounting Jason – Self-employed sales, advertising	Rusty White male, 8/25/93 Elm Grove Elementary – Amy Smith Linda – interior design Pat – Farming (?)
Michael White male, 8/6/94 Oliver Heights Nursery School – Rhonda Paula – Dentist Rod – Vice President, Sales, Marketing	Andy White male, 7/16/94 Elm Grove Elementary – Stephanie Walker Daria – Public relations, marketing Martin – Sales	Sean White male, 2/22/93 Elm Grove Elementary – Wendy Conner Leah Burchill – Lab technician
Nate White male, 8/22/94 University Day Care – Angel, Faye Linda – librarian Howard – educational software producer	Malcolm Biracial male, 4/8/94 Larkspur Elementary – Sena, Lucy Mena – administrative assistant	
	Alan White male, 3/25/94 Larkspur Elementary – Sari, Salli Lena – stay home mom (nursing/library science) John – Physician	

group activities and helped children with tasks. Ethnographic fieldnotes were generated for each visit (Emerson, Fretz, & Shaw, 1995) detailing the focal child's activities, the instructional environment, and the teachers/caregivers actions. In addition, parents, teachers, and children were interviewed about their conceptions of readiness and the transition to elementary school. These semistructured interviews took place at times that were convenient to participants, in homes and schools, and were audiotaped and transcribed for analysis.

This chapter is based on the observation and interview data and is supported by relatively traditional strategies of qualitative inquiry (Emerson et al., 1995). Codes were generated inferentially and deductively, applying theoretical notions to the data and constructing themes from within the data (Graue & Walsh, 1998). I read and re-read the interview transcripts and fieldnotes for themes within a community context and within readiness intervention. I worked to validate these themes by looking for supporting and disconfirming evidence. These themes were then read against the literature of early childhood practice to illuminate traces of developmental thought. I developed memos to illustrate conceptual themes and compared these themes with the fieldnote and interview evidence. I organized a narrative that represents the teaching practices, in which the participating children lived their lives. I present those themes in the next section.

THE ROLE OF INDIVIDUAL DEVELOPMENT

For those advocating extra-year interventions, time provides the ultimate adaptation to individual development. It allows a responsive match of context to child, particularly for those who are not developing typically.

> When elementary schools do not offer options that provide additional learning time, allowing late bloomers and late learners to spend an extra year in preschool can be a very positive alternative to sending them off to kindergarten and waiting to find out whether they will 'sink or swim.' An extra year to grow and learn in a supportive preschool environment can greatly decrease the odds that a child will flounder and need rescuing in the primary grades. (Grant, 1997, p. 7)

This approach makes sense given a view that development, readiness, and therefore educational decisions were inherently individual. While age-related patterns guided expectations and practice, individual expression of development was a concern that echoed through many conversations. Children, and therefore their experiences, were not one-size-fits-all:

I think what I've learned in watching him is that *readiness is very individual*... I guess it isn't a science really, but yet, for a parent watching a child, because I'd had the experience of having the older child and watching how I could tell, he wasn't quite ready for this. Then I was able to see those same things in a younger sibling and say, 'This particular child is not ready in these ways, so let's just play it safe.' (Andrea Waltersloan, Jacob's mother, Redshirt)

If children's development is expressed individually, what is a child-centered response? Do you construct curriculum around the needs of particular children or do you shift children to a curriculum that is deemed more in line with their needs? The approach taken rests on the meanings made of deviations from presumed norms of development and the degree to which teachers and parents can respond to the children in their care.

In the classrooms we observed, there was astonishing coherence in the strategies used in instruction. The instructional practices, the environments, materials, and evaluations enacted *the kindergarten prototype* (Graue et al., 2003). The kindergarten prototype is linked inherently to a preschool prototype. Teachers and caregivers of preschoolers, particularly children aged 4 years, are often keenly aware of the demands of kindergarten and use their perceptions of kindergarten to make judgments about the children with whom they work. As a focal point of instruction, the kindergarten prototype is constructed from a notion of the typical kindergartner, a child with the social, physical, and academic maturity that supports kindergarten pedagogy.

Teaching to a Presumed Norm

Addressing the kindergarten prototype, many classrooms used a general curriculum, in which activities were designed and provided with a generic child in mind, someone typically developing and without the need of much support by the teacher. Teachers designed multiple activities in thematic or skills-based frameworks, often through centers or whole group activities. Teachers were managers who set up materials and were engaged with children when there were conflicts or lack of progress. Limited direct interaction occurred between teachers and students that could be labeled as explicitly instructional. In these contexts teachers designed educational environments with which children interacted. It was through these interactions with materials and with each other that development was supported. In the following sections, I present examples of teaching, first in preKindergarten (preK) settings, and then in Kindergarten contexts, which illustrated the enactment of the kindergarten prototype in teaching.

Child-Initiated, Center-Based, but Passive Teacher Instruction

In almost all of the preschools we observed, teacher-distant, center-based teaching was the norm. For example, in Nate's day care classroom, there were several choice times with activities that addressed a theme. In November there were a number of activities related to owls, including reading books, singing songs, and doing art activities. During choice time, the teachers set out activities from which the children could choose. Teachers rarely interacted directly with children during this time unless to support material use, intervene in problem situations, or to respond to child requests.

> Nate and Ned moved to the table with the science project. The objective is to follow a recipe by mixing warm water, and a flour like substance to make "goop", a molding material. There are three trays containing a flour-like powder. The assistant pours warm water into Ned's tray. She tells the boys to push up their sleeves if they intend to make goop. In the distance Faye (the lead teacher) says, "Have a plan, know what you are going to do."
> 9:55
> The students begin to ask questions about the goop. They ask, "What kind of glue is it? Can we eat it?" Nate says that it is for playing with. He asks if he can stir and the teacher allows him to stir. He starts mixing it with his hands and notices that the consistency is not gooey or sticky. The assistant asked how many cups of water. Ned said two or three, and Nate said one. When the assistant handed the cup to Ned to try the experiment first, Nate said, as if speaking to himself, "I know I can have a turn by the end because I will get to play with it."
> Faye is monitoring Roger who kept drifting to the no zone area, the window. Finally she accommodates him by allowing him to look out the window. She lifts him a bit as he tries to support himself by pulling up on the window ledge. Joel comes to the science project table, but soon loses interest and goes to the window. Another student soon takes his place.
> Nate says that he has played with the science project before, and that his mixture "was just not right." Faye came over to help. They explained what they did. They said that it was supposed to be green, but they added hot water.
> Nate and Ned then moved to a table near a window in the back where two girls sit. There they find crayons, markers, and pictures of an owl to color. They started coloring immediately. They don't pay much attention to each other's work.

This example is fairly typical of the other preK contexts that were observed, where children made choices about what they were doing from a pre-specified set of activities. Teacher–child interaction was on an as-needed basis, with the need defined by student compliance with the potential choices or to support completion of tasks. The generality of instruction is related to norms of development and the assumption that children can best calibrate activity to need. Whether the focus was a specific activity or a set of centers, this general approach led to relatively generic knowledge of individual children. Because teachers did not interact with children on a systematic instructional basis, they had limited opportunities to gather specific developmental information. If children were not on the radar screen (working within the classroom parameters), the assumption was that they fitted within the classroom prototype.

Teaching Social Skills

A different approach could be seen in Jacob's preschool classroom. Jacob was a redshirt seen by adults as socially and emotionally immature. His engagement in dramatic play was labeled as self involved and uncooperative. In January, his teacher Sarah took the opportunity of a puppet play to help Jacob interact in ways that she values with other children in the class:

> There is a puppet theatre set up in dramatic play. The children are grabbing the puppet faces with other puppets. The play is active and louder than usual. The puppet theatre shakes on its foundation. Children are using the puppets in a fairly aggressive manner perhaps. The rowdy play knocks Ginny around. Sarah is coming closer to the theatre after watching if for a few minutes. She steps in to correct the aggressive play. Tyler, Zeke, Jacob and several others grab and pull each other.
>
> Jacob: It is raining butterflies, don't come over! I'll steal the phone! (Sing song voice, Jacob leaves as Sarah enters the area and comes back puppet on hand)
> Sarah: Fighting and hitting with puppets? I remind you–I say, "Jacob, we don't hit"
>
> Sarah conversationally tells the children she has never seen a puppet show with grabbing and hitting between the puppets. She asks the children if they've seen shows like that. Jacob and Tyler continue to discuss their drama while Sarah talks. Ginny was jostled in the drama, but is ok.
> Sarah: I will put on a puppet show for you. You have a seat. I can help....
>
> Sarah enters the dramatic area. She goes behind the screen kneeling. Children gather. Sarah asks for helpers. Jacob volunteers to help Sarah. He appears excited briefly then gets quiet. Sarah suggests to Jacob that he help by handing the puppets to her as she makes up the show. She comments that there is no script. Jacob gets quiet. He gathers the puppets all about him on the carpet. They are soft and his arms are spread wide about them.
> Sarah: Jacob ok, so help me by giving me the puppets. Well puppets are all over. Hitting and always...puppets are usually only behind a stage. [The bee puppet to the children in a high squeaky voice] Hi, what is your name? Brown bear is my name. And I am the busy busy buzzing bee. [Turns to Jacob and says gently] Jacob are you helping me or what? I can't put on the show unless I have the puppets.
>
> Jacob has slumped to the floor with his chest and body over all of the puppets. Sarah makes several requests to Jacob. He does not give her puppets, but remains on the floor covering the pile of soft puppets with his body.
> Sarah: Children I think we will have to make a change of plans. You can just play.

Karlie: No...
Tyler: We need Franklin...[Tyler runs off to get the Franklin puppet]
Sarah: Jacob looks like he is upset. Jake, what are you upset about? Let's find something else to do.
   At this moment Sarah gets out from behind the theatre. Jake lies over the puppets for a few more minutes and gets up. He has all of the puppets. Shortly Jake and the other children are in the theatre again. Their play is excited.
Jake: I can make tables and rockets without ah, ah, ah, no fighting...I need one more show.
Sarah: Jake?
Jake: My name is Beetle Hitter...
Sarah: Would you like to put on a show for us Jake? You have bubble bear...
Jake: No turtles! [in response to Tyler's introduction of the Franklin the turtle puppet] My name is Tug Fat. This is my son. I am going swimming. Dark green...I said no turtles!
Sarah: Why not? I said to work it out with your friends. Talk to Zeke and Ginny.
Jake: I said no turtles!

Sarah continues to coach the kids to talk to each other about the puppets and the show.

In this detailed example, Sarah is doing more than managing student interaction – she is modeling language tools and social skills to facilitate play. She actively enters the play situation, modeling the rules and strategies for play that are valued in this context. She mediates Jacob's experience by showing him how to play with the puppets in an "appropriate" way and succeeds in directing a story line that is less aggressive. Throughout the study year, Sarah worked with Jacob to scaffold his play with other children. Sarah actively entered turn taking games with Jacob, Zeke, and Ginny and she fostered Jacob's interest in puppetry. Sarah told Jacob when his aggressive growly voice or boisterous actions bothered other children, and she frequently described his successful play interactions with others. As he became more skilled in his invitations and interactions with other children, she dropped structured materials and verbal supports out of the play environment. While the content of Sarah's pedagogy could be critiqued, this type of teacher action was very rare in our observations. In other contexts it was more likely for teachers to reiterate rules and to sanction inappropriate behaviors rather than provide examples. The teaching of social skills in most of the settings seemed to be relegated to the mantra of "use your words."

Given the focus of social development in most early childhood settings, I found this lack of direct teacher involvement in its support baffling. What would cause such a gap between the discourse and practice? One idea is that the social development is not seen as teachable – it is instead part of the maturational aspect of the child that comes with indirect patterning and time. It is an extension of the notion of child-centeredness, making the child rather than the teacher the one who leverages development. It privileges child actions as real and true indicators of development and relegates the teacher to the role of manager from the periphery. But in a powerful inversion of the normative model, eligibility for participation is limited to those who already have the desired attributes. The social focus of mainstream readiness concerns (Graue, 1993) with its maturational dimensions, actually mitigates against teacher intervention in social development and marks the ready child as one who does not need support.

Whole Group Instruction

The coherence of the kindergarten prototype model extended to the practice in kindergarten classrooms. The following examples show an active teacher, but I challenge the reader to think carefully about exactly who the learner is. A classic example was seen in Cindy's half-day kindergarten experience in a Catholic elementary school. At the end of October, this kindergarten was focusing on shapes and on Halloween/fall activities.

> After an opening time in which children were given an overview of the day's activities, the children were sent to assigned tables to do a shapes test. They worked through two worksheets with 5 shape problems. Everyone did the worksheets at the same time, focusing on good listening and task completion.
> At 9:10 Mrs. Babbs tells the students when she calls a table's name, they can go get scissors to make shape books. She tells them they can go through the books with their parents and tell them about it.
> The blue crayon table is called. Cindy and her tablemates go to get their supplies. The room gets quiet as the kids cut. Mrs. Babbs tells the class, "That's why you don't have to put your name on the front, because you are cutting the pieces apart."
> Mrs. Babbs walks up and down in between the tables saying, "You might want to put your shapes in 3 piles, one for squares, circles, and one for triangles so you are ready to have me staple them together when you are finished."
> Cindy asks Mrs. Babbs about 2 pieces that she cut that aren't the same size. Mrs. Babbs says it's okay, they are close enough. Mrs. Babbs shows an example of a book of triangles that is finished. She staples it together and says, "I'll come around and check your books." She picks up a pile of orange books and instructs the students to work on those when they are finished. On the front cover she points out that it says, "Pumpkins by" and tells the students to sign their names underneath. She says she will give the students pumpkin stickers to decorate the covers of their books.

In this example, the teacher is a manager – she circulated around the room to help students finish the task rather than to deepen individual experience related to shapes. Each product was alike, which represents the core of this approach – all children do the same thing because developmentally, they should be more alike than different. The kindergarten prototype is extremely strong here. It sets the parameters of normal and feeds a system where children outside this prototype are seen as unready. Redshirting and retention are local practices that reinforce the prototype such that curricular differentiation is not needed. It is exacerbated in a half-day program that often focuses on the need to "get through" instruction – the limited time teachers have in a 2.5 h session promotes an efficient factory model of teaching to make sure that everyone gets the core.

Explicit Teaching through Centers

Richard's full day public kindergarten classroom was run on a modification of a Work Jobs model (Barrata-Lorton, 1972), in which children were required to complete specific skills-based activities, checked by the teacher, before moving on to the next activity. In January, the class was working on a snowman theme:

> Around the room children are working on many different projects with a variety of materials:
>
> - Snowmen materials and worksheets
> - Matching upper and lowercase mittens
> - Snowmen boots (unsure)
> - Geo boards and worksheet replications
> - My number book
> - A dice game with drawing the snowman and all his/her parts
> - Pattern game with cards/individual boards and shapes
> - Sorting game with snowmen similar and different
>
> Each worksheet contains a different type of cognitive task: sequence the events, match halves of pictures, circle rhyming words, etc. As children work, they check with their teacher, Mrs. Schwartz, who gives feedback and evaluates their progress.
> At the second table Mrs. Schwartz tells them how to arrange their shapes to complete the task. Children are to glue 18–20 shapes, triangles, and squares onto a game board. The object of the game is to try to get home by following directions on the game cards. Some children take a lot of time gluing shapes. Others are speedy.
> Children often appeal to Mrs. Schwartz with questions. However, they are expected to work independently most of the time. They often take up the teacher role, giving their classmates feedback. Some children are working on a series of snowmen that are similar but slightly varied – they are to sort them in as many ways as they can imagine. Donny

has grouped the snowmen at least three times, Mrs. Schwartz tells him there is one more way that he can sort them. He screws up his face.

Richard has finished all of the pages of the work. He stands and takes the stack to Mrs. Schwartz. She asks him to repeat the rhyming words to her. She checks his work and gives him directions to cut and make a book out of the individual sheets. He sits back down.

As the afternoon progresses, more and more children stand to have Mrs. Schwartz check their work.

In Richard's classroom, students were presented with a variety of tasks that support a particular set of skills – sorting, sequencing, problem solving, working independently. Students had choice of the order in which they completed these tasks, but they were nonetheless required to have a complete set by the end of a week, regardless of skill level. Mrs. Schwartz monitored student's progress by managing the flow of classroom activity, but also by being a checkpoint. The plus side of this system was that it provided for variability in development in its diversity, and Mrs. Schwartz knew moment-to-moment how students had completed tasks and worked to challenge those who needed an extra nudge. The downside of the system was that students spent much time waiting for a chance to have their work checked and there was always more work. In fact, several children suggested that they should be paid for all the work they did because there was so much.

The normative notion of the ready child served as a guide to instruction and as the standard for judging readiness. This prototype helped teachers think about what is typical for children of kindergarten age, supporting activities for a modal kindergartner. However, this tool was in many ways overextended, allowing teachers to think of generic children who represented the norm rather than children present in that classroom that very year. While recognition of the individual aspect of development was prevalent in teacher and parent discussions, it was rarely present in practice that involved adaptation or generation of activities.

The focus on a prototype set strong parameters for readiness defined by maturation and made difference a matter of deficit (see Burman, 1994). It enabled a global planning strategy in which two practices were prominent. The first had children doing approximately the same tasks at the same time with the same expected outcome. This homogeneity was supported by the idea that children of the same grade were more alike than different. The second strategy defined teachers as those who set the environment and then got out of the way. Teachers monitored student behavior within limited notions of child choice but rarely entered interactions (social, cognitive or physical) to scaffold learning beyond enforcing rules. In giving children time and space to make choices and to negotiate the social and intellectual terrain of the classroom, teachers often missed wonderful opportunities to teach, do powerful assessment of learning or to provide tools for children who might be struggling. This distance between teachers and children missed what might traditionally be seen as the heart of a child-centered curriculum – authentic interaction with children on their own terms. Authentic interaction requires being with children in their play, responding to their calls for support, and intervening responsively. This absence was particularly evident in supporting children's social development.

This discussion would be incomplete if I do not recognize that development can be conceptualized in diverse ways. In the following section, I explore how theories of development set up different readings of how children grow and learn.

Developmental Realists

The first view is focused on the appropriate links between child development knowledge and early childhood practice. From this realist perspective (Schwandt, 1997), *child development* is a concrete entity, identified through systematic inquiry of children, their contexts, and growth. This empirical knowledge of child development is seen as the most appropriate foundation for practice with young children. It is illustrated by Lilian Katz' (1996) definition:

> [W]hen we use the term child development we are invoking a set of concepts, principles, and facts that explain, describe, and account for the processes involved in *change* from immature to mature status and functioning. In other words, we are referring to a particular kind of change: change that is dynamic rather than linear. (p. 135)

This position is promoted by the National Association for the Education of Young Children, which has advocated the use of child development knowledge as a foundation for practice (Bredekamp, 1987; Bredekamp & Copple, 1997). It is also endorsed by scholars whose work has supported professional development for early educators (Katz, 1996). In addition, there is a growing literature that correlates use of developmentally appropriate practice (DAP) with student outcomes (Burts et al., 1992). From this strong developmental perspective, the issue is aligning practice with standards that reflect our knowledge about development.

Strong developmental models related to pedagogy focus on three types of knowledge: general knowledge about child development and learning within a particular age range, knowledge of individual children's strengths, interests, and needs, and knowledge of the child's social and cultural context (Bredekamp & Copple, 1997). The practices described here were focused primarily on typicality by age. (While attention to culture is part of this framework, it is questionable whether activities would be viewed as coming from or representing particular cultural norms.) Age-based expectations were strong, providing momentum and standards for activity. Adaptations for individuals were maturationist, with time being seen as the prime tool for children developing at a different rate. While it could be argued that the gift of time is the ultimate developmental adaptation, it is also plausible that this strategy shifts instructional responsibility away from the teacher, making her accountable only for finding a place for a child rather than making the classroom responsive. From a strong developmental perspective, the teacher-absent, age-focused practices that we observed are partial enactments of *DAP*. Missing is the dialogic function of teaching. It was reactive, rather than responsive:

> Development and learning are dynamic processes requiring that adults closely understand the continuum, observe children closely to match curriculum and teaching to children's emerging competencies, needs, and interests, and then help children move forward by targeting educational experiences to the edge of children's changing capacities so as to challenge but not frustrate them. (Bredekamp & Copple, 1997, p. 15)

Cultural Developmentalists

In this perspective, development is considered to be *constituted culturally*. Culture provides a context for development – opportunities for growth and experience that shape the resources that catalyze and interpret learning. From this interpretivist (Schwandt, 1997) perspective, the norms of development are formed by the norms of culture.

> Adults in a culture symbolically construct an ideal child, and this ideal child is shaped by the culture's goals for child development. However the nature of this ideal varies from culture to culture (Harkness & Super, 1996). Ethnic diversity therefore implies varying definitions of the ideal child. (Greenfield, Quiroz, & Raeff, 2000, p. 93)

When a child walks depends on when a child is allowed to and encouraged to walk within particular social and cultural activities. On the other hand, there is attention to the ways that the notion of development is itself culturally bound (New, 1994). In the United States, the construct of development has reflected norms that are white and middle class (Weber, 1984). Cross-cultural analyses of development have been critical to our understandings of "normal" development, showing it as located, shaped by historical, cultural, and social process (Heath, 1983; LeVine, 1989; Whiting & Edwards, 1988). For cultural developmentalists, development is plural, with appropriate practice defined culturally.

Cultural developmentalists focus on the socially constructed notion of the ready child, defined in terms of the kindergarten prototype. With the focus in early schooling of independence and individualism (Killen & Wainryb, 2000), the ideal child contained in the kindergarten prototype is one that is able to capitalize on opportunities set up in the early education context with little intervention by the teacher. Within this cultural script, children requiring much teacher mediation are lacking readiness and therefore are better suited to a younger set of developmental demands. This model locates problems of readiness within the child (again, a deficit model) and distances educators from actively supporting student learning. It constrains the cultural resources available to enhance development. The cultural developmentalist reading moves attention to the cultural spaces in which children grow and learn, but really is an "additive" approach, attaching the dimension of culture to a developmental perspective.

Postmodern Readings of Development

The third approach to development comes from a postmodern perspective (Schwandt, 1997), and questions the construct as a self-standing entity. For those who *deconstruct development* (Burman, 1994; Cannella, 1997), the notion of development is inextricably linked to modernist views of the world. This notion is described as a social practice that hides issues of power in the cloak of science:

> The investment in portraying development as progress works to deny our histories of the personal costs of "growing up." More than this, turning the complex disorder of individual development into orderly steps to maturity reflects explicit social interest in maintaining social control within and between social groups and nations. (Burman, 1994, p. 19)

Development has normative foundations that put some children and families at the center and others at the margins, is hierarchical in that children move from less to more developed, while also being supremely individualistic. The postmodern critique of development works explicitly to disengage children from a hegemonic model of practice, with the intention of opening new ways to see children and our relationships with them.

Postmodern critiques examine the degree to which the discourse of progress overtakes attention to individual children in the here and now, locating the problem of school readiness in the discursive construction of the child and early schooling. It takes on the tenor of child description but also the general use of developmental psychology to authorize practice. It shows how:

> Developmental psychology makes claims to be scientific. Its use of evolutionary assumptions to link the social to the biological provides a key cultural arena in which evolutionary and biologistic ideas are replayed and legitimised. Closely associated with its technologies and its guiding preoccupations has been its use to classify and stratify individuals, groups and populations so as to maintain class, gender and racial oppression. (Burman, 1994, p. 4)

In these particular instances, the dominating discourse of the prototypical kindergartner comes from notions of development as progress, which places value on maturity. Its classification systems authorize teacher action in ways that are scientifically (or professionally) legitimate, making critique of practice less likely.

DISCUSSION

Are these understandings an end point? I certainly hope not. In an applied field like early education, the *so-what* looms large. The next step question is epistemologically framed, a legacy of what it means to know and the role of inquiry. From a strong developmentalist position, we measure practice against standards that are characterized relative to empirically defined notions of development and enacted through conceptions of professionalism. A shared notion of what is good for kids helps us know what to do on Monday. A cultural perspective focuses on understanding practice in the context of particular cultural models, examining issues like cultural mismatches between home and school, or differences in cultural meaning systems that imply issues of equity. Aligning beliefs and practices or respecting variation guides practice in a cultural perspective. A deconstructive (Burman, 1994) reading highlights the discursive aspects of activity, taking a suspicious stance relative to any suggestions of more varied and inclusive forms of practice on the grounds that we are only substituting one discourse for another.

There is a common assumption that postmodernism is a dead end for practice and that there is no point in deconstruction unless it is accompanied by a reconstructive analysis (Cannella, 1997). When read through a deconstruction lens, the data presented in this chapter provide evidence of significant implications for practice. They challenge us to re-think daily classroom practices for children seen as readiness risks who are located in classrooms where curriculum practices are guided by developmental discourses. These "at risk" children become invisible in classrooms guided by developmental philosophies, and re-emerge through the use of deconstruction and the identification of the kindergarten prototype. Like the layering of tracks of music, not all things can be seen and heard using the track of developmental realism alone. The addition of a second track, a cultural perspective, provides further information, but not everything is discernible. However, a third track (deconstruction) makes audible and visible some of the silences, some of what is missing from only one or two tracks. For me, deconstruction enables a focus on history and the combination of developmental and cultural perspectives that draw attention to the silences of developmentalism.

I have found myself working from each of these perspectives over the course of my career and have only begun to recognize that I bring all of them to my practice. Bringing all these theoretical positions to my work simultaneously means that I am thinking about measures of development, meanings of development, and discourses of development all in one thought. I am not the only one working this hybrid identity, given our history as researchers.

What has been inescapable so far is some concept of development – clearly I am a very well socialized, early childhood educator. But I do not think of the concept of development developmentally or evolutionarily, with one conception seen as more mature, more complex, or at some higher level than the others. I focus on the simultaneity of these perspectives, in much the same way that Denzin and Lincoln note the coincident nature of the seven moments of qualitative research – they constitute each other mutually even when we try to think of them as separate (Denzin & Lincoln, 2000). Conceptions of development are relational and it is in the interpretive space between them that I find myself pondering what to make of these children's experiences.

What this recognition provides is a window for a different kind of implication, one that straddles boundaries and remakes itself in varied contexts. It forces me to think about the kinds of actions I pursue in response to empirical assertions. The action this project brings me to is to ask more questions, but questions that I hope prompt some kind of action. I wonder what it means to be child centered if the child at the center is a chimera? I am reminded of my son Sam, who is fond of telling me that the average is not a real number – it is something imaginary to help you see lots of other things. But in this case, the child that is the focus of the child-centered classroom actually obscures the view of the children in the room. Who is this modal child and how does s/he allow the teacher to remain disengaged from interaction? And how does this disengagement further reproduce the value of the modal child? How do we deal with very concrete reality of variability in development – whether it is in terms of behavior and norms, cultural meanings, or the discursive apparatus that leads discussion to ideas of variation or development? What does this variability mean in today's context of standards, accountability, and the rhetoric of "Leave no child behind"?

My hybrid reading, which says that focusing only on development, or culture or deconstruction, limits what we can know about the other perspectives, and is a form of postmodern practice. It recognizes the historical forces that shape conceptions of children; it acknowledges the cultural variation in ideas about development; and it illuminates the discursive functions of professional guidelines and parenting practice. But I am not forced to declare myself a citizen of one developmental enclave while denouncing another. I need all the tools I can muster to make sense of complex learning environments.

For me, the hybrid reading highlights the invisibility of individual children in the classrooms observed; and it shows how the teachers' lack of interaction robs them of opportunities that might finetune the links between child and activity, and cement relationships between child and teacher. Further, it contrasts the pervasively held kindergarten prototype with the locally held notions of appropriate practice to show their common foundations. In doing so, it provides an opportunity to re-establish interactions and relationships between teachers and children as the foundation for practice.

NOTES

1. I am grateful to Janice Kroeger, Dana Prager, and Ruth Latham for their fieldwork and to Janice Kroeger and Christopher Brown for their work on initial data analysis.

ACKNOWLEDGMENTS

I am grateful to the Spencer Foundation for its support of this project and to Sharon Ryan & Sue Grieshaber for their expert suggestions and support in writing this chapter.

REFERENCES

Barrata-Lorton, M. (1972). *Workjobs.* Menlo Park, CA: Addison-Wesley.

Bredekamp, S. (1987). *Developmentally appropriate practice in early childhood programs serving children from birth through age 8.* Washington, DC: National Association for the Education of Young Children.

Bredekamp, S., & Copple, C. (Eds) (1997). *Developmentally appropriate practice in early childhood program – Revised edition.* Washington, DC: National Association for the Education of Young Children.

Burman, E. (1994). *Deconstructing developmental psychology.* London: Routledge.

Burts, D. C., Hart, C. H., Charlesworth, R., Fleege, P. O., Mosely, J., & Thomasson, R. H. (1992). Observed activities and stress behaviors of children in developmentally appropriate and inappropriate kindergarten classrooms. *Early Childhood Research Quarterly,* 7(2), 297–318.

Cannella, G. S. (1997). *Deconstructing early childhood education: Social justice and revolution.* New York: Peter Lang.

Denzin, N., & Lincoln, Y. (Eds) (2000). *Handbook of qualitative research,* (2nd ed.). Thousand Oaks: Sage.

Emerson, R. M., Fretz, R. I., & Shaw, L. L. (1995). *Writing ethnographic fieldnotes.* Chicago: University of Chicago Press.

Grant, J. (1997). *Retention and its prevention. Making informed decisions about individual children.* Rosemont, NJ: Modern Learning Press.

Graue, M. E. (1993). *Ready for what? Constructing meanings of readiness for kindergarten.* Albany, NY: State University of New York Press.

Graue, M. E., Kroeger, J., & Brown, C. P. (2003). The gift of time: Enactments of developmental thought in early childhood practice. *Early Childhood Research & Practice,* 5(1).

Graue, M. E., & Walsh, D. J. (1998). *Studying children in context: Theories, methods, and ethics.* Thousand Oaks, CA: Sage Publications.

Greenfield, P. M., Quiroz, B., & Raeff, C. (2000). Cross-cultural conflict and harmony in the social construction of the child. *New Directions in Child and Adolescent Development,* 87, 93–108.

Harkness, S., & Super, C. M. (Eds) (1996). *Parents' cultural belief systems: Their origins, expressions, and consequences.* New York: Guilford.

Heath, S. B. (1983). *Ways with words: Language, life, and work in communities and classrooms.* Cambridge, MA: Cambridge University Press.

Katz, L. (1996). Child development knowledge and teacher preparation: Confronting assumptions. *Early Childhood Research Quarterly,* 11(2), 135–146.

Killen, M., & Wainryb, C. (2000). Independence and interdependence in diverse cultural contexts. *New Directions for Child and Adolescent Development,* 87, 5–21.

LeVine, R. A. (1989). Cultural environments in child development. *New Directions for Child Development,* 8, 71–86.

New, R. S. (1994). Culture, child development, and developmentally appropriate practices: Teachers as collaborative researchers. In: B. Mallory & R. S. New (Eds), *Diversity and developmentally appropriate practices* (pp. 65–83). New York: Teachers College Press.

Schwandt, T. (1997). *Qualitative inquiry. A dictionary of terms.* Thousand Oaks, CA: Sage.

Shepard, L. A. (1990). Readiness testing in local school districts: An analysis of backdoor policies. In: S. F. B. Malen (Ed.), *The politics of curriculum and testing: 1990 Yearbook of the Politics of Education Association* (pp. 159–179). New York: Falmer Press.

Shepard, L. A., Graue, M. E., & Catto, S. F. (1989). Delayed entry into kindergarten and escalation of academic demands. Paper presented at the American Education Research Association, San Francisco.

Weber, E. (1984). *Ideas influencing early childhood education: A theoretical analysis.* New York: Teachers College Press.

Whiting, B. B., & Edwards, C. P. (1988). *Children of different worlds: The formation of social behavior.* Cambridge, MA: Harvard University Press.

Zill, N., Loomis, L. S., & West, J. (1997). *The elementary school performance and adjustment of children who enter kindergarten late or repeat kindergarten: Findings from national surveys* (Statistical analysis report No. NCES 98-097). Washington, DC: U.S. Department of Education, Office of Educational Research and Improvement.

TEACHING NOTES

Felicity McArdle

ABSTRACT

This chapter works to provide a space beyond the predictable discourses of early childhood education in order to interrogate the social practices of teachers and children. What is presented in this chapter is not a collection of dispassionately observed facts but one person's reconstruction of some important language 'moments', in the lived experience of a few Year One children. Through the use of pastiche and collage as the medium for 'displaying' the data, this work of interrogation involves pulling apart the tried and true, established mechanisms for reading the classroom. The result is a much untidier picture of the lived experience of Year One children than the traditional educational discourses have allowed.

INTRODUCTION

Toby's mother told me that he came home the other day and he had had the best day OF HIS LIFE!

He went swimming AND rode to swimming IN A BUS!

(From my "teacher" point of view, I must add that I think this was the same day we did quite a lot of work on the letter 'S', explored the properties of the number 3, put some bean seeds in a jar to follow their growth, and discussed families, and the concept of family differences and similarities. Strange that Toby didn't mention any of these matters).

Teacher talk is sprinkled liberally with such anecdotes. In staff rooms, meetings, seminars, and conferences, teachers frequently engage in this swapping of stories, lending rich color and texture to their thoughts on education. While often amusing, and accompanied by shakes of the head or rolling of eyes, the tales mostly dramatize points of view, and parts of the knowledge acquired by every experienced teacher. Frequently, the stories are decontextualized, untheorized, with no accompanying analytical or academic utterance. This is not to say that the stories do not function as a reflection on practice. Indeed, reflection is often tacit, implicit rather than overt.

For instance, in choosing to recount that remark of Toby's to me, his mother makes a point without being explicit. Our shared amusement over his words, and my later sharing of the story with colleagues, are illustrative of the partiality of our own understandings and the ways we represent the understandings of others. Toby, of course, says a lot more things to his mother on any afternoon, but it is this story that gets repeated. The source of interest or amusement to his mother and, in turn to me, is the unspoken 'other' of school.

Much debate around early childhood settings has been centered on resolving the work/play binary that is central to the thinking of many educators as well as parents. Similarly, discussion in many curriculum areas includes the binary notion of process/product. There are other examples of binary thinking: teacher/student; story/data; theory/practice; classroom/real world and so on. They pervade the discourse of teachers and academics. There is a proliferation of understandings of the word discourse. For the purposes of this chapter, discourse is used in the sense of "practices that systematically form the objects of which they speak... discourses are not about objects: they constitute them and in...doing so, conceal their own invention..." (Foucault, 1980, p. 49).

Indeed, liberal humanism, which has been the dominant post-war discourse in early childhood education, is seen as being in direct opposition to "the old ways" of, for example, corporal punishment and a denial of "personal liberties". In recounting Toby's words, I make, in brackets, the comparison with the more visible categories of school learning (i.e., reading, science, and other 'formal' curriculum areas). There is a boundary between 'school learning' and what Toby learned, and it is this blurring of the boundary which is the source of interest. This story provides a useful illustration of the poststructural point that each side of the binary needs the other, to clarify properties and positionings. Indeed, ironic readings of school allow for spaces at these sites of 'border wars' where *both or all* (work *and* play; old *and* new; theory *and* practice; structure *and* freedom) are necessary and true (Haraway, 1991).

A "GROOVY" CLASSROOM

I began the school year with a missionary zeal. I was assigned to a class of 27 year one students...in Australia, this is the first year of formal schooling, and the children are generally aged 5–6 years. I designed the classroom and curriculum to reflect play-based, child-centered principles, and was determined to "put my theories into practice", and take early childhood principles into the more structured school environment. I congratulated myself on how well I was achieving this goal, but this is not a story of how successful my mission was.

My recent reflections on my professional work in the classroom have directed me to seeking out children's talk as discourse, by listening to the language, by scrutinizing spoken language as texts which speak the speaker. My classroom is never going to look the same. I have lost the earlier picture I had of myself as the "groovy" teacher in a "democratic" classroom, where the children were so lucky to be having all the wonderful experiences I was providing. Now I have another tale to tell. My reading of these texts now informs my practice to a much greater degree, and it is this reading which this chapter endeavors to make visible.

What is presented in this chapter is not the objective truth – a collection of dispassionately observed facts – but my reconstruction of some important language 'moments' in the lived experience of a few year one children. I am now aware of power relations, positionings, multiple texts in the setting, and the various agents acting on me, and the tyrannies that I also impose on others.

At the same time, the voice of a practical teacher asks: "But how would you get anything done in a classroom, if you're constantly concerned with these matters?" A short answer would be to revisit what is supposed to be "done" in the classroom, and the strategies employed in achieving these objectives.

For instance, many of the stories I have collected are about differences. Children notice it, they remark on it, they fear it, they correct it, they worry about it; they seem to be forever vigilant when it comes to difference and transgression. A teacher might conduct research on the anti-bias programs and equity principles, in order to "correct" the harmful effects of issues such as these in the classroom. It might also be useful for the teacher to ask some new questions, which might make a new space for thinking and speaking practice. Other possible readings of the same stories might look at evidence of alternate discursive practices operating within the same framework to further explore the evidence gathered. This awareness of the multiplicity of readings can be empowering to early childhood educators. For example:

- How do children learn about these "rules" and about not breaking them?
- What are they fearful of, and how is this taught?
- How does it become so internalized that we are no longer aware that it is something we have had to learn?
- Why is school the site of this, and when does difference/sameness become so important?

Just as the mantra of play is applied in much of the early childhood literature as a means of meaning making for children, teachers too can benefit from the introduction of some blasphemy (Haraway, 1991), some playful irreverence, and some questioning of the taken-for-grantedness of much that is held sacred in early childhood.

The downgrading of play has resulted in taboos and barriers limiting the richness of discourse, in order to control its most dangerous elements (Foucault, 1980). This study does focus on play, looking not only at children engaging in learning through play, but also at a theoretical reading of play, and its possibilities in the disruption of discourse. Early childhood educators have been "permitted" play as a learning device, but it is with the implication that this be confined to young children...moving on to the more academic tones for the "grown-up" learning. Plato's suspicion of play continues in educators today who assign "play" to "entertainment" or "fun"(Ulmer, 1985). Piaget recognized the part of play in learning, but relegated it to the readiness stage. Students then moved on, and when knowledge "progressed" to a higher plane, play was no longer needed.

Through play, children make meaning of their world (Weber, 1984, p. 45). Jokes can do the same for adults. Humor or playfulness is not generally considered the most suitable style with which to examine a topic which is deemed "serious", "significant" or "big". Yet Rowan Atkinson as Mr. Bean can make the same points about religion in a 10 min silent comedy sketch, as a 45 min investigative documentary which might present serious analytical terms ... how we are positioned by church texts, and uncomfortable pews. This is not to say that the one approach rates against the other. Rather, we are multiple, and can learn or acquire knowledge through various channels, depending on mood, predisposition, social conditions, or numerous influences.

TEACHER STORIES

Stories such as my "Toby" story are not usually subjected to detailed scrutiny in everyday contexts such as school staffrooms. This is not to say that teachers as listeners are not aware of the illuminatory elements contained in the story. It could be said that teachers, through this talk, are engaged in doing research or theory all the time. These stories are a means of generating more knowledge about children and what they are learning. They are a means of teasing out theories, questioning, finding meaning, making comparisons, sharing knowledge, investigating, wondering about what's happening. The fact that the ideas and concepts under discussion are not necessarily articulated in academic terms, does not mean that the teachers are not knowledgeable in the sense of being able to theorize their work.

In terms of scholastic research, however, the sharing of stories in this folkloric way is often understood to be crass anecdotalism, the opposite of hard data, rigorously theorized. Poststructuralists would view this notion of valid scholarship as founded on a binary formulation of tales *or* data. For many empiricists, anecdotal evidence is viewed as an oppositional category to, say, research findings of a more systematic, scientific or even serious classification. The very openness and partiality of stories renders them oppositional to more "valid" (academic?) evidence and language. Further, recounting children's words does not carry the authority that is presumed with adult opinions. And any blurring of these boundaries and disruption of categories creates panic, and resistance (Davies, 1994). The problem that remains is that, in converting these stories to a more "weighty" or authoritative form, the richness of the language is lost, and the voice is altered. The interpreter, without actually erasing or rewriting the text, excavates, and in the process, can alter the original (Sontag, 1990). We hear and see less, and much of the feeling is lost.

At the same time, it must be said, practical understanding is not an origin for knowledge in the sense of a foundation. It is not enough to say, for instance, that only practising teachers can know about children, and that it is this experience alone that is enough to provide a full picture of what happens at school. The risk of sliding into subjectivism and relativism, allowing for no other possibilities, is not to be ignored. What counts as an observation depends on current theory. In making this point Silverman (2001) emphasizes the importance of seeing data as a starting place for interpretation.

The "data" on which this chapter is built, are a collection of vignettes that focus on the school voices of children in their first year's encounter with formal schooling in Australia. I began to collect stories as I worked with my class of school beginners, attempting to turn a reflective gaze on what the children were learning, and how this learning occurred. The question of whose knowledge, for what purpose, is a crucial one for feminists (Caine & Pringle, 1995). New approaches to reading, especially the idea of *reading against the grain*, provide a variety of critical vantage points, in which to locate my research. Feminist's thought led to a broadening and questioning, looking for the range, diversity and complexity in the stories I was collecting. Although the analysis accompanying some of the stories is not strictly confined to issues of gender, race, or class, I place it in the context of the more general feminist project of arguing that social relations need to be viewed in terms of plurality and diversity rather than unity and consensus (Weiner, 1993).

Anyone who has ever visited a school even half an hour after the last child has gone cannot fail to realize that there are a lot of voices to be heard in a functioning school. The silence is eerie, the absent presence of the noise which filled the space such a short time ago — shouts of joy, tears over scraped knees, teachers asking, children answering, laughing, singing, cheering, whispering, running, jumping, yelling, chasing, falling, catching, squealing, yawning, hiding, dancing, stamping, tramping and colliding.

Now, if we turn a poststucturalist eye, or ear, to the activities here, we must add metaphorical voices to the cacophony (Belenky, Clinchy, Goldberger, & Tarule, 1986; Gilligan, 1982). The voices of theorists and educators, politicians and parent bodies, administrative bodies and even the physicalities of the setting itself (Preston & Symes, 1992), must all be included in this view, as well as the silences as absences of words and language.

Adults' words about educating children carry a lot more weight than children's. Yet, this adult/child binary thinking excludes a range of possibilities. To speak with the voice of a child carries cultural connotations of perhaps sweetness, innocence, naivety, amusement, being uninformed. While children's utterances are definitely heard at school, the discourse is not always made visible or legitimate.

Much has been written out of the "professional" voice...which could be described as the informed voice of educators, adults, talking to other educators, engaging in dialogue, dealing with knowledges about children. We listen to this voice and consider carefully the words, and add our own interpretations in the interests of improving our practice, and presumably, improving the lot of the children in our care.

There are multiple voices in this chapter. This inquiry is about listening to that voice I hear when Toby talks about himself and school. In the process of displaying children's language and discursive practices, I need to blur some of those boundaries that exclude some forms of discourse while allowing others. I do not wish to disguise the children's words in academic language, for the sake of lending weight to my opinions, or providing indicators of validity, if this is done at the expense of capturing the richness of their own expressions. Nor do I presume to have "gone native", nor found a window to the children's minds, nor experienced "school" as a child does. None of these notions are possible, and I do not attempt them. In Heidegger's (1974) terms I seek to provide a boundary, that is "...not that at which something stops, but, as the Greeks recognized, the boundary is that from which something begins its presencing" (quoted in Hebdige, 1988, p. 228). My voice tells my story, but I do not want to reduce the children's voices to objects for thinking about the subject. I want to leave them be as they are, radiant and self-showing, and perhaps open to possibilities for other interpretations by other listeners.

Multivocal ethnographic methods (Tobin, 1988) enable the collecting of a number of voices, which can display multiple ways of speaking. In my case, in this chapter, I speak with a number of different voices. My teacher's voice is heard alongside the children's in the anecdotes. I use another voice to sometimes make an aside (St. Pierre, 1997) as I recount a fairly typical teacher story. And there is a more formal voice, when I call on what Kirby (1996) refers to as the expert talk to add a layer of analysis to this chapter. Children use a voice with friends, a voice with parents, a voice with teachers, and so on.

Arguments over research paradigms are ongoing and, for many of us, passé. The production of evidence-based research is essential to supporting calls for change, developing new theories, and advocating and collaborating with policy-makers and other stakeholders. However, when research in education is restricted to the measurement of outcomes, test results, and purely quantitative empirical methods, many areas of educational concern can be excluded from closer contextual examination. Various facets of the classroom that could and should be explored cannot be expressed in positivist terms. For instance, how can we measure or come up with conclusive findings to explain the different atmosphere which exists in every classroom? Creating a few "categories" cannot hope to do this.

This chapter is a poststructural inquiry into the first year of schooling as a set of linguistic and social practices. I work to provide a space beyond the predictable discourses of early childhood education (in particular, liberal humanist) in order to interrogate the social practices of teachers and children. My analysis and reflection draws considerably on the works of Foucault (Foucault, 1980,1983,1985,1986), among others. Poststructuralist analysis recognizes the importance of agency as well as structures in the production of social practices. If a story is analyzed in terms of subjects, power, and situating devices, such a reading can highlight different perceptions of practices, or simply language, perhaps previously transparent or invisible. Such analysis is concerned with the effects of systems of language use in the production of social practices. By focusing on the complexity and diversity of language use, I present a fragmented picture but, as Jones (1993, p. 158) puts it, this can be a positive uncertainty, and a more acceptable explanation than a grand theory that has as many qualifications as exemplifiers.

The methods of collecting data that I used were diverse. However they were very close to strategies used by most early childhood teachers as part of the teaching process – that is, making written observations of what I consider significant experiences for individual children; keeping a journal; photographing; collecting samples of children's work (e.g., analysis of drawings); group conversations and individual conversations (Goodwin & Goodwin, 1996; Silverman, 2000). In subjecting these to poststructuralist analysis, I look for ways to understand what learning the children are engaged in by hearing their language and their "silences". My understanding as a researcher is informed by Foucauldian notions of power and powerlessness, regulating bodies and behavior (Rose, 1990), rules and the breaking of them, sameness and difference, learning and internalizing, ways we organize our desires (McWilliam, 2000), the forming of self.

The stories that make up this chapter are not presented in any cogent sequence according to timelines or some logical developmental pathway. Things did not happen systematically in my classroom. I did not always take advantage of every learning opportunity as it occurred. I offer some reflections and analysis, and sometimes just the stories, as I read them. Sometimes my reflections do not reveal anything spectacular, and sometimes they do, but the moment has passed. It is this atmosphere of complexity, randomness, and concurrent yet contradictory events and dramas, which situated me and the children, and to convey the context is as important as analyzing the content. The form that my writing takes as a whole piece is another context, leaving room for the reader to engage in a new reading, to negotiate their own audience response. Whilst this interplay presents many school voices, I attempt to refine the focus of my study to the children's voices that I hear, and making them audible to another audience. To make the children's voice powerful enough to demand serious consideration and attention, I sometimes underline the story with a feminist/poststructuralist reading, but the children's actual words are the starting point. However, by contextualizing them, and in the very process of choosing the stories to tell, I editorialize, and so distort the picture.

The use of collage appeals to me in my attempts to present a picture or story of my involvement with children beginning school. When you look at a collage, Berger (1985) notes, you can view each tiny little piece, but you are always aware of the whole work. Like a person's kitchen notice board, the placings and choices give context to the items. Whatever is placed nearby, can add to detract, contrast, highlight, submerge, overshadow other pieces. Indeed, the overall choices and placings give a picture of the composer as well. While the piece as a whole presents a picture, it is made up of more than one viewpoint. These can be looked at in any order - the viewer chooses to see.

So it is with my teaching, and the children in my classroom. In documenting some of the language of the children, and then subjecting this documentation to poststructural analysis, I looked for ways to understand some of the 'uneasy moments' (Luke & Gore, 1992) that occurred daily. As a researcher I remained engaged in the passionate and creative process of teaching. Thus my research remained dynamically engaged with my practice, reconstituting it as a praxis (Lather, 1986).

The children in my class talk about friends (having lots of them; not having any; playing with them; and so on). They also talk about being hurt, and they worry about things, with discomforting frequency. My intention here is not to generate another "Oh dear, isn't school awful for kids?" story either, because they, for the most part, say they like it. They like having so many friends to play with; they like doing "hard work"; they like the monkey bars (which incidentally have been removed from every playground, for reasons of health and safety). The case to be made about lost innocence and ruined childhood has been better made by others, like Postman (1983) in his work "The Disappearance of Childhood".

My interest was in exploring current understandings about the curriculum as a set of discursive practices which constructed difference...girls and boys, teacher and children, and any number of categories and "others". The classroom and the playground are sites where relationships of power are continually reproduced, in continual struggle and constantly shifting

(Walkerdine, 1981). The normalizing aspects of dominant discourse are visible in the interactions between very young children, and using the principle of discourse to show how power relationships and subjectivity are constituted, we can address some of the traditional concerns of early childhood educators from a new perspective.

The experiences of the children in my class were unique and non-linear, as can be said of any classroom and teacher and group of children. Rather than attempting to infer some commonality in the experience of induction of year ones, this uniqueness is insisted upon in the refusal of this work to generate 'findings'. This poststructural analysis is an attempt to display differences and how they are constituted through the social setting of school. It can provide a framework for thinking, which might assist other teachers in their ways of thinking and speaking practice, and their ways of seeing, hearing and speaking to the children with whom they work.

TELLING TALES

Peter Likes to Play with Dogs

A teacher from the middle school "borrowed" one of my year one students, to interview him as part of an In-service Course we were involved in (looking at Early Literacy). The teacher was relating some of Peter's answers, as part of his "findings" about children's language. He commented on how articulate Peter was, how confident and positive he was. As an illustration of this, he related how he had asked him what sort of things he liked to do, and he thought Peter said "Play with dolls." So he said "WHAT? DOLLS?" and Peter quickly corrected him and said "No. I said DOGS." and we all smiled about that.

What interests me as the child's teacher is that I suspect Peter *would* have said "dolls". In fact, he brings a collection of G.I. Joe dolls, and an assortment of dinosaurs, cars, and so on to school. He and his friends play with them quite a lot, making castles and roads and things, in rather involved dramatic play, which often extends into their lunch hour play. They have never seemed self-conscious about it, and I have certainly never considered it problematic. Thus Peter was very astute to pick up on his "mistake" so quickly, and, I suspect, did an excellent job at covering up or saving face in front of the other (male) teacher. I wondered how he "knew" to do that, and I wondered why I felt so defensive on his behalf. I hesitated to set the teacher straight, in case he thought less of Peter.

A feminist poststructuralist reading of this story could, at this point, search for the multiplicity of discourses that have informed it, and this could be extended to an infinite and unmanageable degree.

While everyone can hear lots of voices in schools, I feel I have an advantage in being able to hear the children's voice from a unique vantage point. As their classroom teacher, I have built up a large bank of "knowledge" about this little group of children. And this is assisted by the relationship which develops between us over time, as it is enacted in each classroom, according to the subjectivities of those involved.

In my classroom, I have attempted specifically to apply my interpretation of early childhood thinking in a primary classroom. Much of the day is spent in activity-based learning, which allows me many opportunities to listen and talk with the children, making frequent observations and informal assessments, as they also have many opportunities to listen and talk with each other. In a sense, I am "doing" research on them all the time and this is a unique opportunity to collect information which will add to the picture of the formation of identity.

When Peter corrected himself about the dolls, he grabbed the chance to retell his story so that he could place himself in the best position possible in his interaction with the male teacher, who had signaled that he could not accept that a boy liked playing with dolls. My silence supported this fiction of Peter's, and contributed to the perpetuation of the story. But my correcting the perception might have damaged Peter's status in the future with that teacher and the others who were listening. Peter would probably not thank me for using him as an example to further the cause of gender equity. An analysis of my reaction would also introduce the myriad of social factors influencing the teacher voice, the complexity of gender education as a lived experience for teacher and student.

Chrissie on Hurt

C: "I hate it when people bully me and all that."
Me: "How do they do that?"
C: "All they do is they chase you and all that...and they just tease you...and catch you and don't let you go...sometimes they trip me and I fall over, but I don't cry...I don't tell the teacher...I just hide where they can't find me."
Me: "Why don't you cry?"
C: "Because they might be just playing games."

C: "I'm drawing a boy bullying me. He's having fun bullying me...that's why he's smiling...people like bullying little kids, but little kids don't like it. You can dob on higher grades can't you?...they say you can't."
(In Australia, if somebody reports another's 'misdemeanour' to an adult or person of authority, they are said to be "dobbing". Being called a "dobber" is a derogatory term).

Although the neofeminist deconstruction of current regulatory practices generally point to the absence of physical coercion in the liberal humanist school culture (Weiner, 1993), fear of physical hurt and violence certainly seems ever present in the language of school beginners. The notion that the production of normalized behavior in children is manufactured and infused with power connotations is explored by Weiner (1993). This concept of power draws on Foucault, and does not rely on physical threat or overt ambition to dominate, but rather it produces the willing subject, according to Weiner (1993).

Listening to the language and interactions of school beginners leads me to question this notion of physical coercion having been replaced as the dominant discourse. I wonder if another reading could look at the possibility that the children learn so well and so early that difference in the playground can result in hurt and pain. Then, as Davies (1993) proposes, the lesson is so internalized that we are no longer conscious of the agent of coercion. We just "know" with our bodies. I am not so sure that the physical threat is absent.

When I asked the children in my group to tell me about what they did not like about school, every one of them mentioned being hurt. Notwithstanding the fact that I invited negativity in my question, and previous discussions we have had about such matters, it occurred to me to consider the implications if I were positioned in such a way that, every day as I walked out the door to go to work, I had the very real hope that I might not be hurt today.

This story might also be read as providing a glimpse of the hierarchy and organization in which children are engaged. Power is distributed according to relations of expertise, in this case, age and experience. Individuals are being located in chains of allegiance and dependency, empowering some to direct others and obliging others to comply (Rose, 1990). The "truths" seem to be inherently persuasive, and the anxieties are quite obvious. I have tried on a couple of occasions to question children further about this "dobbing rule", but no matter how hard I try to indicate that I have no motive but curiosity in finding how the rule gets "taught", I am met with blank silences. Either the children are genuinely unable to articulate how they have come to learn this truth, or we do not share a language in this realm. When I persisted in asking Chrissie about whose rule it is, eventually, after many uncomfortable and puzzled silences, she reluctantly came up with an answer: "Mr Capp's." (the principal...who else?)

Drawing on Foucault, Weiner (1993) connects the power and knowledge, so that they are used as a single configuration of ideas and practice, and that constitutes a discourse. In this case it is a discourse the children are engaged in, but one that adults do not share or generally access. The knowledge that is produced as truth is the knowledge that is linked to the system of power which produces and sustains it.

Monique

Monique..."I don't know how to be good."

In desperation, the teacher next to me was appealing to one of her "recalcitrants", when Monique sadly admitted that she did not have the necessary knowledge. Anthropologists and historians recognize that different cultures and different historical times specify human capacities differently and individualize humans in ways foreign to our own. The notion of free, rational conscious choosing and an autonomous self is a creation of western capitalist democracies (Jenks, 1996). The popular behavior management technique which aim to have children considering the consequences of their actions must work on some presumption that children have the ability and knowledge to choose the "good" option.

The new sociology, as Wexler (1990) proposes, must include an awareness of the deeply socio-political concrete character of knowledge, science and education. Using this framework, Wexler says it must then be asked what is it that implies public social practice. In a semiotic even more than an industrial society, knowledge is power.

Stewart

February (close to the start of the school year in Australia)
I was pinning some drawings up on the wall today.
About three kids were talking to me all at once.
So, I took a deep breath, and said something like:
"If you just wait a minute Adam, I'll answer David first, and then I'll help you, but I can't do everything at once, can I?"
I made a special effort to use pleasant tones, and not sound short, as this was very early in the year, and I know they are still feeling that everything is strange.
But straight away, Stewart, who must also have been waiting for a look in, said:
"Yes, hmm, do you sometimes get tired of working here?"

While I was taken aback by Stewart's sensitivity, and how immediately he felt "a something" going on, I was also reminded of Walkerdine's (1981) point about the teacher's training making her powerless. Stewart's ability to spontaneously express his reading of the situation was something I wanted to see myself as encouraging, since this was part of my training. This training would not permit me to "stifle" his self-expression, either by insisting that he be quiet, or even by showing that I was tired, frustrated, or finding it difficult to meet all the children's demands of me.

At the same time, this now added to my tasks, since I had to attempt to alleviate that anxiety he was so clearly communicating to me. Soon, if Stewart learns that such utterances are "bad manners" or that he "needs permission" to speak, he will no longer make such observations. For a lot of time in these first years of schooling, and for a range of reasons informed by their varying beliefs, teachers are involved in what Davies (1993) terms the mind and body bending exercise of bringing the children into line with what they take to be the real world. This will make the teacher's job more manageable, since the child will become more controllable, when tied to the liberal humanist rules of consistency and predictability (Walkerdine & Lucey, 1989).

One way to "make things more manageable" is to make the children more "disciplined". And this means the spontaneous expressions and insights disappear...voices are silenced. If Stewart had learned that saying "the wrong thing at the wrong time" brings some sort of trouble, I would not have heard his concern. A poststructuralist reading of this story illustrates not only the constitutive force of the discursive practices in the schoolroom, but at the same time recognizes the subject as capable of having agency in relation to those practices (Davies, 1993).

To "learn school", subjects are provided with positions, and they see their world from the vantage point of that position, and in terms of the particular story lines and concepts relevant within the discursive practices of school. Agency or choice arises because there are many and contradictory discursive practices in which the subject engages (Davies, 1993). Stewart's mother encourages his spontaneity, his "rights" to express himself and to have an attentive hearing. I use a whole language approach to learning in my classroom, so it would seem most contradictory to me to insist that children raise their hands, or seek some form of permission before they speak. My progressive, child-centered training also prevents me from dictating to children (overtly), what they should and should not say. We have both taken up agentic subject positions within the discourses, having positioned ourselves or been positioned by the various discourses of school.

Maxine's Proposal

Maxine always sidles up to me as everyone is going out to lunch or something, slips her hand in mine, and says "I love you Ms McArdle!" to which I always reply that I love her too. One day after we'd professed our love for each other, she said "Will you marry me?" So I "accepted", and she was delighted, and rushed off to tell the others.

Peter reacted immediately, laughing and looking accusingly at me, and declared "You can't do that!" Maxine and I looked at each other, wondering what to do next. So I merely explained that Maxine had asked me and I had said Yes, and anyway, why couldn't we? Peter quickly replied: "You can't do that. What about the babies?" I looked at Maxine, and she said: "Alright, we'll have to have a father, but we'll have two mothers."

Maxine is engaged in fluid movement between the two existing genders (Davies, 1993), but Peter's subjectivity is constructed and maintained around, or in relation to, that discursively produced difference (Kristeva, 1986; Moi, 1985; Weedon, 1987). For Peter, maleness and femaleness are taken as the unproblematic base on which masculinities and femininities are constructed, whereas Maxine has no problem with being inconsistent or contradictory in moving between sex/gender roles.

Peter has to immediately apply some category maintenance work, which Davies (1993) also observes to occur wherever any individual is seen to be misinterpreting. In playing with the story-line myself, I hope to give the children freedom to innovate with or reject the dominant interpretations. That is to say, by positioning myself, not as the ultimate authority and holder of knowledge, the children can take up alternative positions which are not centered on coming up with the answer I want to hear. If, through play, we can create a new story line for Maxine which is independent of sex/gender roles, then this can be empowering to all the children, allowing for diversity and variations, reducing the tyranny of "normalness".

Play, drama, and humor can be powerful tools in disrupting discourses, making inconsistencies obvious, underlining the ridiculous, questioning why something is accepted unquestioningly, allowing new explanations and possibilities, creating innovative solutions to serious matters in a non-threatening way. Social comment and disruption of the dominant discourse can be effectively addressed through play and humor, as many writers and performers have always known, from court jesters to the cast of Monty Python. Such performers are engaged in presenting an examination of the current "commonsense" relation between self, language and society, replacing this with a model that encompasses the constitutive force of language (Davies, 1993).

Jennifer/on what School should be Like

I asked Jennifer to draw me a picture of herself when she's feeling happy at school. She described what she was doing as she drew:
"Sitting at a desk. That's what I really want to do. You could turn them around, and get some more desks...and we could all sit at our own desk...and we could write our name underneath it. This is the blackboard (with 6's on it) and T's. Now...7's. And you could give us sums to do."

Throughout this year, I have observed Jennifer as extremely imaginative, expressive, creative, uninhibited, adventurous. Her choice of activity on any day would be dramatic play, without a doubt.

Since Jennifer's penchant for fantasy and dramatic play is immediately obvious to all, her views on school could easily be explained as another of her "pretend games", perhaps informed by the view of school presented on television, say "The Simpsons." Or perhaps her older sister, or other family or friends discuss their pictures of school, and this is what she is relating. In that case, I can feel comfortable in dismissing her remarks, since I can believe that, armed with that extra knowledge I have of Jennifer because I am her teacher, I know better than she does, what sort of school experience is best suited to her needs. I can "see" that if Jessica was suddenly placed in such a classroom situation, she would soon realize how much she enjoys learning through play, and that she is only describing the other as desirable because she doesn't know any better.

A deconstruction of this story however looks for the power and the subjectivities constructed. I am opposing the tyranny of desks and chairs in rows, so as to free the children from restrictions such a classroom text imposes. So that the children do not feel regimented into a confined area with clear lines of demarcation, and very little room for movement around the space, I have removed most of the chairs, and they are not considered exclusive to anyone in particular. My hope is that a reading of the text of my classroom would convey ideas of free movement, more choices, less teacher direction. However, in reaction to what I view as problematic in a more traditional classroom, I replace this with my own tyranny, and Jennifer has as little say in my running of the classroom as she would have in a more traditional room.

After this, I asked a friend's 12 year old daughter, Shannon, what she thought about school, and her immediate and only response was: "I like to sit on chairs...I don't like to sit on the floor." Once again, subjects see themselves constituted within the discourse from the vantage point of their particular position, and the particular images and metaphors that constitute that position (Davies, 1993). To me, the idea of sitting on the floor/carpet has never seemed problematic, as I have always viewed it as something even liberating, since it has connotations for me of informality and casual style. Shannon's remark makes visible another position, and another absence of choice.

The Grey Shirt

> Peter hates school on the days he has to wear the grey shirt (synthetic, buttons down the front, not soft material). On sports days (Thursdays) when he can wear the white cotton T-shirt, well that's OK.

I have never heard anyone else mention this problem of the grey shirt, but Peter's Mum told me about the issue, and Peter often refers to the days by whether it's a grey shirt day or the other. Foucault's interest in such non-discursive practices, points out that, even though the discourse is not articulated as such, nevertheless they constitute material processes that concretely mark human bodies, while enmeshed with discourses (Gunew, 1990). The practice of strictly enforcing uniform policies, down to the different days each variation is to be worn, results in the production of docile, observable, or resistant bodies, groups, populations (Gunew,1990, p. 14). Difference and non-conformity is rendered conspicuous and difficult, until it is eventually beyond consideration. Corporate control over the school population is established, according to Preston and Symes (1992, p. 188), through such matters as clothes and the actual movement around the schools, which are all subject to strict regulation and control.

Toby Crying

> March
>   I returned from the staffroom where I'd had my lunch to find Toby in absolute distress ... sobbing uncontrollably, taking great gasps of air, seemingly severely traumatized. The teacher "on duty" there had him sitting beside her and was trying to talk with him about what the matter was, as she had just come across him in that state, and couldn't find out what was bothering him.
>   This was such a surprise to me as he is such a cheerful little boy, who loves to play to the crowd, and do little performances for us. His extreme distress made me momentarily fearful that he had been severely bullied, abused, or something. I looked around for any guilty looking parties or someone ready to shed some light. But there was nothing of the

sort - no clues. I could tell it was not just a matter of having hurt himself, or that he'd been hurt by someone–the most commonplace upsets!

Anyway, he was beside himself, gasping for air, and incapable of speaking. So I put him on my knee and just hugged him and waited till he calmed down. This took a good few minutes, and then he would go to tell me and start up crying again. Eventually we got down to it. "MY PANTS ARE WET!" (Hmmmm! Great idea to put him on my knee, as I now notice that damp feeling on my lap!) Apparently he had been playing a game and was just caught short.

A critical reading of this story might look at, amongst other things, how tenuous is the children's hold on things at school, and how scary everything is, how much they struggle for survival and for their sense of dignity, how much they must feel at the mercy of the catastrophes that can befall them. Toby's distress could be attributed to a feeling of humiliation and being totally overpowered by the absolute control others have over all his actions and even his most basic needs, all the power being perceived as residing in the institution and the adults who are in charge.

Poststructuralist analysis can provide another reading of Toby's experience, understanding his anxiety, at least in part, as a product of the forces he applies to himself. As Toby's teacher, I have some access to and information about his parents, and I have good reason to believe that they are loving and supportive parents, who care about his well being. It would be highly unlikely that he had ever been severely punished by them for such an "accident". Equally, progressivist and humanist ideas about teaching prevail in these times. One enduring idea which persists in early childhood classrooms can be traced back to John Dewey's (1938) ideas on the progressive classroom. While his original ideas placed emphasis on participative democracy and responsible citizenship, the idea of a progressive classroom today has come to be interpreted as a room full of busy children, learning through play and discovery, and engaged in hands-on experiences. The teacher is even reluctant to use the word "teach" in relation to the work in the classroom, preferring to speak of guiding, facilitating, caring and nurturing (McArdle, 2003). With this picture that Toby has already begun to build up of me, and the other teachers he has encountered, it would seem unlikely that he would have reason to fear any severe sort of punishment from anyone over this incident. Why then does he become so seemingly disproportionately distressed?

Just as citizens who live in liberal democracies are no longer hanged, children in our schools are no longer beaten, or punished for such an "offence" as Toby's. There were no other children or adults aware of what had happened, so he was not being teased or controlled by his peers. He has positioned himself as controller. As Rose (1990, p. 10) explains, an expertise of subjectivity has become fundamental to our ways of being governed and of governing ourselves.

Everything Toby is learning about school, from the physical layout and the routines, to the hierarchy of age and experience, is teaching him the importance and desirability of "fitting in", being normal, being an ideal sort of person. The government of the soul, according to Rose (1990, p. 131), depends on our recognition of ourselves as potentially certain sorts of persons, the unease generated by a normative judgment of what we are and what we could become, and the incitement offered to overcome this discrepancy by following the advice of the experts in the management of the self. The experts in Toby's case could include his parents, other children with more "experience", teachers, television images, literature, and perhaps countless other agencies, all combining to present a picture of the ideal person and the behaviors which are the manifestations of such ideals.

This effect is achieved, not through the threat of violence or constraint, but rather by way of the persuasion inherent in its truths, the anxieties stimulated by its norms, and the attraction of the images of life and self, it offers us (Rose, 1990, p. 10). While Toby's distress serves to direct my attention to this area of concern, it can also point out the silences, both in others, and in Toby, over other aspects of his forming of self. Until this day, he had seemed to me to have every confidence in himself, happily making friends, enjoying school activities, and even volunteering to do performances for us on his toy piano. With all these indicators of a healthy self esteem, I was at a loss to explain his extreme distress over something I felt did not warrant such a reaction. But then my lived experiences have helped to form my opinion of what constitutes normal behavior, and these standards can and do form the basis of what I consider to be areas of concern, and degrees of extremity in behavior indicators.

Margaret's Spelling

Margaret was relating what had happened on "Neighbours" the previous night:
"...and so...Well, just before that, Mark and his girlfriend were...you know...K-O-N-E-Y."
Me: "Sorry, Margaret...what was Mark doing?"
Margaret smirks, and rolls her eyes, and nods knowingly:
"You know...K-O-N-Y.."
Me: "Oh...do you mean kissing ?"
Margaret: "YES!" and everyone nods knowingly.

Adults wishing to exclude listening children from the conversation will often spell out the key words, since young children can not spell. But Margaret demonstrates here that the lack of spelling skills does not necessarily mean absence of knowledge. She has worked out that whenever the adults around her want to talk about kissing and such matters, they spell rather than come out with the words.

Margaret refuses to be positioned as a nonentity at the best of times, and spelling is certainly not going to be enough to keep her out of things! Language might be all we have, as Davies (1993) states, but there is nonverbal or para-language which children also understand to a great degree of sophistication, even if they are not obviously participating. The other concern that this story might serve to highlight is the very early connotations Margaret is constructing around the language of sex. Knowing her parents, I feel sure that this is far from their ideal introduction to sex education, as they are both abreast with all the current literature on child-rearing and related issues, both being social workers. And yet, Margaret is clearly of the opinion that sex is not part of the "normal" discourse of school or home.

Kids Hurting each other

　　*I won't be your friend anymore.
　　*You can't come to my birthday.
　　*He kicked me...because I wouldn't play with him.
　　*She hit me in the back...because I sat down in front of her.
　　*He whacked me...because he couldn't see.
　　*Me: "David, look here, Sam is so upset...He says you don't like him. But I'm sure that's not true..."
　　David: "Yes, it IS true! I don't like him!"

At this very early stage of their formal schooling, all children have not yet learned that language of psychology that Rose (1990) refers to. When they inflict physical pain on each other, it appears shocking behavior in schools and is dealt with immediately. When this power is not available to them, they find power in language. They inflict pain on each other through words. Still this is not acceptable (to adults) at school, so again the children must develop new means of empowerment. Teachers and other adults find such blatantly hurtful comments ("I don't like you!") problematic, and set about eliminating such language from the children's use. Children are urged to "consider other people's feelings"; or "think how you would feel if someone said that to you". Eventually the children are left with little choice other than to acquiesce, at least when around teachers. Children struggle for quite a long time to learn the liberal humanist concept of the person as fixed and unitary, since this does not accurately capture their experience, which is of multiple, diverse and contradictory ways of being (Davies, 1994).

These liberal humanist rules of predictability and consistency make people more controllable (Walkerdine & Lucey, 1989). The story of David and Sam is a case in point. Having to constantly deal with the arbitration of disputes requires patience and energy which cannot always be summoned, and one's personal resources can at times be spread quite thinly. So sharing the discourse of liberal humanism means that the children are left with little room for explanation or negotiation, since basic premises are simply learned as common sense, and therefore undeniable. Any deviant behavior then is problematic, and must be corrected. To articulate that experience of diversity as normal and acceptable would be quite empowering (Davies, 1993), and saving them from the awful task of trying to render rational and consistent which is not so. The children are positioned as wrong; the discourse is not questioned, nor is the societal standard demanded here. The constitutive force of language is not part of the model of teaching in this situation.

Cubbies/Outdoor play

> Jim: I'm the genie and this is my magic surfing carpet ride.
> Brad: I'm a pirate, and so is Peter. Are you a pirate, Jennifer? Yes! Jennifer's a pirate too, and so is Jade. This is our place here. Peter, I sleep in here...oh...yes, you sleep in here too. Peter and I...we sleep in here. Jennifer, you and Jade...you sleep in that one. Hello...right...we're going to sleep now...Goodnight.
> Jim: Peter...what is your wish?
> Peter: What?...oh yeah...um...I wish for an eyeball...this one here,...where my patch is.

There is a small area outside our classroom where the children can play cubbies whenever we are having "activity sessions". The play that develops in this space is unique. It is often something like a pirate game, or castles, or houses...and involves visiting the different spaces which are allotted to specific inhabitants. This is the first thing that gets organized in the play – which space belongs to which occupant.

This outside play is more active than any inside activity, and often becomes quite boisterous. At the same time there is usually much evidence of all the "cooperative skills" i.e., negotiating roles, turn-taking, collaborative work, group dynamics, shared constructions, and so on.

This outside "cubby" play is not the same as the play children engage in at the designated "play times" – little lunch and big lunch. The children have made some clear distinction, not only between outside and inside activities, but also between outside cubby play, and outside "playground" play. We have had no discussion about this directly, although the noise concerns have meant that I have frequently asked them to "keep the noise down".

The "problem" of noise dictates a lot in schools. In allowing the children to engage in noisy play during the "work" times of the day, the teacher has to consider the disturbance to other classes around – namely, I suspect, that the other children will hear the "fun", and "not be able to concentrate on their hard work".

Here again the complexities of the situation influence my actions. I do not wish to invite conflict or criticism from other staff members or parents, and my experience leads me to pre-empt this. The idea of children having "too much fun" is "all very well, but are they actually learning anything??" While I am very much engaged in disrupting that work and play binary, to be continually justifying the point can become exhausting, and sometimes detrimental to the eventual outcome. The moral panic about disruption of boundaries (Davies, 1994) often results in a return to the other, since it is so often easily articulated, and can sound so much more reasonable.

To disrupt or break open binary thought requires an energy and purpose which is often difficult to summon with confidence, especially if localized and particular discursive practices strongly oppose such disruption. This makes a strong case for practice which is confidently informed by "sound" theory, thereby making it possible to articulate the other, making it visible, and so able to be considered.

In any case, the children seem to have decided on some sort of distinction, and the two styles of play are quite distinct.

Stewart/Arts Council

March...8 weeks at school

A group of Arts theatre performers came to school today and their show was based on a Medieval theme, with musical instruments, and costumes, and the language of such dramatic presentations for schools. My class went to their first performance of the day, in the school hall, with about 200 other children from various year levels.

This in itself was a fairly daunting experience for them so early in the school year, and many of them seemed to find the mass of children overwhelming. The performers didn't seem all that comfortable, at times. I suspect that the range of ages in their audience made things a bit difficult. Anyway, they performed a mixture of story telling and

Teaching Notes 81

instructional material about timelines, history, music, etc. I found it a bit confusing, but the year ones were spellbound, or perhaps, awestruck.

So, at the end, they invited questions from the audience. This is always a pretty risky business with little kids, because they haven't yet grasped the conventions of questioning. Well, Stewart had a lesson in them today!

Since the play was about medieval times, even though I hadn't discussed this with them at all previously, Stewart's question (???) was:

"I have the Lego Knights."

I thought this was a great connection he made, since no-one had mentioned knights, though they were in that time. The actors were really thrown by his "unconventional question" and merely nodded, mumbled or grunted something unintelligible, and then waved dismissively over his head, inviting a question from an older child...they didn't even comment on what he had said! Just like he hadn't said anything! I felt it was so cruel, and he just ducked his head, and made no further mention of his idea.

A critical theorist can read in this story an illustration of the point made by Cleave, Jowett and Bate (1982) in their study of school beginnings, about the effects of mass events on small children, and how this contributes to their forming of self concept. Stewart speaks up with confidence and self-assurance, only to be rendered small and insignificant, in fact, almost invisible.

This is at the same time a story about silences. Stewart will learn quickly that when you are invited to ask questions, it is not a curiosity that is being encouraged, but rather you are expected to follow certain conventions in what you ask. Indeed, in similar circumstances in a classroom, you are really invited to second guess what the teacher wants to be asked so that certain knowledge can be delivered. Those who anticipate correctly are swiftly rewarded, be it with smiles, a tone of voice, time and attention, or some distinct signal of approval.

The large massing of the children also silences. The restriction of bodies, the noise and the sea of faces all silence the voice of school beginners, leaving them no choice but to join in the "roar" before the performance begins, and then to be silenced by the drama and the anticipation at the appearance of the actors. At question time, the actors maintain this silence with the brusqueness of their speech, and by the tone they adopt when answering – a sort of no nonsense message, with no time for "shilly shallying". This rush and bustle is a technique often used as a means of control or coercion, carrying people along with the momentum.

And children who ask "suitable" questions are rewarded with an animated answer, and even verbal approval of their question.

Stewart read himself into the text, but there was no room for his reading in what the actors considered the text. Part of Stewart's lesson then is that texts have intrinsic meanings and you must seek them out to be correct. He is seeing text differently because he is seeing detail differently. As Davies (1994) proposes, children should be encouraged to do this, not to learn that there is one correct reading, and all others are incorrect.

Another contributing factor to the silencing is that Stewart, unlike some other children in my group, has a very strong sense that adults are right and rational and consistent. It would not have been an option to him to read that incident as rudeness or ignorance on the part of the actors. Instead, he physically ducked his head and avoided eye contact with anyone for some time, until the incident had faded and the impetus of surrounding events carried him along. My first reflection was that the actors had been cruel and dismissive, and I wondered how many times I unknowingly do the same thing in the classroom.

In addition, the complexity of deconstruction reveals subjectivity and positioning. On reflection, I have realized that had a similar incident occurred, say in another classroom, another massing of children, but with other teachers, I would not have remained silent myself. I am confident that I would have interjected on Stewart's behalf, and detailed his point, relating it to the "lesson". But in this case, I positioned myself in a silent, powerless position, giving the actors all power and control. To stand up and speak out in such a situation would have been frightening to me, and possibly an affront to the actors.

The boundary between performer and audience is clearly marked, and enormous courage is required to blur this boundary. Stewart just was not aware of all these rules. So he was actually positioned with more power than I could muster. While Stewart is operating on the premise that adults are rational and right, a deconstruction of this scenario can show him the multiplicity of positions which are available to adults, not all of them powerful in a pedagogical situation.

Michael/Having Fun

> Michael was making life difficult for the student teacher, taking no notice of her instructions, and generally refusing to cooperate. I had forgotten that he could be like that...(I must have applied some behavior management techniques with some success early in the year!) I took him aside, put my arm around him, and had a "man to man" chat:
> "Michael, old pal...why are you acting like this?"
> and he very confidently explained to me:
> "Because I'm having fun!"

"But, you don't usually act like this," I reasoned with him.
And he answered me quite swiftly:
"Yes, and I'm not usually having fun!!"

He seemed, more than the others, not to have cottoned on to the fact that even though I was supposedly handing my authority over to the student teacher, my rules still applied – well, at least if I was materially present. I would in fact give some little nonverbal signals to "miscreants" (?) every now and then. But I think Michael was having none of such hypocrisy – either she was in charge, as I said, or I would have to be a bit more honest.

Michael's agency or choice arises because of contradictory discursive practices at work in a pedagogical event. He is taking up a position of resistance partly in response to the contradictions within and between discourses (Haug, 1987). Through his experience of the usage of these discourses in everyday life, he chooses to position himself according to the discourse which is saying that the student teacher is the figure he must now answer to. In the face of evidence to the contrary, namely that I am still in the background imposing restrictions on behavior, Michael is enjoying the experience of a new set of boundaries which are making it possible for him to have more "fun" than usual. He is also able to exploit the fact that my positioning of myself in a "supportive" role for the student teacher prevents me from maintaining my categories of acceptable behavior, if this puts me in opposition to her positioning (Kristeva, 1986; Moi, 1985; Weedon, 1987). He knows that I will eventually speak with him, but for the moment, he makes his choice. (Similarly, a colleague had said to her five year old son, "*Clean up your room, or I'll give you a smack.*" The child looked at the state of the room, quickly weighed up the situation, and replied, "*I'll take the smack.*")

The difficulty in recognizing actual irresolvable contradictions in our own and others' discursive productions is highlighted here, because Michael's understanding is not strongly linked to rationality and consistency (Davies, 1993). Teachers often relate such stories with a shake of the head and amusement at the failure of the children to comprehend the hidden rules. It is this humor which serves as the device to make visible those contradictions, and that naming of the boundary which is being transgressed.

This is not to say that contradictions should not exist. In fact, according to Davies (1993), they are necessary because of the contradictory nature of the various realities we inhabit.

Michael's attempt to exercise a freedom to innovate with adult interpretations could not continue, if the student teacher's positioning of ownership of the management was to be maintained as the dominant discourse. The presentation of this complexity is important, especially in the light of Walkerdine's (1981) notion that we cannot be comforted by the thought that "progressive education" will free children to explore their own experience, without understanding precisely how that experience is understood and how that produces children as subjects.

Doing Stuff

> Terry tells me David spat water in his face...So I have to have "the investigation", but I'm trying to help them figure some of this out for themselves...probably not through particularly noble ideals. They both carry on all the time, and basically, I'm sick of it–all the "let's be friends" strategies aren't working. So I ask David "Why did you do that?"
>
> Children find it very difficult to answer questions like that–either, it's pretty darn obvious why they did it, or, they don't know what they're supposed to say–and they just come up with something so that you'll get on with it.
>
> Anyway, David says: "I did that because he does stuff to me all the time." We both look at Terry then, and he says that he does do stuff to David, because David often does stuff to him. So I adopt their language: "Why don't you both promise each other that you'll stop doing stuff to each other?" They think this is quite funny, and end up laughing with each other.

In pursuing the ideals of child-centered education founded on liberal humanism, teachers try to arm children with "conflict-resolving" strategies as an alternative to physically violent means of settling disagreements. Progressive pedagogies, according to Walkerdine (1992), mark a shift from overt to covert forms of regulation. Children are taught with the language of psychology, which disguises the school's involvement in the calculated management of human forces and powers in pursuit of the objectives of the institution (Rose, 1990). Management of subjectivity has become a central task of modern institutions, but this is often disguised in more socially acceptable notions, such as those introductory group dynamic sessions, aimed at team building, bonding, caring and sharing, and similar phrases which are all beginning to wear a bit thin.

This story of David and Terry exemplifies what Walkerdine (1992) refers to as the construction and active creation of "context". I am engaged in regulating the boys' behavior, but I am concealing this beneath an apparent intentionality of child-centeredness, to extend "freedom" and "creativity". Meanings that the children will make of certain words will be shifting and elusive, reliant on various social factors (Weiner, 1993). My insistence that the boys examine their actions, and my eliciting confessional admissions from both parties, are in Wexler's terms (1990) primary mechanisms for knowing the subject, allowing control, in accordance with the knowledge/power nexus.

By introducing humor into this exchange, I can make the situation visible to the boys from another vantage point. The teacher does not usually use the language the boys were using, and such a transgression on my part was enough to startle the boys, and then enable them to step away from their positioning. To break the seriousness of the discourse, and even grasp a sense of the ridiculous, all the subjects are free to take up alternate positions. As Davies (1994) advocates, if the children could articulate, or in this case, appreciate the experience of diversity as normal and acceptable, this could be quite empowering for them.

When children turn to adults to mediate on disagreements, there is an expectation of a particular sort of engagement. Walkerdine (1981) looks at the utilization of language organized round the power relations of the moment. On this basis of the teacher "sorting things out", teachers establish a convention that purportedly gives everyone a fair hearing. However, who is in what position, who is allowed and permitted to say what to whom, and using what sort of language, all affects and controls the outcome. The conventions surrounding "dobbing" provide another illustration of this point.

If we accept that power resides in all social relations, this opens up the possibility of a multiplicity of forms of resistance (Barrett & Phillips, 1992). David, Terry and I all choose to resist our positionings – each boy wants to be declared the person who should be listened to, and I want to extricate myself from the position of arbitrator, since I have very little conviction about the importance of the disagreement, or commitment to its resolution. I am also hoping to discourage the boys from bringing such incidents to me, as I am not always able to summon the energy required to turn such an exchange into a lesson on cooperation.

Democracy/Leaders

I have always hated a lot of things associated with having children walk in two straight lines. It just seems to create unnecessary problems:
Who's turn is it to be leader?
Who won't have who for a partner?
Who's last?
Who does nobody want?
And besides, it seems such an unnecessarily difficult ask: to expect people to move from one point to another side by side, but not talking. My solution is to just insist that

we all keep together, and not disturb others. We still get there, with about the same amount of noise. Everyone stays together, and it all seems more human to me.

The other day, we were getting ready to go somewhere and Peter said:

"You know, Brad's never had a turn at being leader with me?"

We've never even discussed this, but they've been going to other teachers for a P.E. class over the last few weeks. So I commented (whilst secretly patting myself on the back for being so democratic) that I don't worry too much about leaders, do I? And Tom immediately concurred by saying:

"No, you're just always the leader!"

Hmm! Not exactly what I'd had in mind.

The very process of "learning school" (Cleave et al., 1982) especially in the early years, means learning the drills and routines, the social habits and daily practices. Foucault sees training institutions like schools and prisons as the points where the power practices of modern life are instilled (Preston & Symes, 1992, p. 9). This is an issue frequently wrestled with by teachers as they attempt to reconcile the contradictions which must arise if one believes in encouraging children to make "democratic choices" whilst learning to function successfully in an institution such as school. In the past, I have positioned myself as resisting forms of social control, and rejected the idea of imposing such strict guidelines for behavior on little children. However, my choosing *not* to teach these "practices" has sometimes been detrimental to the children, since they have inevitably encountered those who have strongly insisted on certain "codes of behavior", and been reprimanded without any forewarning that their behavior would invite such responses.

Since coercion by physical force is no longer acceptable in liberal democracies, the control mechanisms involved in this learning of daily habits have been relocated. The language of psychology has made the mind accessible, as Rose illustrates (1990). But Foucault also sees control centered on the body, not simply on mental processes. Teachers are involved in controlling the anatomy rather than our belief systems (Preston & Symes, 1992, p. 189). Control over gestures, for instance, resulting in the production of docile bodies, is almost considered a prerequisite to the "success" of a "lesson", and teachers will sometimes, for instance, insist on their students repeating a "Good Morning" greeting, since it had not been done in acceptable unison. This served to set the tone, and "let them know who's boss", which was what I was strongly advised to do when I was a trainee teacher. A poststructuralist reading views this exercise as establishing (and thereby limiting) subjectivities and positions.

Foucauldian (1980) thinking does not hold that power is an external force which is containable and locatable as a single entity which can then be either exerted or resisted. Rather it permeates all of society, determining our actions and desires in small and very detailed ways (Preston & Symes, 1992, p. 134). Davies (1993) talks of how we know things so strongly that they are no longer described, but inscribed. We internalize that knowledge so that it is no longer visible.

As well as examination and confession, surveillance is another application of bio-power. Behaviors which would interfere with productivity are easily observed and detected as deviances (Preston & Symes, 1992, p. 182). So bodies are placed in restricted spaces and with codes of conduct, even to the physical movements which are permissible, making variance or difference clearly recognizable. Normalizing becomes the objective of all involved, students and teachers.

Teacher voice
Tuck your hands in your lap
Put your hand up
Hands down
Walk in two straight lines
Cross your legs
Sit down
Sit up straight
Stand up straight
Hurry up
Slow down
Move quietly
Speak up so everyone can hear
Be quiet

Shhh shhhh
Out of bounds
Tidy up
Tuck your shirt in
No hat; no play
We'll see
If we have time

Open shut them, open shut them,
Give a little clap.
Open shut them, open shut them,
Fold them in your lap.
Creep them, creep them,
Creep them, creep them,
Right up to your chin.
Open wide your little mouth,
  but...
DO NOT LET THEM IN!

Child
I can't see
Can I please go to the toilet?

Shirley Temple is a star
S–T–A–R
She can do the rumble

Can I please have a drink?
I'm dobbing
Are we going to do hard work?
Can we....?
Can I play?
Nobody plays with me
Is there school tomorrow?
When is it lunch time?
She said she wasn't my friend.
She said she won't play with me
Are you allowed to play there at lunch time?

She can do the splits
She can do anything
Just like this.
Firecracker firecracker
boom boom boom
Firecracker firecracker
boom boom boom
Queen does the curtsey
King does the bow.
Boys go ⟨kiss kiss⟩
Girls go Woah! (lifting up skirts to show knickers.)

CONCLUSION

From Rousseau's time, educators in this field have strongly advocated the importance of acquiring knowledge of children through observation and reflection, to the extent that this is considered an essential element of early childhood education. This chapter then makes a contribution to this field in the sense that it adds to our knowledge of children, providing methods and tools with which to observe and disrupt discursive practices in an early childhood setting. Since theory structures what we see, poststructuralist analysis can add a dimension to the observations we are making about the children in our classrooms...and the actions we plan, based on the observations and knowledge.

The cubists depict the visible as not just what confronts the single eye, but the totality of possible views taken from all around the subject being depicted (Berger, 1985, p. 18). When a painting is reproduced by a film camera it inevitably becomes material for the film maker's argument. It is helpful to consider the classroom and school with the aid of a framework which recognizes the multiplicities of positionings acting on the construction of knowledge. The school and classroom, are, in some sense, loosely bounded territories where cultures, subjectivities, identities, impinge on each other (Hebdige, 1988). To isolate any small areas becomes a form of 'reproduction', creating new contexts and arguments about the authority of my choices. While I cannot pretend to being objective in my observations, I can, through the concept of a textual collage, experiment with the form of this narrative, in the hope of making the various discourses and spaces of school visible, and, so, talked about.

Mine is a unique and localized tale, but there are wider implications. Since I was engaged in the process of revisiting my stories as I worked with the children, I sometimes found my research "paralyzing", as issues of power and oppression, and opportunities for resistance were made visible to me as the teacher. Sometimes these were the "uneasy moments" referred to by Luke and Gore (1992), and I came to recognize them as a signal that discourses were competing and colliding in my construction of my classroom.

At the same time, I found the ideas of multiple readings and discourse analysis freeing for my students and myself. In "Shards of Glass", Davies (1993) works with older children, leading them to see themselves constituted through discourse, and to provide them with tools and the means to disrupt the dominant discourses. Some of my stories are about the possibilities of addressing this same issue with still younger children through play.

It is not enough simply to observe children in our classrooms, and treat issues of difference, gender, and equity as add-ons to more traditional early childhood frameworks for curriculum planning. At this time of global unease and instability, there is a temptation to retreat from the discourses of multiculturalism to the more fundamental and romantic humanist discourses of essential goodness, and a simplistic way of organizing the world into good and bad (Lampert, 2003). The case for helping children to engage critically with difference is put strongly by many contemporary theorists, including the influential New London Group (1996). We live in multiple communities, each with their own 'rules', conventions. If we are committed to truly democratic principles of education, then this is about meaningful success for all, and that success is not just defined in economic terms. What we want for our children is that they live successful lives, and participate as citizens in a future that we cannot know. It is important that children consciously develop their ability to read and understand differences, in relation to the historical, social, political and value-laden systems of knowledge and social practice. Through critical framing, children can gain the necessary distance from issues of difference, constructively critique, extend, and creatively apply what they have learned in new ways (New London Group, 1996).

My theorizing also leads me to extend this idea of disrupting discourse through play to further reaching applications, not limited to an educational setting. Humor, drama and play are devices which have been long used to make visible, the boundaries, categories, and social practices acting as agents in our constructions of knowledge.

I have not come up with a new set of instructions, of "never-fail" teaching techniques, that will result in a classroom of happy, well adjusted children, brimming with self esteem and confidence, expressing themselves with astonishing creativity, being democratic at the same time as they all pursue their individual interests. I would love to be able to say all those things are happening in my classroom, and I feel a certain amount of dissatisfaction that I don't do enough. Walkerdine (1992) alludes to this when she writes of "impossible fictions". The ways in which I describe my classroom weave a picture – often romantic – of myself into the text. My struggle with my own story lines about me as a teacher is illuminated by Davies' (1993) point that we are fictionalizing our lives all the time.

Boundaries cannot be transgressed until they are made visible. By presenting my study in this form, I attempt to illuminate and reveal how power is exercised through discourse, in an early childhood classroom and the playground, and how resistances might be possible. I do this with an eye for the ironies, humor, and *fun* to be found in teacher stories about their work. And I *play* with the stories by using them to ask some blasphemous (Haraway, 1991) questions.

> We know nothing of childhood; and with our mistaken notions the further we advance the further we go astray. (Rousseau, 1991,1762)

REFERENCES

Barrett, M., & Phillips, A. (Eds) (1992). *Destabilizing theory. Contemporary feminist debates.* California: Stanford University Press.
Belenky, M., Clinchy, B., Goldberger, N., & Tarule, J. (1986). *Women's ways of knowing.* New York: Basic Books.
Berger, J. (1985). *Ways of seeing, based on the BBC television series.* London: BBC Corporation and Penguin Books.
Caine, B., & Pringle, R. (Eds) (1995). *Transitions: New Australian feminisms.* St Leonards, NSW: Allen & Unwin.
Cleave, S., Jowett, S., & Bate, M. (1982). *"... And So to School" A study of continuity from preschool to infant school.* Windsor, Berks: NFER-Nelson.
Davies, B. (1993). *Shards of glass. Children reading and writing beyond gendered identities.* Sydney: Allen & Unwin.
Davies, B. (1994). *Poststructuralist theory and classroom practice.* Melbourne: Deakin University Press.
Dewey, J. (1938). *Experience & education.* New York: Macmillan.
Foucault, M. (1980). *Power/Knowledge: Selected interviews and other writings, 1972–1977.* New York: Pantheon.

Foucault, M. (1983). The subject and power. In: H. L. Dreyfus & P. Rabinow (Eds), *Michel Foucault: Beyond structuralism and hermeneutics*, (2nd ed.) (pp. 208–226). Chicago: University of Chicago Press.
Foucault, M. (1985). *The history of sexuality, Volume Two*. New York: Vintage Books.
Foucault, M. (1986). *The care of the self* (English edition). New York: Pantheon.
Gilligan, C. (1982). *In a different voice*. Cambridge: Harvard University Press.
Goodwin, W. L., & Goodwin, L. D. (1996). *Understanding quantitative and qualitative research in early childhood education*. New York: Teachers College Press.
Gunew, S. (Ed.) (1990). *Feminist knowledge. Critique and construct*. London: Routledge.
Haraway, D. (1991). *Simians, cyborgs, and women. The reinvention of nature*. London: Free Association Books.
Haug, F. (1987). In: E. Carter (Trans.), *Female sexualization*. London: Verso.
Hebdige, D. (1988). *Hiding in the light: On images and things*. London: Routledge.
Heidegger, M. (1974). *Identity and difference (Introduction and translated by Joan Stambaugh)*. New York: Harper & Row.
Jenks, C. (1996). *Childhood*. London: Routledge.
Jones, A. (1993). Becoming a "Girl": Post-structuralist suggestions for educational research. *Gender and Education*, 5(2), 157–166.
Kirby, K. (1996). *Indifferent boundaries: Spatial concepts of human subjectivity*. New York: The Guilford Press.
Kristeva, J. (1986). Women's time. In: T. Phillips (Ed.), *The Kristeva Reader*. Oxford: Basil Blackwell.
Lampert, J. (2003). Is there anything we can do to make the world right again? The privileging of humanism and the troubling of multiculturalism and globalisation in 2 picture books about 9/11. Paper presented at Performing Research Conference, Queensland University of Technology, Faculty of Education, 24–25 October, 2003.
Lather, P. (1986). Research as praxis. *Harvard Educational Review*, 56(3), 257–277.
Luke, C., & Gore, J. (Eds) (1992). *Feminisms and critical pedagogy*. New York: Routledge.
McArdle, F. (2003). The visual arts: Ways of seeing. In: S. Wright (Ed.), *Children, meaning-making and the arts* (pp. 35–62). Sydney: Pearson Prentice-Hall.
McWilliam, E. (2000). Stuck in the missionary position? Pedagogy and desire in new times. In: C. O'Farrell, D. Meadmore, E. McWilliam & C. Symes (Eds), *Taught bodies* (pp. 27–38). New York: Peter Lang.
Moi, T. (1985). *Sexual textual politics*. London: Methuen.
New London Group, The. (1996). A pedagogy of multiliteracies: Designing social futures. *Harvard Education Review*, 66(1), 60–92.
Postman, N. (1983). *The disappearance of childhood*. London: W.H. Allen.
Preston, N., & Symes, C. (1992). *Schools and Classrooms*. Education Australia series. Melbourne: Longman Cheshire.
Rose, N. (1990). *Governing the soul*. New York: Routledge.
Rousseau, J. (1991). In: A. Bloom (Trans.), *Emile: Or on education*. Hammondsworth: Penguin. (Original work published 1762).
Silverman, D. (2000). *Doing qualitative research: A practical handbook*. London: Sage.
Silverman, D. (2001). *Interpreting qualitative data. Methods for analysing talk, text and interaction* (2nd ed.). London: Sage.
Sontag, S. (1990). *Against interpretation and other essays*. New York: Anchor Books.

St. Pierre, E. (1997). Nomadic inquiry in the smooth spaces of the field: A preface. *International Journal of Qualitative Studies in Education, 10*(3), 363–383.
Tobin, J. (1988). Visual anthropology and multivocal ethnography: A dialogical approach to Japanese preschool class size. *Dialectical Anthropology, 13*(2), 173–187.
Ulmer, G. (1985). *Writing and reading differently*. Kansas: University of Kansas Press.
Walkerdine, V. (1981). Sex, power and pedagogies. *Screen Education, 38*, 14–26.
Walkerdine, V. (1992). Progressive pedagogy and political struggle. In: C. Luke & J. Gore (Eds), *Feminisms and critical pedagogy* (pp. 15–24). New York: Routledge.
Walkerdine, V., & Lucey, H. (1989). *Democracy in the kitchen: Regulating mothers and socialising daughters*. London: Virago.
Weber, E. (1984). *Ideas influencing early childhood education: A theoretical analysis*. New York: Teachers College Press.
Weedon, C. (1987). *Feminist practice and poststructural theory*. Oxford: Blackwell.
Weiner, G. (1993). *The gendered curriculum – producing the text: developing a poststructural feminist analysis*. Paper presented AARE Conference, December, Perth.
Wexler, P. (1990). *Social analysis of education. After the new sociology*. New York: Routledge.

THE AMORPHOUS PRETEND PLAY CURRICULUM: THEORIZING EMBODIED SYNTHETIC MULTICULTURAL PROPS

Richard Johnson

ABSTRACT

Early childhood education is a visual field. Much of our work begins with observing and documenting children's talk and actions. The knowledge gleaned from looking is then used to plan curriculum, much of which involves the creation of materials-rich environments to engage children's learning. Yet, quite often we do not question what we see. This chapter uses visual cultural theory to examine the multicultural props used in dramatic play with young children. By examining these images for what is both seen and not seen, I illustrate how these props create a specific discourse in early childhood education.

The historical and current work of many early childhood educators is grounded in visual culture (Devereaux, 1995). Much of our training begins with learning how to look at and observe children's learning as the basis for planning responsive curriculum. As the field has expanded, teachers have learned to observe and study children even more meticulously. We systematically observe much earlier in the life cycle (e.g., *in utero* via ultrasound technologies and at the moment of birth via standardized APGAR tests), and we look much more intensely, all the time (Billman & Sherman, 2003). Moreover, with the latest electronic technologies we can now access and use observation systems online (e.g., Work Sampling System, 2003) that make documenting children's learning more efficient and easier to administrate.

The knowledge about children produced through these observational technologies informs the ways in which educational environments are structured and curriculum experiences are enacted. Just as the methods and systems of observing children have become more refined over time, so have the materials and the physical environments in which children learn. Now, teachers can choose from a myriad of commercially available materials, and many classrooms house numerous learning centers where children can explore subject matter from early numeracy and literacy concepts to social skills. Thus, the educational environments that are based on our ever-increasing knowledge of young children's learning also encourage children to engage with the visual.

The improved ability to look and the pedagogies promised by these new observation systems, however, also enhance the ready consumption and further reproduction of traditional ways of knowing children (Gandhi, 1998; Johnson, 2005). While systematic study using new technologies may produce more accurate knowledge of children's learning and therefore contribute to improving classroom materials and environments, it also makes it more difficult to question what is problematic about such systems and what they enable us to see.

In the very recent past, I have become enthralled by visual culture theory and critiqued my long-held interests in video, in learning technologies, in the environment, in the current and historical study of children and childhood (Jenks, 1995), and in my recent work on touch/no touch (Johnson, 2000) and how this work is visually perceived and received (Banks, 1998). Visual culture theory helps with further understanding the extent to which the cultural formations we inhabit have become increasingly saturated by visual images entailing a multiplicity of purposes and intended effects. As Britzman (2000) notes,

> Looking is an act of choice. Through looking we negotiate social relationships and meanings. Looking is a practice much like speaking, writing, or signing. Looking involves learning to interpret and, like other practices, looking involves relationships of power. To willfully look or not is to exercise choice and influence (p. 10).

Using visual culture theory has pushed me to search beyond normative analyses and to begin to understand what the field of early education chooses to see and not see. This focus on the visual is what pushed me to analyze play and early childhood curriculum materials and their links to multicultural education – which is what the remainder of this chapter critiques.

VISUAL CULTURE AND EARLY EDUCATION

Many years ago, I was conducting a longitudinal study of several preschools in Hawaii and the primary assessment instrumentation included the *Early Childhood Environment Rating Scale* (ECERS) (Harms, Clifford, & Cryer, 2004). While initially finding this tool useful as an overall observation instrument and talking point for post-observation reviews with the center staff, what I found to be especially helpful was the item "Cultural awareness" on the ECERS. This particular study was being conducted at a time when multicultural studies were gaining widespread acceptance. I found that the usage of the Likert-type scaled terms which ranged from "Inadequate" ("No attempt to include ethnic and racial variety in dolls, book illustrations, or pictorial bulletin boards") to "Excellent" ("Cultural awareness evidenced by liberal inclusion of multiracial and nonsexist materials plus cultural awareness is part of the curriculum") was invaluable for the staff to consider how their physical environment and the explicit curriculum responded to cultural issues in early education.

While, the "Cultural awareness" item drew our attention to cultural issues in the environments where we worked (Clark, DeWolf, & Clark, 1992), a more retrospective read helps me now to see that it probably did not assist us in looking much beyond the physical environment itself to consider more critically, issues of culture, racial identity, ethnicity, and gender (Narayan & Harding, 2000). By assuming that the inclusion of diverse images of people through the use of multicultural toys and books (see Figs. 1 and 2) will socialize children about difference, we did not go any further in examining the meanings that were being conveyed to children by our daily talk and teaching actions (Johnson, 2004). Thinking back to that study in light of recent research on visual culture and representation (Fischman, 2001; Jenks, 1995; Metz, 1982), it is easy now to see the inherent danger of imposing simplistic, additive structures (i.e., more racially "correct" dolls and puzzles equals attendance to multicultural education; see Figs. 1 and 2) into action research and professional development models.

Fig. 1. Multi-Cultural Children Puzzle.

This additive practice is similar to the use of tourist curricula (Au, 2001; Richards, 1993) in an attempt, honest or otherwise, to honor multicultural education. Only recently did schooling include a wider diversity of experiences of racial and ethnic groups in the United States (Hidalgo, 1993), and responding to that push, Marsh (1992) has commented that too many teachers, in their politically correct zeal to teach multiculturally, fell into the trap of teaching a tourist curriculum that uses a less authentic approach. "Tourist curriculum" is the term used to define the teaching of cultures through the use of "food, traditional clothing, and household implements" (Derman-Sparks, 1989, p. 7). Like others, Marsh stated that through a tourist curriculum "multicultural activities become isolated or contained in one unit rather than being infused into the daily curriculum. Students are misled into thinking that various cultures are based on holidays and celebrations rather than being a part of everyday life" (1992, p. 270). Clark et al. (1992) addressed parallel issues when they reviewed "Play kit" approaches to multicultural education, in which,

> Students brought out material elements of culture, such as tepees or war dances, for a few days, rather than the essence of a people's beliefs and way of life. They told a story, sang a song, or constructed an art project, and then got back to the 'regular' curriculum, without ever having touched on important issues and ideas. Near thanksgiving we still visited school after school where headbanded children threatened to scalp us (Clark et al., 1992, p. 5).

Quite often, multicultural props and manipulatives are used as a kind of tourist approach to address diversity issues. By adding these materials to the

The Amorphous Pretend Play Curriculum

Fig. 2. Multi-cultural Children Doll.

dramatic play area, it is assumed that children will be socialized into understanding that there are many different kinds of people all of whom are equal. Visual culture theory urges teachers to look carefully at these props and manipulatives (see Figs. 3–7), and to examine these images beyond the pointed advertising slogans or comments that support the use of these products as part of a multicultural curriculum (e.g., other captions report that the use of these particular toys: "Foster[s] a positive awareness and inclusive attitude towards individuals with physical challenges even during block play;" "Role playing is made easy with these 7 occupational hats;" and "These 8 wonderful play hats let kids assume so many imaginative roles;" Constructive Playthings, 2003, p. 15). The next section illustrates how visual culture theory can be used by teachers to consider both the explicit and hidden meanings associated with various multicultural props.

Fig. 3. House, Furniture and Black Family.

(RE)READING PRETEND PLAY IMAGES THROUGH VISUAL CULTURAL LENSES

In her acclaimed critical work on British paintings, Beth Tobin (1999) suggests that "one way to recover subaltern subjectivity from an elite text is to read the imperial text symptomatically – that is, reading what is not there but is implied and called into existence by a series of oppositions" (1999, p. 12). She goes on to discuss how she reads a set of particular 18th century

The Amorphous Pretend Play Curriculum

Fig. 4. Posable Asian Family.

paintings as colonial discourse "for they participate in specific practices and ideologies that circulated" (p. 12) in and about that period. Much like Tobin's work, here I am interested in a particular set of images, how they represent a field of study, and how they too speak to a dominant discourse in early childhood education. I recognize that as a poststructuralist reading, "words and images do not merely reflect the world, but mediate, even create, what we believe to be reality" (Tobin, 1999, pp. 13–14).

The focus here is to incorporate multiple interactional analyses to assist in the critique of multicultural pretend play props. In doing so, I consider some of Lather's (1998) critical work that encourages a "multiplicity of readings by demonstrating how we cannot exhaust the meaning of the text, how a text can participate in multiple meanings without being reduced to any one, and how our different positionalities affect our reading of it" (p. 125). By looking at and analyzing both the visual images (i.e., photographs) that these ethnic families represent (e.g., the Hispanic, Asian, African-American, and White pretend play family from the Constructive Playthings catalogue and website) and the physical props themselves, I provide alternative interpretations of the multicultural curricula aids that are meant to help teachers and children navigate and consider an increasingly diverse world (Jameson, 1990; Mirzoeff, 1999).

Fig. 5. House with Furniture/Asian Family.

The aim of the analysis of these photographs and depictions of multicultural toys and props is to look, and look again and again at these images and what they represent (Tonkiss, 1998). That is, by incorporating visual cultural analytical techniques into this critique of multicultural play objects, one is able to look well beyond the static nature of these plastic toys as they are advertised and typically added into classroom activity settings (Cohen, 1998). Visual culture theoretical and analytical techniques assist in envisioning these images in deeper ways (Rose, 2001), understanding further how these curriculum tools, as presented, and typically critiqued, add very little to a revitalized multicultural movement.

The following pictorial samples (see Figs. 3–7), like the example presented earlier (see Fig. 1) include several typical catalog pictures or images, images which in their familiarity represent the early childhood education field. The

The Amorphous Pretend Play Curriculum

Fig. 6. Pliable White Family.

following analyses offer a way of exploring how the images present and construct particular ways of seeing the world. This particular type of discourse analysis critiques "how images construct accounts of the social world ... paying careful attention to images, and to their social production and effect" (Rose, 2001, pp. 140–141). To understand what discourses are at play in these images, I employ Cowling's (1989) methodologies of looking for textual and visual commonalities.

In this regard these images or artifacts can be seen as constitutive because they speak to the notions of the natural child, the romantic, unthreatened, enlightened being who appears very much at one-with-nature (Buckingham, 2000; James & Prout, 1997). Children depicted in these curriculum content catalogues constitute the normative child who is doing what the field of early education demands s/he do – learning by doing/hands-on learning, actively involved in discovery-based learning, at one with nature, peaceful, joyful, and pure. All that even while these multicultural props and toys represent so many people(s) who have witnessed and experienced so much pain, oppression, suffering, humiliation, death, and betrayal by the very persons addressing and playing with them in the catalog, the colonizer him/herself.

Fig. 7. Pretend Play Family/Hispanic Family.

Looking across the images depicted in Figs. 2–6 it is possible to see common themes that counter the intent of the props as conveyers of multicultural meanings (Davey, 1999; Hayes, 2002). The first theme is that of happiness as every image, whether a real-life character holding a plastic or cloth doll or the doll(s) itself, to a character (and there were close to 40 in these few pictures) are all depicted with happy expressions which are readily visible on their faces. Similarly in each image, the characters are surrounded by an abundance of family members; and all seem to have afforded the confines of middle- to upper-class type housing (i.e., two and three story structures with a lot of furniture). Moreover, many of the children depicted in the images are being tended to and cared for by adults – there is always a mother and a father present, seen holding hands and seeming to watch over and care for the younger characters. What is also apparent is how easily the characters are depicted in certain natural positions. The family size of seven people is deemed *natural*, despite the ethnic or cultural background, as family size and composition are statically portrayed – all families shown have the same number of members. Living in a large house with a wide range of identical furniture seems equally likely, no matter your family size and/or ethnic background. Together, these images negate the wide range of diverse circumstances of the many children who live in quite different situations (e.g., homeless, more than one family sharing living space, different socio-economic circumstances), and belong to an array of family structures (e.g., single parent, step, interracial, gay families). In this global era (Trouillot, 2002) all apparently belong to one and in that collapse and act of containment, in that normative translation, they lose particular unique aspects of their identity (Young, 2002). In a similar manner, they also locate Asian, Hispanic, and African-American families in identical contexts such as two and three storied houses (and associated furnishings) that are connected with white middle- and upper-class families, whilst potential African-Americans and Hispanic homeowners are denied bank mortgages based on their ethnic identity (Mohanty, 1995).

Another related issue is how highly *interchangeable* these respective multicultural characters appear to be. In terms of gender, everyone is well-matched. For every girl present exists a boy; for every family of one ethnic group (e.g., Asian) there was an identical variation of a family of another ethnic group (e.g., Hispanic or African-American). Alongside the displays of houses available, there is a choice from a wide array of interchangeable characters. As well, the materials themselves (hardplastic or soft cloth) can be physically manipulated as they are "pliable" or "posable".

In short, these renditions of family are not only stereotypical, but the stereotypes are static and essentialized across ethnicity, race, and socio-economic circumstances. Every family depicted consists of equal number of children and there is ALWAYS a mother and father present, and usually grandparents as well. Family size is consistent across ethnic lines, from Asian to White, and all families are housed similarly.

Representation and Fetishism

The few images from popular early education catalogs that have been traced here, interpolate the classic child(ren) of early childhood education – that romantic, natural child, the unthreatened, enlightened being who is portrayed unproblematically in the larger field of early education. Children – regardless of race, socio-economic circumstances, culture, and gender, and whether a prop or the child manipulating the materials – are always portrayed as naturally happy, safe, and members of stereotypical families (Johnson & Sumsion, 2004). The normative figures visualized in these images – the 'multicultural' dolls, puzzles, and curriculum props are doing precisely what the field demands they do – offering themselves as potential materials, which can assist the dramatic play process while embedded in a context said to reflect "real life." As such, these props do what is demanded by the field of early childhood education in that they facilitate learning by doing, and stimulate discovery-based learning about multicultural issues which are visualized as peaceful, joyful, intentional, and pure.

Like so many other disciplines, culture has become an instrumental part of the early education field. The additive nature of how culture and diversity are addressed as evidenced in these images continues to be a repetitive, atheoretical, fetishistic operation (Hight & Sampson, 2002; O'Loughlin, 1992). Additive "neutral" pedagogical processes, like the placement of Asian dolls or a Black or "posable" White family into the dramatic play curriculum without further critical interrogation, indicate a "present without depth" (Eco, 1986, p. 53), and remain problematic because of the lack of accompanying histories of colonization, slavery, and other humanitarian circumstances. Hight and Sampson (2002) suggest that the very present danger in these types of simplistic actions is that they "perpetuate myths ... and in the process are consigned to a condition of relative invisibility" (p. 7). The ongoing lack of recognition and the pretense that happiness, safety, and interchangeability are normative aspects of childhood continues to marginalize alternative understandings of children and their many lived circumstances (Burman, 1994; Jenks, 1996; Stainton Rogers & Stainton Rogers, 1992), early childhood theoretical positions (Canella & Viruru, 2004; James, Jenks, & Prout, 1998; Tobin, 1997, 2001), and restricts the field from advancing intellectually.

Rather than seeing these images and the products they support and wish to sell as helpful, easily added and integrated into a dramatic play and a multicultural curriculum to enhance interactions and understanding of the world, an alternative read, or a "supplemental" interpretation, notes the restrictive, confining manner in which these very props operate. While they are meant to "Foster a positive awareness" and "assume so many imaginative roles," a more interrogative, critical, oppositional look suggests that they are in fact nothing more than "controlled imaging aimed at controlling controlled imaginations" (Hunt & Frankenberg, 1997, p. 118).

"LOOKING" FORWARD

Over the past decade or so, the field has strived to make inclusive changes (Kessler & Swadener, 1992; Tobin, 1992), so much so that the National Association for the Education of Young Children (NAEYC) added culture to their Developmentally Appropriate Practices (Bredekamp & Copple, 1997) framework. Similar adjustments were made in the popular curriculum products available, so that curriculum vendors now have a multicultural index designation as part of each catalog.

However, as this analysis illustrates the multicultural materials we use represent multiple and interwoven layers of control of imaging and imaginations (Hunt & Frankenberg, 1997). Challenging the dominance of the essentialized and romanticized images of children and childhood that constrain teachers to additive approaches in addressing issues of diversity in the classroom requires that we all learn to look critically as we actively make sense of the world. This looking is "about constructing particular versions of truth, questioning how regimes of truth become neutralized as knowledge ... thus pushing the sensibilities of [teachers] in new directions" (Britzman, 2000, p. 38). Had I not looked hard here, with intentionality(s) and through alternative critical lenses of visual culture, I would have failed to see so much, as I have failed so many times before, and continued to visualize these particular photographs and objects with rapt purpose as a fervent spectator.

If we envision our collective theoretician/practitioner selves and the greater field from a critical, action-oriented research perspective (Gruenewald, 2003), then we have to self-consciously and collectively incorporate resistant methods of studying (Mohanty, 1995), interpreting and further understanding the various disciplines, materials, and methods we encounter in our individual and collective work. These potentially emancipatory methods could assist us in moving past the simple replaying of typical ways of seeing early childhood practices and assist us in reworking (Loomba, 1998) and renegotiating the past and the present (Tompkins, 1995). These research methods can actively assist us in our respective discipline(s) as we seek to "open [up], disinterring the repressed and troubling questions ... that loosen the ties that bind" (Pajaczkowska, 2001, p. 4). Visual culture theory offers early childhood educators tremendous opportunities for rewriting culture.

REFERENCES

Au, W. W. K. (2001). What the tour guide didn't tell me: Tourism, colonialism, and resistance in Hawaii. In: B. Bigelow (Ed.), *Rethinking our classrooms Volume 2: Teaching for equity and justice* (pp. 76–80). New York: Rethinking Schools Ltd.

Banks, M. (1998). Visual anthropology: Image, object and interpretation. In: J. Prosser (Ed.), *Image-based research: A sourcebook for qualitative researchers* (pp. 9–23). Philadelphia: Falmer Press.

Billman, J., & Sherman, J. (2003). *Observation and participation in early childhood settings: A practicum guide.* San Francisco: Allyn and Bacon.

Bredekamp, S., & Copple, C. (1997). *Developmentally appropriate practice in early childhood programs* (Rev. ed.). Washington DC: National Association for the Education of Young Children.

Britzman, D. (2000). "The question of belief": Writing poststructural ethnography. In: E. A. St. Pierre & W. S. Pillow (Eds), *Working the ruins: Feminist poststructural theory and methods in education* (pp. 27–40). New York: Routledge.

Buckingham, D. (2000). *After the death of childhood: Growing up in the age of electronic media.* Oxford: Polity Press.

Burman, E. (1994). *Deconstructing developmental psychology.* New York: Routledge.

Canella, G., & Viruru, R. (2004). *Childhood and postcolonization.* New York: Taylor & Francis.

Clark, L., DeWolf, S., & Clark, S. (1992). Teaching teachers to avoid having culturally assaultive classrooms. *Young Children, 7,* 4–9.

Cohen, J. (1998). *Spectacular allegories: Postmodern American writing and the politics of seeing.* Virginia: Pluto Press.

Constructive Playthings. (2003). *Constructive playthings catalogue.* Missouri: Constructive Playthings.

Cowling, M. (1989). *The artist as anthropologist: The representation of type and character in Victorian art.* Cambridge: Cambridge University Press.

Davey, N. (1999). The hermeneutics of seeing. In: B. Sandywell & I. Heywood (Eds), *Interpreting visual culture: Explorations in the hermeneutics of the visual* (pp. 3–29). New York: Routledge.

Derman-Sparks, L. (1989). *Anti-bias curriculum: Tools for empowering young children.* Washington, DC: National Association for the Education of Young Children.

Devereaux, L. (1995). An introductory essay. In: L. Devereaux & R. Hillman (Eds), *Fields of vision: Essays in film studies, visual anthropology, and photography* (pp. 1–18). Berkeley: University of California Press.

Eco, U. (1986). *The search for the perfect language.* J. Fentress (Trans.). Cambridge: Blackwell.

Fischman, G. F. (2001). Reflections about images, visual culture and educational research. *Educational Researcher, 30*(8), 28–33.

Gandhi, L. (1998). *Postcolonial theory: A critical introduction.* New York: Columbia University Press.

Grueneworld, D. A. (2003). The best of both worlds: A critical pedagogy of place. *Educational Researcher, 32*(4), 3–12.

Harms, T., Clifford, R. M., & Cryer, D. (2004). *Early childhood environment rating scale.* New York: Teachers College Press.

Hayes, M. (2002). Photography and the emergence of the Pacific cruise: Rethinking the representational crisis in colonial photography. In: E. M. Hight & G. D. Sampson (Eds),

Colonialist photography: Imag(in)ing race and place (pp. 172–187). New York: Routledge.
Hidalgo, N. (1993). Multicultural teacher introspection. In: T. Perry & J. Fraser (Eds), *Freedom's plow* (pp. 99–108). New York: Routledge.
Hight, E. M., & Sampson, G. D. (2002). Photography, 'race', and post-colonial theory. In: E. M. Hight & G. D. Sampson (Eds), *Colonialist photography: Imag(in)ing race and place* (pp. 1–19). New York: Routledge.
Hunt, P., & Frankenberg, R. (1997). It's a small world: Disneyland, the family and the multiple re-representations of American childhood. In: A. James & A. Prout (Eds), *Constructing and reconstructing childhood* (pp. 107–125). Washington, DC: Falmer Press.
James, A., Jenks, C., & Prout, A. (1998). *Theorizing childhood*. New York: Teachers College Press.
James, A., & Prout, A. (Eds) (1997) Re-presenting childhood: Time and transition in the study of childhood, In: A. James & A. Prout (Eds), *Constructing and reconstructing childhood: Contemporary issues in the sociological study of childhood*. London: Falmer.
Jameson, F. (1990). *Signatures of the visible*. New York: Routledge.
Jenks, C. (1995). *Visual culture*. London: Routledge.
Jenks, C. (1996). *Childhood*. London: Routledge.
Johnson, R. (2000). *Hands off!: The disappearance of touch in the care of young children*. New York: Peter Lang.
Johnson, R. (2004). (mis)Representations of identity in pretend play props: Critiquing pretend play from a visual cultural perspective. Paper presented at the annual meeting of the American educational research association. San Diego, CA.
Johnson, R. (2005). The naturalization of the early childhood citizen in a global world. Paper presented at the international globalization, diversity, and education conference. Pullman, WA.
Johnson, R., & Sumsion, J. (2004). Picturing early childhood education as imperialist entity. Paper presented at the annual reconceptualizing early childhood education conference. Oslo, Norway.
Kessler, S. A., & Swadener, B. B. (Eds) (1992). *Reconceptualizing the early childhood curriculum: Beginning the dialogue*. New York: Teachers College Press.
Lather, P. (1998). Staying dumb? Feminist research and pedagogy within the postmodern. In: H. Simons & M. Billig (Eds), *After postmodernism: Reconstructing ideology critique* (pp. 101–132). Thousand Oaks: Sage.
Loomba, A. (1998). *Colonialsm/postcolonialism*. New York: Routledge.
Marsh, M. (1992). Implementing antibias curriculum in the kindergarten classroom. In: S. Kessler & B. B. Swadener (Eds), *Reconceptualizing the early childhood curriculum: Beginning the dialogue* (pp. 267–288). New York: Teachers College Press.
Metz, C. (1982). *Psychoanalysis and cinema: The imaginary signifier*. London: Macmillan.
Mirzoeff, N. (1999). *An introduction to visual culture*. New York: Routledge.
Mohanty, S. P. (1995). Colonial legacies, multicultural futures: Relativism, objectivity, and the challenge of otherness. *Publications of the Modern Language Association of America, 110*(1), 108–118.
Narayan, U., & Harding, S. (Eds) (2000). *Decentering the center: Philosophy for a multicultural, postcolonial, and feminist world*. Indianapolis: Indiana University Press.
O'Loughlin, M. (1992). Rethinking science education: Beyond Piagetian constructivism toward a sociocultural model of teaching and learning. *Journal of Research in Science Teaching, 29*(8), 791–820.

Pajaczkowska, C. (2001). Issues in feminist design. In: F. Carson & C. Pajaczkowska (Eds), *Feminist visual culture* (pp. 123–128). New York: Routledge.
Richards, J. J. (1993). Classroom tapestry: A practitioner's perspective on multicultural education. In: T. Perry & J. W. Fraser (Eds), *Freedom's plow: Teaching in the multicultural classroom* (pp. 47–63). New York: Routledge.
Rose, G. (2001). *Visual methodologies.* Thousand Oaks: Sage.
Stainton Rogers, R., & Stainton Rogers, W. (1992). *Stories of childhood: Shifting agendas of child concern.* Toronto: University of Toronto Press.
Tobin, B. F. (1999). *Picturing imperial power: Colonial subjects in eighteenth-century British painting.* Durham: Duke University Press.
Tobin, J. (1992). Early childhood education and the public schools: Obstacles to reconstructing a relationship. *Early Education and Development, 3*(2), 196–200.
Tobin, J. (1997). *Making a place for pleasure in early childhood education.* New Haven: Yale University Press.
Tobin, J. (2001). *"Good guys don't wear hats": Children's talk about the media.* New York: Teachers College Press.
Tompkins, J. (1995). "Spectacular resistance": Metatheatre in post-colonial drama. *Modern Drama, 38,* 42–51.
Tonkiss, F. (1998). Analysing discourse. In: C. Seale (Ed.), *Researching society and culture* (pp. 245–260). London: Sage.
Trouillot, M. R. (2002). The perspective of the world: Globalization then and now. In: E. Mudimbe-Boyi (Ed.), *Beyond dichotomies: Histories, identities, cultures, and the challenge of globalization* (pp. 3–20). New York: State University of New York Press.
Work Sampling System. (2003). http://www.worksamplingonline.com/ Accessed September 8, 2003.
Young, R. J. C. (2002). Ethnicity as otherness in British identity politics. In: E. Mudimbe-Boyi (Ed.), *Beyond dichotomies: Histories, identities, cultures, and the challenge of globalization* (pp. 153–167). New York: State University of New York Press.

IMPLEMENTING *TE WHÀRIKI* AS POSTMODERNIST PRACTICE: A PERSPECTIVE FROM AOTEAROA/NEW ZEALAND

Jenny Ritchie

ABSTRACT

Since 1998 New Zealand early childhood educators have been required to implement programs consistent with Te Whàriki (Ministry of Education, 1996), a bicultural early childhood curriculum that validates and enacts kaupapa Màori (a Màori theoretical paradigm reflected through the medium of the Màori language). This curriculum document affirms and validates the status of Màori, the indigenous people of this country so that Pàkehà (New Zealanders of European descent) early childhood educators now need to reposition themselves alongside Màori whànau (families) and colleagues who remain the repositories of Màori knowledge. This means a decentering of the "mainstream" curriculum to develop models that parallel Màori language and content inclusively alongside western knowledges in all facets of the early childhood curriculum. This chapter utilizes data from a recent study to illustrate some ways in which the bicultural requirements of Te Whàriki, are being understood and experienced by early childhood teachers, teacher educators, and professional development facilitators. In particular, this chapter considers how Te Whàriki challenges non-Màori teachers' to confront the power relations that have historically positioned them as curriculum 'experts' and marginalized indigenous cultural knowledge.

INTRODUCTION

There is now general consensus within the early childhood field, which is also supported by a growing body of literature (Clark, 1995; Creasor & Dau, 1996; Derman-Sparks & Force, 1989; Genishi, Dyson, & Fassler, 1994; Hyun, 1998; Kendall, 1996; King, Chipman, & Cruz-Janzen, 1994; Mac Naughton, 1998; Stonehouse, 1991) that implementing child-responsive curricula requires paying attention to the ways in which culture and context mediate development. In the U.S.A., for example, the National Association for the Education of Young Children (NAEYC) document, "Developmentally appropriate practice in early childhood programs serving children from birth through age 8" (Bredekamp, 1987) has been revised to "explicitly acknowledge the powerful influence of [social and cultural] context on all development and learning" (Bredekamp & Copple, 1997, p. 41).

Critical and post-modern theorizing has focused on enhancing awareness of the socially constructed, contestable nature of cultural meanings, which are shaped by dominant discourses available and the power relations that underlie these. Stephen May's (1999) discussion of cultural hybridity theory, part of the wider postmodern critique, recognizes the fluidity and malleability of culture(s) and knowledges as historically situated social constructions. In this conceptualization, contingent local narratives and identities replace totalizing meta-narratives and essentialized or "museumised" (p. 23) identities. Meaning-making is thus situated within localized cultural and linguistic settings inscribed within these specific discourses (McLaren, 1995). In contrast to this view, most of the literature on teaching for diversity in early childhood education advocates a type of 'level playing field' multiculturalist approach. It is assumed that teachers can enact culturally responsive pedagogies that recognize and validate all cultures equally. In doing so, many teachers continue to assume that the practices they employ within their educational settings are culturally universal (May, 1999), ignoring the reality of a plurality of 'truths' (McLaren, 1995) and the existence of multiple cultural identities. Moreover, postmodern theories also challenge the universalistic hegemonic dominance assumed by western cultures to the detriment of indigenous and other non-western ethnic groupings within societies. Multicultural approaches that seek equal inclusion of cultures ignore the historicity of colonization and its impact on indigenous peoples.

In this chapter, I examine some of the experiences of early childhood educators when they are required to implement a bicultural curriculum that places primary emphasis on indigenous culture and knowledge. In the next section I use postmodern theories to further explore why a level playing field approach to culture is not equitable.

POSTMODERN CONSIDERATIONS OF CULTURE, IDENTITY, AND CURRICULUM WORK

It is necessary to consider the role of power relations and effects in any discussion of culture and identity politics, since some ethnic groups are clearly positioned where they have fewer choices than others (May, 1999). This is particularly evident in Aotearoa/New Zealand, where Màori continue to assert to have the colonialist society recognize their rights and validate their knowledges. McLaren (1995) asks us to interrogate the workings of these power relations, and to consider who has the power to exercise meaning, and whose culture is signified through educational practices. Postmodernist theorizing of difference cannot only create a space from which marginalized groups can speak, but can also enable people to move beyond essentialized identities and cultural representations (McLaren, 1995).

The challenge for educators is to pursue critically reflective, non-essentialized ways of understanding identity by engaging in "reflexive self-critical distancing from their own cultural discourses", which enables the validation "of other discourses/communities of language" (Werbner, cited in May, 1999, p. 23). In this process, previously subjugated knowledges "can be revalued and simultaneously employed as counter-hegemonic critiques" of the dominant discourses (May, 1999, p. 32). The western cannon of knowledges is supplemented and critiqued by repositioning our gaze to the very many other ways of reading and knowing the world. The modernist search for grand narratives is replaced by respectful recognition of the existence of a wide range of complex and contrasting parallel journeys of learning, and the challenge to western educators becomes one of accessing and validating these multiple pathways, while maintaining a stance of "permanent critique" (Foucault, 1984, p. 43, cited in Jones & Brown, 2001, p. 714).

Educators, then, can work to become aware of the ways in which certain discourses have been internalized and are therefore privileged, informing the ritualization of their practice (McLaren, 1995). They can question whose voices are heard and validated, and how these discourses are located within the wider positionings of power/knowledge and hierarchies of socio-economics, class, ethnicity, and gender (McLaren, 1995). Educators can focus on gaining understandings of the complexities of children's social and cultural identity, reflecting upon the nature of the life experiences that have shaped it, and the power relations behind children and families' socio-cultural positioning (Rosaldo, 1989, p. ix).

There have been a range of pedagogies documented that may be viewed as attempts to acknowledge a philosophy of difference, situating these differences within the power relations of the wider community. These include culturally relevant pedagogy; culturally responsive pedagogy (Osborne, 1991); culturally sensitive approaches (Gonzalez-Mena, 1992; Mangione, Lally, & Singer, 1993); culturally consistent and inclusive programs (Booze, Greer, & Derman-Sparks, 1996); and culturally congruent critical pedagogy (Hyun, 1998). With any attempt at generating such pedagogies, educators need to embrace difference, complexity, uncertainty, and even confusion (Grieshaber & Cannella, 2001) as part of the process.

Fundamental to the enabling of these alternative pedagogies is the recognition that no longer can western pedagogical expertise be taken as given. Instead, the new pedagogies that are to be generated can only represent the ways of being and knowing of those involved in their conceptualization and delivery. In order to enable alternative voices to be represented, educators have the pedagogical responsibility to promote dialogue with children and families, rather than attempting to speak for them, being conscious of how western educators' positioning and discourses are privileged and authoritative (McLaren, 1995).

It has been suggested that ethnic relations need not necessarily be hierarchical, exploitative, and conflictual (May, 1999). Skilled educators may be able to create openings, "prying open semantic spaces" (McLaren, 1995, p. 187) to enable a range of discursive positions to emerge, beyond the totalizing narrative of the majority ethnic group. As Homi Bhabha (1994) has written:

> What is theoretically innovative, and politically crucial, is the need to think beyond narratives of originary and initial subjectivities and to focus on those moments or processes that are produced in the articulation of cultural differences. These 'in-between' spaces provide the terrain for elaborating strategies of selfhood – singular or communal – that initiate new signs of identity, and innovative sites of collaboration, and contestation, in the act of defining the idea of society itself. (p. 2)

In moving beyond dichotomized positions of 'dominant' and 'other', into new hybrid, 'third spaces' (Bhabha, 1994; May, 1999; McLaren, 1995, p. 213; Meredith, 1998), it is important to consider issues of cultural essentialism and the question of "Who is defining whose culture and identity?" Peter McLaren (1995) asks, "Who has the power to exercise meaning, to create the grid from which Otherness is defined, to create the identifications that invite closures on meanings, on interpretations and traditions?" (McLaren, 1995, p. 213).

As we tiptoe into complex cultural territories, negotiating cultural terrains, not just our own but other people's, our motivation needs to be ethically guided and constrained:

> As educators we need to be exceedingly cautious about our attempts to speak for others, questioning how our discourses ... position us as authoritative and empowered speakers in ways that unwittingly constitute a reinscription of the discourse of colonization, of patriarchy, of racism, of conquest. (McLaren, 1995, p. 224)

It should be acknowledged that people "have a deep bond to their own historical cultural and linguistic communities" (May, 1999, p. 26). Further, cultures inevitably change over time. In legitimizing knowledges of cultures other than the western mainstream, there is a danger that these knowledges are redefined and essentialized by western educators. Marginalized or colonized people themselves must retain control over this process, in order to sustain the integrity of their culture (Smith, 1999), since their "identity is bound up with their sense of belonging"... and "their self-respect is affected by the esteem" with which their ethnic group is held in the wider community (Margalit & Raz, cited in May, 1999, p. 26). The development of *Te Whàriki* is one example of how educators from indigenous and non-indigenous backgrounds have worked together to validate indigenous knowledge and challenge the dominance of Eurocentric views of knowledge.

TE WHÀRIKI: A BICULTURAL DOCUMENT

Aotearoa/New Zealand is a country in which the indigenous people have experienced two centuries of colonization. Colonization not only involves economic exploitation of the indigenous people and their resources, but also the colonization of their minds (Jackson, 1992). Education as one of the main conveyors of mainstream values has been a key tool of the colonizer (Viruru, in Cannella, 2000). Consequently, Màori knowledges have been subjugated and devalued. Màori have faced the task of continually reasserting the validity of their knowledges and world view in the face of the colonialist onslaught, in which education has been a key instrument. Linda Tuhiwai Smith (1999) has written that:

> The colonization of Màori culture has threatened the maintenance ... and the transmission of knowledge that is 'exclusively' or particularly Màori. The dominance of Western, British culture, and the history that underpins the relationship between indigenous Màori and non-indigenous Pàkehà, have made it extremely difficult for Màori forms of knowledge and learning to be accepted as legitimate. (p. 175)

The bicultural model as demonstrated in *Te Whàriki* derives from Te Tiriti o Waitangi/The Treaty of Waitangi, the 'founding document' of our country that allowed for the governance by the British Crown (and by extension all those who have immigrated here under government policies), while providing significant guarantees to Màori, as tangata whenua (original people of the land). Te Tiriti o Waitangi, signed in 1840 between Màori chiefs and the British Crown, allowed the subsequent settlement and colonization of Aotearoa by Europeans, in exchange promising Màori self-determination over everything that they valued. *Te Whàriki* reflects this partnership between Màori and the majority culture, not only in its development, but also in its structure (Carr & May, 1993; May, 2001). It is innovative in that it is the first bicultural and bilingual curriculum document for our country. It reflects a bicultural partnership on the part of the writers by means of collaboration among Helen May and Margaret Carr from the University of Waikato, and Tamati and Tilly Reedy appointed by the National Te Kòhanga Reo Trust (May, 2001, p. 245), the parent body of the Kòhanga Reo movement for Màori language revitalization and whànau (family) development. It further represents the perspectives of a wide range of early childhood educators, since the development of the document involved extensive consultation with the early childhood community (Carr & May, 1993).

The bicultural orientation of *Te Whàriki* is clearly seen in its introductory statement that "all children should be given the opportunity to develop knowledge and an understanding of the cultural heritages of both partners to Te Tiriti o Waitangi" (Ministry of Education, 1996, p. 9). The document also contains a parallel Màori text providing Màori perspectives of the Kaupapa Whakahaere (Principles) and Taumata Whakahirahira (Goals or "Strands") (Ministry of Education, 1996, pp. 31–38). Tilly Reedy, one of the key contributors to the development of *Te Whàriki*, has described the bicultural paradigm expressed in the document as encouraging "the transmission of my cultural values, my language and tikanga, and your cultural values language and customs. It validates my belief systems and your belief systems also" (Reedy, 1995, p. 17). She considers *Te Whàriki* to offer "a theoretical framework which is appropriate for all.... A whàriki [flax mat] woven by loving hands that can cross cultures with respect, that can weave people and nations together" (Reedy, 1995, p. 17).

Te Whàriki explicitly requires early childhood staff to inclusively implement the Màori language and culture "making them visible and affirming their value for children from all cultural backgrounds" (Ministry of Education, 1996, p. 42). This is to be achieved by including "Màori people, places, and artifacts" and providing "opportunities to learn and use the Màori language through social interaction" (p. 43) when it is "included as a natural part of the programe" (p. 77) (see the appendix for more examples from *Te Whàriki*).

The bicultural focus of *Te Whàriki* document has had huge implications for early childhood education in this country, since very few early childhood educators are Màori, and very few non-Màori speak Màori or have an indepth understanding of Màori culture and values settings (Ministry of Education, 2004). Helen May, one of the *Te Whàriki* project directors, recognized that this bicultural emphasis would be a significant challenge for mainstream early childhood education:

> ... the holistic and bicultural approach to curriculum of *Te Whàriki*, inclusive of children from birth, was a challenge to staff who were more familiar with the traditional focus on play areas and activities for children in mainstream centres. (May, 2001, p. 248)

The theoretical paradigm of *Te Whàriki* draws eclectically not only upon Màori epistemologies but also upon a range of western early childhood ideologies including cognitive-psychological developmentalist theories, as well as sociocultural perspectives (Nuttall, 2002). The sociocultural and bicultural orientation of the document is evident in the core principles of Empowerment/Whakamana; Holistic Development/Kotahitanga; Family and Community/Whànau; and Relationships/Ngà Hononga. In an effort to incorporate local narratives and to prevent teachers from essentializing Màori culture, the curriculum also incorporates several pedagogical emphases relevant to our discussion of postmodern approaches.

First, the curriculum and therefore necessarily, associated professional development, has a reflexive orientation that invites educators to critique their practice and programs. Consequently, many early childhood teacher educators and professional development facilitators employ pedagogical strategies that aim to develop in teachers the competence of reflexivity, an ability to reflectively critique prior and ongoing assumptions, knowledge, and understandings (Siraj-Blatchford & Siraj–Blatchford, 1997). The objective is, through critically examining the history of colonization and racism in education and society generally, to generate a sense of commitment to bicultural development as a process for restorative social justice. "Bicultural development" (Metge, 1990; Royal Commission on Social Policy, 1987) is a social change process generated from a commitment to social justice and Te Tiriti o Waitangi. The implication of development is that of an ongoing process of change toward an equitable bicultural society (Metge, 1990). According to the Royal Commission on Social Policy (1987):

> Bicultural development has been proffered as an important element of any programe which has as its objective the advancement of the social and economic status of Màori people. It is an option which derives from the principles of the Treaty of Waitangi. (Royal Commission on Social Policy, 1987)

Postmodernist critique of the connotations and limitations of the concept of 'development' is noted here (Morss, 1996). Transformative change to address and redress social equity issues arising from the legacy of colonization will inevitably confront challenges arising from the multiplicities and complexities of culture, politics and historicity, and should not be conceived as some kind of simplistic, straight-forward "developmental" process.

The curriculum, in addition to providing some explanations of adults' responsibilities for each strand, and examples for the various goals, demonstrates its reflexive orientation by inviting educators to critique their practice and programs. Some examples of 'questions for reflection' posed in the document are as follows:

- In what ways do the environment and program reflect the values embodied in Te Tiriti o Waitangi, and what impact does this have on adults and children? (Ministry of Education, 1996, p. 56)
- In what ways is Màori language included in the program? (Ministry of Education, 1996, p. 76)
- What opportunities are there for children to experience Màori creative arts in an appropriate way and at an appropriate level? (Ministry of Education, 1996, p. 80)

The existence of these reflective questions threaded throughout the document offers the possibility and challenge of the ongoing critique required by reflexive practice.

A second tier of the pedagogical approach implicit in *Te Whàriki* is the need to develop in teachers a metacultural and metalinguistic awareness, a process that involves generating an understanding of the distinctiveness and relativity of their own and other cultures and languages (Skutnabb-Kangas,

1991). The illumination that "we know ourselves to be faced with multiple realities" (Edge, 1996) has been recognized as a key pillar of postmodernist pedagogical practice. This orientation facilitates "multiple and multi-ethnic perspective taking" (Hyun, 1998) and can also enable people to "recognize limits beyond which one's own sense of reality may not reliably transfer" (Sleeter, 1992). This awareness can be enhanced through the opportunity to learn, in as great a depth as possible, at least one other language and culture. In Aotearoa/New Zealand, Màori is nominally an official language, yet very few non-Màori have had the opportunity to learn the language. In order to deliver a bicultural early childhood curriculum, teachers need to be competent to incorporate te reo Màori (the Màori language) respectfully, appropriately, and authentically. As the revitalization of the Màori language continues, it is possible that this challenge will become less daunting for future generations, who may have had more exposure to and hence a more positive attitude to learning Màori than their forbears. However, at present outside of the kaupapa Màori education movement and Màori broadcasting, early childhood education is one of the few sites where there is an espoused commitment to sustaining te reo.

A third example of implementation of postmodern theories occurring under the mantle of *Te Whàriki*, is the shifting of power dynamics within early childhood settings. Since there are few Màori educators (only 6.9%) teaching in mainstream early childhood settings (Ministry of Education, 2004), and Màori average about 15% of the total population, an obvious way for educators to obtain this expertise is to recruit Màori families to contribute their expertise in tikanga and te reo Màori. Educators do, however, need to be sensitive to such issues since many Màori have been denied opportunities to become fluent in their own language (Henry, 1995), and have felt alienated by the education system (Awatere, 1984). Another aspect of change in power relations is evident in early childhood centers where bicultural development is ongoing, in that children, both Màori and non-Màori, can be observed to be seeking access to dual knowledge and linguistic paradigms, requesting both Màori and Western terms, explanations, and perspectives.

Despite these efforts, there is a danger that in their efforts to 'normalize' bicultural practices that have not historically been included in the curriculum, teachers will grasp at what is readily available in the public domain, and do this without recourse to Màori co-constructors of these new discourses. It is therefore also possible that teachers will present 'Màori' as a stable, essentialized identity or discourse in their practices, which can reaffirm their culturally bounded positionings and reinforce culturally transmissive practice (Jones & Brown, 2001; Nuttall, 2002). However well-intentioned (Simon, 1996) this may be, it will founder if it remains a representation of Màori knowledge as portrayed by non-Màori without the relationship and dialogue with Màori that enables legitimization and authentication attained through the shift in power relations necessary to genuinely respect and validate Màori positioning as arbitors of their languages and knowledges. The experiences of members of the early childhood community implementing this bicultural curriculum forms the focus of the rest of this chapter.

CONTEXT AND PROCESSES OF THE STUDY

The data reported here are drawn from a study of an early childhood teacher education program that had a long-standing commitment to preparing teachers who would be biculturally competent (Carr, May, & Mitchell, 1991; Ritchie, 2002). The study aimed to give voice to a range of participants, both Màori and Pàkehà, as they explored their understandings of concepts and processes related to the implications of the bicultural curriculum. Attention to postmodernist critiques of research suggests that methodology might address matters such as the partiality of understandings (Denzin & Lincoln, 1998; Sleeter, 1996); the valuing of localized, situated knowledge (Constas, 1998; Lave, 1993); and the need to create openings so that previously silenced voices are heard (Lincoln, 1995; MacNaughton, 1998; Simon, 1987). To achieve this aim, an emergent, eclectic, qualitative methodology was utilized, a key feature of which was the co-theorizing by the researcher and Màori participants of key meanings from the data, giving voice to Màori perspectives, and repositioning their discourse as central to the project. In addition, as researcher, I aimed to work as collaboratively as possible within the constraints of the circumstances around the participants. This collaboration was cognizant of an "ecological" research perspective (Schensul & Schensul, 1992, p. 197), which recognizes that the complexities of our lives and ways of operating are inextricably bound up with those of others. The collaboration was also a way of generating shared meanings that privileged the understandings of participants and aimed to recognize and diffuse the power differential within the researcher/researched dynamic.

Data were gathered from interviews with 18 early childhood educators with fairly even representation of both Màori and Pàkehà (of European descent) colleagues. These included two group interviews with Màori colleagues who preferred this option. Participants included eight university colleagues (four Màori and four Pàkehà), four professional development facilitators (three Màori and one Pàkehà), and six graduates of the teacher education program (three Màori and three Pàkehà). Additional data were gathered from 13 observations of different early childhood center programs; audiotaped discussion from 2 years of one university class; a collection of 12 samples of student assignments; and an open-ended written survey completed by 28 graduates of the teacher education program.

Initial coding utilized NuDist, a qualitative software program. Coding was recognized as being about making sense of the data, identifying patterns of meaning that had been negotiated and illuminated during interview discussions (Aubrey, David, Godfrey, & Thompson, 2000, p. 126). This method of coding as analysis has been described as "paradigmatic analysis of narrative data" (Wideen, Mayer-Smith, & Moon, 1998, p. 162). It was an emergent process through which codes were generated from and in response to the raw data, rather than being imposed from a previously identified framework. Some codes identified from the transcripts of interviews with Màori lecturing colleagues, for example, included under the overall heading of 'Màori knowledges', the importance of these for non-Màori, and the danger of these being compartmentalized and therefore marginalized within the overall teacher education program. Coding generated around the node of 'pedagogy' identified that pedagogy needs to be informed by lecturers' own research, incorporate critical thinking, and integrate te reo and tikanga (Màori language and culture). Additional codes for pedagogy concerned the issue of Pàkehà taking responsibility for the implementation of Màori content while consulting Màori; and the recognition of emotions felt by Pàkehà confronted with the challenge of their inadequate knowledge of te reo and tikanga. Further codes included tino rangatiratanga (Màori self-determination) as a central organizing principle, bicultural development goals and strategies, and racism as a barrier within the institution and as manifest in students within the program.

The process utilized was one of identifying key meanings for each statement/cluster of statements, which were then presented back to the participants for their consideration and comment. Further and more profound analysis was generated through co-theorizing with Màori participants. For example, a code generated was "goals of bicultural development", and the following is an excerpt from notes that were taken back to a co-theorizing hui (meeting) with Màori participants for discussion about the code of bicultural development.

Statements generated from interviews about the goals of bicultural development in early childhood education included:

- Tino Rangatiratanga (self-determination as guaranteed in Tiriti o Waitangi): Màori self-determination, Màori control over Màori domain
- Taonga Katoa (everything of value to Màori as protected by Tiriti o Waitangi): language revitalization, tikanga, Màori determine what is made available to mainstream in "public domain"
- Responsibility of Crown agents, e.g., early childhood teachers to: support and work toward tino rangatiratanga, respect and protect taonga, value ritenga Màori [Pania]: Goal of bicultural development "To empower Màori to take control and to empower Pàkehà to 'let go' of that power and work collaboratively toward equity. In many cases this process should be worked out cooperatively between both parties."

Part of the discussion from the hui critiqued power "sharing" issues implied by the bicultural goals of the curriculum:

Moana: You know there are varying ways of getting bicultural development.
Erina: Yeah but that support too is still not allowing Màori to determine, they're still not handing over, they still want to have the control. They see the support as the controlling still. ... they are not endeavouring to bring Màori forward and put Màori into those positions to actually determine their own pathway collaboratively.
Hiria: And they probably never will.
Erina: Well we can't get tino rangatiratanga until we work collaboratively anyway.

This co-theorizing strategy was a means of privileging Màori voices in a project lead by a Pàkehà researcher, not only within the data collection, but in the theorizing of the significance of those data. This process of creating shared meanings (Aubrey et al., 2000), of "making sense" through "a complex back-and-forth process of negotiation" (Shotter, 1990, p. 164) has been variously termed transformative "co-exploration" (Noddings, 1995, p. 93), "whitiwhiti korero" (Holmes cited in Bishop, 1996, p. 104), and spiral or koru discourse (Bishop, 1996; Bishop & Glynn, 1999). Dialogue becomes a tool for mutual construction of the frames of reference, being mindful that "this is always a sensitive task that involves total receptivity, reflection, invitation, assessment, revision, and further exploration" (Noddings, 1995, p. 191).

VOICES

In this section, contributions from participants are analyzed and links made to some of the postmodern theorizing outlined previously. In particular,

I focus on how participants were dealing with the challenges of enacting early childhood education in the context of the bicultural curriculum in this country.

Pàkehà Student Assignments

Written assignments by some of the year three Pàkehà students in the early childhood teacher education program indicated that they were conceptualizing their roles in early childhood as one of reflecting upon complexities, rather than delivering pre-determined packages. A student chose as her assignment topic in a level three course "The Professional Educator", to focus on her professional responsibility in terms of delivering te reo Màori within the early childhood curriculum:

> At the centre of any dilemma that I as a Pàkehà may have are of course the children. It is important to note that children are subject to values and attitudes of adults around them and society as a whole. Children must be given the right to choose their own values and ideas.
> Early childhood educators must provide children with a variety of learning opportunities, this includes opportunities to learn and discover in a positive way that Te Reo is a living and meaningful language that reflects a unique culture of the Tangata Whenua of Aotearoa/New Zealand. It is important that children are given the power to make their own decision about how they portray and treat people from other cultures. [Sandra]

Sandra appears to be resisting prevailing early childhood discourses that narrow the discursive possibilities available to teachers and children by reifying the child's interests as central and determining of the focus of early childhood programing. She seems to be aware of tensions that accompany her desire to position the subjectivities of children as central to her discourse, whilst her awareness of the complexities of the historically derived situation of denial of Màori knowledges implores her to enable these to be accessible to children. She is torn between her desire to recognize children's rights to "choose their values and ideas", having acknowledged that they are continually influenced by those discourses privileged (and/or devalued/ignored) by the adults who surround them. For many Pàkehà children and communities, Màori knowledges are neither valued nor accessible. She suggests that unless early childhood educators take the proactive stance of providing access to Màori language and cultural knowledges, children will not have "the power" to access this choice.

It has recently been acknowledged that "the strong free-play tradition of New Zealand's early childhood programs has meant that practitioners have been slow to move away from a narrow interpretation of 'interests' as children's self-selection of activities" toward project-type approaches involving "sustained learning experiences around shared interests in the socio-cultural contexts of home, community and centre" (Anning, Cullen, & Fleer, 2004, pp. 12–13). This narrow and individualistic focus on children's interests also inhibits the teacher from introducing parallel knowledges, such as Màori, in augmentation of those already demonstrated or expressed by children. Requirements to include te reo me ōna tikanga (Màori language and culture) may be sidelined by adherence to an educational philosophy that requires teachers to follow the child's lead and respond with an 'emergent' curriculum that is child-centered based on the ideology of 'free' play, the 'freedom' of which is inevitably constrained by the dominance of mainstream discourses as portrayed and sustained by adults including educators.

Glenda MacNaughton (2004) asks us to consider relations of power that exist in education settings and how these distort and silence some meanings and privilege others. Unless teachers have the tools to critically reflect upon the theoretical bases of their programing and interactive decision-making, the outcome is likely to be uncritiqued cultural transmission of dominant discourses (Nuttall, 2002). Teachers operating from this discursive position may not recognize that in fact, their teaching approaches are not culturally neutral, but are culturally situated. They derive from progressive western educational thinking, and have been given credence in the advocacy for 'developmental', 'child-centered' programs that have been an important counter to the insidious demand for teacher directed, instructional, structured 'preschool' programs. The student above seems to be aware of her role in providing children with an awareness that there are multiple rather than singular ways of being (Jones & Brown, 2001). She recognizes that children's dependence upon the adults around them can limit their access to power, reducing their available positionings to a mere "illusion of choice" (Cannella, 1999, p. 41).

Awareness of the ways culture plays into everyday practices raised by another third-year student in the excerpt below highlights how cultural differences apply to even the most routine practices such as meal times.

> The centers I have attended on practicum and placement have all had different expectations of appropriate meal time behavior. In most centers children are not permitted to share their food with others, but in one child care centre toddlers were allowed to swap and share with their peers (and teachers too). Our attitudes to 'appropriate' behavior with food can perhaps be linked to our cultural views – with Màori and Polynesian communities having a focus on providing for the collective group. Other issues at the meal table include the appropriateness of conversation. While I feel that this is a good time to encourage conversation and sharing within the group seated at the table, some teachers appear to focus more on getting through the process of eating as quickly as

possible so that the children can move on to more 'productive' activities, preferring that children eat in silence. Again, clear communication with family/whànau regarding our different expectations can help to determine the way our routines are implemented. Looking at the sociocultural principle of learning taking place within social contexts, I feel that meal times can be used as another learning experience. There are opportunities to initiate adult/child conversations, to encourage child/child interactions, and promote small group discussions. Conversations may be based around how meal time rituals are different in other people's homes. [Nola]

This student's comments show a reflective approach, which recognizes the centrality of culturally situated ways of being and knowing (Hooks, 1994, p. 43) to such everyday matters and rituals as the varying mealtime routines that this student has observed during her practicum experiences. Her use of inverted commas around the word 'appropriate' indicates an awareness of the problematic nature of assumptions of appropriateness, and the underlying power dynamics that enable teachers (and others) to privilege certain cultural values over others. She also touches on the differences between the western individualistic and indigenous collectivist orientations (Ritchie, 2001). This student also appears to have taken a broadly sociocultural perspective that involves recognition of the complexities of the discursive elements that surround such daily rituals. Her valuing of children's and their families' voices is a potentially useful strategy for addressing differential power effects created by the historical positioning of teacher as 'expert'. This student's discussion can be seen as indicative of a preparedness to recognize the limitations of her 'expertise', now repositioned alongside her respectful validation of te ao Màori, and its expression in the ways of knowing and habits of being of whànau Màori. In her validation of Màori and other perspectives, she has repositioned the dominant Pàkehà culture as only one possible set of cultural representations and practices, demonstrating a reflexive self-critical distancing from her own cultural discourses (Werbner, cited in May, 1999). Further, her focus on utilizing mealtimes as an opportunity to encourage discussion of different rituals may enable her to facilitate children toward "multiple and multi-ethnic perspective taking" (Hyun, 1998, p. 42).

These students' writings provide some indication of postmodern disquiet with fixed and universalist "recipes" for their future practice as early childhood educators. They are seeking to reconcile their learnings from university studies with the reality of early childhood center practice that they have experienced, and are willing to critique this with a view to applying a socioculturally based awareness of the need for children to have opportunities to be exposed to and have validated a range of discourses including those of te ao Màori.

Kindergarten Teachers

Dealing with multiple perspectives is a challenge to mainstream early childhood discourse that traditionally has treated cultural diversity in tokenistic ways, despite specific programs that have been developed to move our pedagogy beyond this limited scenario (Derman-Sparks, 2004). Graduates of the teacher education program in the study demonstrated some of the ways that they were reframing their understandings to embrace the status of the indigenous Màori while at the same time, they were grappling with balancing the required emphasis on Màori ways of being and knowing with the need to demonstrate respectful and responsive practice about cultural differences generally. For example, one of the Pàkehà kindergarten teachers made a distinction between a bicultural focus that gives primary recognition to Màori as tàngata whenua, the indigenous people of this land, and multiculturalism whereby all people require respect for their ethnic ways of being and knowing.

> *I still incorporate and encourage a lot of multiculturalism in the program, but you can use tokenism and get away with it, you can't with Màori... . And if I have got say a Samoan child I will try a bit harder, but I have all sorts of different things around and it is respecting the human race sort of thing... . You just sort of have little bits, whereas bicultural is not little bits, it's the whole thing. [Camille]*

This comment highlights a particular tension in early childhood programs in Aotearoa/New Zealand, particularly in large urban settings where there may be many diverse ethnic groups present. The privileging of Màori perspectives may seem inequitable in this situation, but then, of course, the pervasiveness of the dominant Pàkehà discourse is seldom questioned! This teacher's use of the phrase "little bits" could be read as disparaging of her attempts to address individual children in terms of their ethnicity, or alternatively as an honest reading of the reality of working in a situation where the demanding teacher/child ratios mean that in many early childhood settings "not all voices are equally valid" (McLaren, 1995, p. 195). Her dilemma appears to be focussed around the dual demands of recognizing the need to validate the cultural paradigm of all the diverse ethnicities of participating children at the individual level, whilst maintaining a programmatic-level integration of te reo and tikanga throughout her curriculum implementation. *Te Whàriki* itself recognizes the need for affirmation and celebration of cultural differences, and contains the expectation that children will gain a positive awareness of their own and other cultures (Ministry of Education, 1996).

For another kindergarten teacher, an understanding of bicultural development focused on the importance of the Màori language, recognizing that language is intrinsic to cultural expression:

> *I think because the staff [at this kindergarten] are actually dedicated towards te reo Màori and because te reo Màori is New Zealand's second language – well it's New Zealand's first language really isn't it? – then we look at things and we sort of think if we want a society that is ... able to get on with each other and have an understanding of each other's languages and cultures then what we do is we actually will go ... bicultural first and from there will extend ourselves out to multiculturalism. Probably what I am looking at is that for now you are in New Zealand and there are two languages in New Zealand you know. That's a very strong point of view. I think we are flexible enough to actually ... try to acknowledge everything, but our main focus is biculturalism. What actually happens is that we are strong enough to be committed to our biculturalism but also be flexible enough to allow other things to come in. [Andy]*

This teacher describes how he and his colleagues have reflected upon their aspirations for a society that is respectful of difference. He is also exploring ways to reconcile the competing discourses of biculturalism and multiculturalism. In addition, he recognizes the challenge of trying to "acknowledge everything" that is required to genuinely deliver a programe that recognizes and supports the culture and ethnicity of all attending children and families. However, from his perspective, bicultural development is a first priority that will eventually lead to multiculturalism, rather than seeing the two discourses as simultaneously compatible processes operating at different levels of the individual and/or program.

Another contrasting view of the bicultural/multicultural tension was offered by one of the Màori professional development facilitators, who saw the bicultural paradigm as inclusive of multicultural diversity. Her view derives from Te Tiriti o Waitangi, which validates two parties, Màori as the indigenous people, and the British Crown, under whose auspices all subsequent immigrants derive their legitimacy as citizens:

> *Moana: I have to endorse the bicultural kaupapa (paradigm), and I do totally, because I don't believe it excludes a multicultural perspective, I think it embraces ...*
> *Jenny: ... so that when we are talking about bicultural we are not talking about just purely Pàkehà and Màori?*
> *Moana: No, we are talking about all our wider whànau [families, used here in an inclusive general sense to refer to citizens]. Because they are descendants of the Crown.*
> *Jenny: They have come in on the Crown immigration policies.*
> *Moana: That's an inclusive model.*

This validation of indigenous culture alongside settler and immigrant ethnicities appears to provide a framework that acknowledges the competing agendas for affirmation and inclusion, thus potentially moving discursive possibilities beyond the limitations of a "laissez-fare pluralism" (McLaren, 1995, p. 195) that merely serves to reify the discourses of the dominant culture.

Another Pàkehà teacher was attempting to move beyond a sense of tokenism in the treatment of Màori content within her program planning. She described how she had begun to build her program around the particular context of the local Màori families involved in her kindergarten. After reflecting upon what she had gained from attending a professional development course focussing on bicultural development, she describes how her emphasis has shifted to focussing on children's families and the local cultural context:

> Susan: I think looking at their families as individuals. And looking at who they are now and where they have come from and the people that are relevant to them ... Our big focus is trying to find information about people in the area from the past and important figures in Màori history.
> Jenny: You are talking about very local, specific to your hapü [sub-tribe]?
> Susan: Yes, very local, and we have approached one of our grandparents, and she is sort of our kuia [female elder]. We don't want to impinge on her too much because she is a very busy lady ... And yeah, she is sort of helping us ... to find out about relevant people, relevant events which we can incorporate into stories, books, pictures, whatever we want to do so that it is part of our program.

Expectations expressed within *Te Whàriki* include the statement that "Activities, stories, and events that have connections with Màori children's lives are an essential and enriching part of the curriculum for all children in early childhood settings" (Ministry of Education, 1996, p. 41). By empowering people such as this Màori grandmother from within the local kindergarten community to be resources and supports for programing, the teacher is also ensuring that "Decisions about the ways in which bicultural goals and practices are developed within each early childhood education setting should be made in consultation with the appropriate tangata whenua [indigenous people]" (Ministry of Education, 1996, p. 11). This teacher is moving beyond a reliance on formulaic unitary discourses, or 'absolute truths' within her early childhood care and education practice, toward organic, 'local truths' (Noddings, 1995), which represent the subjectivities and power/knowledge discourses of Màori children and their whànau (families) legitimately within that early childhood community. This is an example of a practical attempt to incorporate local, contextualized narratives (May, 1999) instead of the widely available public domain stock myths and legends that many teachers rely solely upon. In this way, meaning-making is also handed over to an appropriate Màori linguistic and cultural expert

(McLaren, 1995), whilst care is taken to ensure that this burden is not unreasonable.

All three teachers recognized the benefits of inviting Màori people to support bicultural development within their kindergarten programs. One had Màori friends whom she had invited into her kindergarten:

> I have called on Màori friends at times to help me in that too. A couple of times they have come into the class just doing some things like telling some legends, so that I can hear how they tell it, because I still have problems where I'm thinking, "I'm telling the story about Maui [a legendary supernatural ancestral hero] and who am I to tell that sort of thing?" So if I have had a Màori person come in and help me with that, and we have all heard the story together and then I say: "Remember when [her friend told her] story?" and so I do use that. [Camille]

This teacher demonstrates her understanding that some Màori may consider it inappropriate for a Pàkehà to represent Màori cultural knowledges. A Màori colleague in the study had, for example, expressed concerns about non-Màori representing Màori knowledges:

> The worst thing that can happen is that there's a Pàkehà who stands to represent me on behalf of me and the way I see the world. ...For me as a young Màori mother, the message is that that Pàkehà knows more about being Màori than I ever could, therefore I failed straight away ...[Kahu]

This sentiment is echoed by other Màori, such as academic Ella Henry (1995), who, whilst acknowledging the validity of Pàkehà support for kaupapa Màori, has sometimes experienced negative emotions, finding it "spooky and ironic" when Pàkehà speak Màori (p. 16). She has said that, "On a bad day, it pisses me off. On a good day I think, Well, it's one way of surviving. I mean, I find it frustrating when I meet Pàkehà who speak better Màori than me" (Henry, 1995, p. 16). Indigenous Hawaiian academic Julie Kaomea (2004) has also criticized non-indigenous people with superficial understandings of Hawaiian culture attempting to represent indigenous understandings. It can also be daunting for even well-intentioned Pàkehà educators to stand before Màori and attempt to speak a second language that they are not confident in using. A Pàkehà student in this study wrote in an assignment that: "I am guilty of 'clamming up' in the presence of Màori parents, for fear of offending by speaking their language of which they may or may not have knowledge of". [Sandra]

In summary, the Pàkehà teachers in this study had found ways of circumventing the potential difficulty of (mis)representing Màori perspectives, by fostering relationships with Màori whànau (family members) within their centers and also calling upon Màori friends. They therefore exercise caution about their role as 'expert' in Màori cultural matters, allowing Màori to speak for themselves (McLaren, 1995). This represents a shift in power dynamics that affords status to both Màori people and knowledges, repositioning Màori content and pedagogies from the margins to the center of the curriculum (Banks, 1996; Hooks, 1984).

Professional Development Facilitators

A Màori professional development facilitator described a scenario from her work in a particular kindergarten setting, where 90% of the children were Pàkehà and 10% Màori. With her encouragement, the Pàkehà teachers had written a story in te reo Màori and introduced it with the children, to an enthusiastic response:

> All the kids in that whànau [literally family, used here to refer to the whole center] love that korero [story], they loved it so much that they made another pukapuka [book] on a similar theme. The kids would predict the pages, say the te reo, and one of the choice things was that the kids wouldn't just go and pick it because you thought they should, they would actually go and get that book when their parents brought them in and take it to their parents, and share the pukapuka with their parents from themselves. So to me that's like magic. Because that's kids validating kaupapa Màori because those practitioners they set that ball rolling, so they are very important as change agents. So you had the teachers, the kids, the families, all awhiing [embracing] the kaupapa [philosophy]. I thought it was just so powerful, awesome. [Moana]

This colleague illustrated how, through being introduced to the existence of a parallel, alternative world view, that of te ao Màori (the Màori world), Pàkehà children were now seeking this knowledge, and claiming it as a right to have access:

> And a really neat thing was the way kids up and ask for te reo Màori, they'll say "What's the Màori name for that bird, cause we were in the bush", and I think that's choice. It's non-Màori asking kaiako [teachers] for, "Can you find out what that word is in Màori?". Powerful depth, it's like saying "We want to know, it's valuable". [Moana]

These examples of Pàkehà children specifically choosing to share with their parents a book written in Màori, and further requesting translations into Màori indicate a shift in awareness. Perhaps these children, in their pursuit of access to kupu Màori (Màori words), are no longer operating from a singular, monocultural, monolingual paradigm, but are becoming reoriented to the existence of a parallel way of reading the world, that of te ao Màori (the Màori world). Furthermore, they are not only aware of this as an alternative conceptual framework, but are actively demanding access to furthering their knowledge of it, this in turn placing expectations on their non-Màori teachers to share in this journey of discovery. As these children and their teachers expand their knowledge of te reo Màori and apply it in learning-relevant experiential contexts they are meeting the *Te Whàriki* goal that children develop "an appreciation of te reo as a living and relevant language" (Ministry of Education, 1996, p. 76). From the children's point of view, they see no reason to limit their understanding of Màori to one particular context, such as a particular story. They are keen to take this new awareness of the existence of a parallel world of te reo, te ao Màori further on an ongoing basis. Teachers, having instigated this process with the support of the professional development facilitators, are now being gently urged by the children, to venture beyond their own limited knowledge of Màori, shifting out of the safe cocoon of standard semantic understandings as expressed through ritualized early childhood practices derived solely from the western cannon of knowledge to augment these with those from te ao Màori (May, 1999; McLaren, 1995). As long as this is done ethically, respectfully, and in consultation with Màori sources, for Màori children and whànau present, this positive co-exploration may re-inscribe their language and culture as a valid and desirable discursive arena, resulting in a transformative shift in power relations (McLaren, 1995; Noddings, 1995).

At a co-theorizing hui with Màori participants, another Màori colleague related how the staff at a center she had been supporting decided to focus on the Màori creation story of Rangi and Papa, Sky Father, and Earth Mother. The teachers had sent the story home in a newsletter for the parents to read before introducing it to the children. Màori colleagues reflected on the reasons that this initiative had been so successful:

> Hiria: *Preparation and being creative about how we can deliver that message and make it tangible enough for non-Màori to see 'Okay, we can belong to that'.*
> Aroha: *That's right, and so it was a non-threatening way of including all the families.*
> Hiria: *And it's also like seeing the face of Màori through their tūpuna [ancestors], through Rangi and Papa.*
> Aroha: *The connection to that was to the whole whakapapa [geneology].... But the thing that also came out alongside of whakapapa ... and understanding that wairua [spirituality] is something that you carry anyway and that that wairua is all about connecting and the connections that you make in those relationships are whanaungatanga [family connectedness]. That's just so awesome, and the important thing is that they are actually articulating it and they are talking about moving it out beyond the staff and into their whànau [the wider family of parents and children attending that center].*
> Moana: *Bringing Te Whàriki together.*
> Aroha: *An indicator of that is the child role-modeling Maui [a legendary supernatural ancestral hero] out in the playground. So something really great is happening, eh. It's becoming part of their knowing. It's a natural part of it.*

Although postmodernist thinking cautions against pedagogical representations being described as 'natural', this colleague's use of this term is indicative of her perception of a major shift having occurred. She recognizes that the inclusion of Màori content within the early childhood program to the extent whereby Pàkehàchildren are voluntarily acting out Màori legends represents a shift in what has been 'normal' for early childhood settings in Aotearoa/New Zealand. Their discussion around Màori concepts of connection with mythological heroes as ancestors, and the wairua (spirituality) of this interconnectedness indicates that these Màori participants had witnessed far more than a superficial essentialized representation of cultural meanings: there was movement beyond dichotomous othering into a third space where Màori knowledges were being shared with Pàkehà children and families in that early childhood setting (Bhabha, 1994; May, 1999; McLaren, 1995, p. 213; Meredith, 1998).

These Màori colleagues are theorizing a transformative process of curriculum implementation, whereby they have supported teachers to an acceptance that it is their professional responsibility to initiate learning opportunities that actively recruit children from non-Màori families and their parents to participate in early childhood education programs that validate indigenous worldviews, knowledges and languages, sometimes provided with the support of Màori whànau members. This is a working model of an alternative to uncritiqued acceptance of the normalization and universalization of the cultural knowledge of the majority ethnic group (May, 1999).

CONCLUSION

As a comparatively and deliberately non-prescriptive document that has an intrinsic focus on critical reflection (Ritchie, 2003), *Te Whàriki* has the potential to represent and validate multiple realities rather than being a tool for imposition of regimes of power and knowledge. It is deliberately envisioned as a *Whàriki* or woven flax mat, which can be woven by different groups of teachers and families to create their own "distinctive patterns", derived from different cultural perspectives, philosophical emphases, community priorities, and organizational differences (Ministry of Education, 1996, p. 11). Its focus on reflective questions encourages a genuine responsiveness to children, families, educators and their specific circumstances. Joy Cullen (2003) recently described *Te Whàriki* as "a catalyst for change" (p. 288). The examples provided in this chapter indicate that *Te Whàriki* has the potential to be employed as a tool to challenge regimes of truth and discursive dominance generated from the historical context of colonization, through its re-validation of previously subjugated knowledges of Màori children and whànau.

Links with postmodern theories have been made to some of the shifts in thinking and in practice identified in the study. These include the need for educators to operate from a position of reflexivity, a "disposition of continual critique" (Cannella, 1999, p. 42) that incorporates a respectful understanding of the complexities of multiple realities and cultural perspectives, based on an understanding of the historical embeddedness of cultural and political relations in Aotearoa/New Zealand. From this positionality, teachers can invite the participation of whànau Màori (Màori families) to become more fully involved with the lives of their children within the early childhood setting, and also to support teachers in their ongoing commitment to bicultural development. As Màori knowledges and practices are incorporated inclusively within the everyday environment, resources, and interactions of early childhood settings, children (and adults) present have opportunities for enrichment through enhanced metacultural and metalinguistic awareness and respect for different ways of knowing and being in the world, co-creating the potential for new collectively co-constructed world views (Shotter, 1993).

Examples have been given here of educators working with Màori families to create their own *Te Whàriki*-based programs, reflecting the values and world views of Màori children and their whànau, as well as those of other children and families. The bicultural modalities that are being created may not constitute a dialectic of two opposing cultures, Màori and Pàkehà, but instead are blossoming as new entities of their own, or third spaces (Bhabha, 1994) which have also been termed "te whai ao"[1] by Huata Holmes (Bishop, 1996, p. 102). This whai ao/third space comes from the pursuit of new shared understandings, created from the validation of local Màori knowledges alongside mainstream perspectives. Each early childhood center is thus generating its own discourses of bicultural curriculum, which are necessarily shifting and complex as educators and whànau (families) continually weave and reweave the fabric of their 'whàriki'.

NOTES

1. Whaiao is a poetic term for 'daylight'. "Ka puta koe ki te whaiao, ki te aomarama" (Williams, 1971, p. 485). This refers literally to emerging into a world of light.

REFERENCES

Anning, A., Cullen, J., & Fleer, M. (2004). Research contexts across cultures. In: A. Anning, J. Cullen & M. Fleer (Eds), *Early childhood education. Society and culture* (pp. 1–15). London: Sage.

Aubrey, C., David, T., Godfrey, R., & Thompson, L. (2000). *Early childhood educational research. Issues in methodology and ethics.* London and New York: Routledge/Falmer Press.

Awatere, D. (1984). *Màori sovereignty.* Auckland: Broadsheet.

Banks, J. A. (1996). Transformative knowledge, curriculum reform, and action. In: J. A. Banks (Ed.), *Multicultural education, transformative knowledge and action. Historical and contemporary perspectives* (pp. 335–348). New York: Teachers College, Columbia University.

Bhabha, H. K. R. (1994). *The location of culture.* London: Routledge.

Bishop, R. (1996). *Collaborative research stories: Whakawhanaungatanga.* Palmerston North: Dunmore.

Bishop, R., & Glynn, T. (1999). *Culture counts: Changing power relations in education.* Palmerston North: Dunmore.

Booze, R., Greer, C., & Derman-Sparks, L. (1996). Creating culturally consistent and inclusive early childhood programs for all children and families. *Child Care Information and Exchange, 1,* 60–62.

Bredekamp, S. (1987). *Developmentally appropriate practice in early childhood programs serving children from birth through age 8.* Washington, DC: National Association for the Education of Young Children.

Bredekamp, S., & Copple, C. (1997). *Developmentally appropriate practice in early childhood programs.* Washington, DC: National Association for the Education of Young Children.

Cannella, G. (1999). The scientific discourse of education: Predetermining the lives of others – Foucault, education, and children. *Contemporary Issues in Early Childhood, 1*(1), 36–44.

Cannella, G. (2000). Critical and feminist reconstructions of early childhood education: Continuing the conversation. *Contemporary Issues in Early Childhood, 1*(2), 215–221.

Carr, M., & May, H. (1993). Choosing a model. Reflecting on the development process of *Te Whàriki:* National early childhood curriculum guidelines in New Zealand. *International Journal of Early Years Education, 1*(3), 7–21.

Carr, M., May, H., & Mitchell, J. (1991). *The development of an integrated early childhood programme.* Paper presented at the 5th early childhood convention, Dunedin, New Zealand.

Clark, P. (1995). Culturally appropriate practices in early childhood education: Families as the resource. *Contemporary Education, 66*(3), 154–157.

Constas, M. (1998). The changing nature of educational research and a critique of postmodernism. *Educational Researcher, 27*(2), 26–33.

Creasor, B., & Dau, E. (1996). *The anti-bias approach in early childhood.* Pymble: Harper Educational.

Cullen, J. (2003). The challenge of *Te Whàriki*: Catalyst for change? In: J. Nuttall (Ed.), *Weaving Te Whàriki i. Aotearoa New Zealand's early childhood curriculum document in theory and practice* (pp. 269–296). Wellington: New Zealand Council for Educational Research.

Denzin, N., & Lincoln, Y. (1998). Introduction. Entering the field of qualitative research. In: N. Denzin & Y. Lincoln (Eds), *Strategies of qualitative inquiry* (pp. 1–34). Thousand Oaks, California: Sage.

Derman-Sparks, L. (2004). Early childhood anti-bias education in the USA. In: A. van Keulen (Ed.), *Young children aren't biased, are they? How to handle diversity in early childhood education and school* (pp. 13–22). Amsterdam: B. V. Uitgerverij.

Derman-Sparks, L., & Force, A. B. C. T. (1989). *Anti-bias curriculum. Tools for empowering young children*. Washington, DC: National Association for the Education of Young Children.

Edge, J. (1996). Cross-cultural paradoxes in a profession of values. *TESOL Quarterly, 30*(1), 9–30.

Genishi, C., Dyson, A. H., & Fassler, R. (1994). Language and diversity in early childhood: Whose voice is appropriate? In: B. Mallory & R. New (Eds), *Diversity and developmentally appropriate practice* (pp. 250–268). New York: Teachers College Press.

Gonzalez-Mena, J. (1992). Taking a culturally sensitive approach to infant-toddler programs. *Young Children, 47*(2), 4–18.

Grieshaber, S., & Cannella, G. (Eds) (2001). *Shifting identities in early childhood education: Expanding possibilities for thought and action*. New York: Teachers College Press.

Henry, E. (1995). Chapter one: Ella Henry – executive director of Greenpeace New Zealand. In: H. Melbourne (Ed.), *Màori sovereignty. The Màori perspective* (pp. 13–22). Auckland: Hodder Moa Beckett.

Hooks, B. (1984). *Feminist theory: From margin to center*. Boston: South End Press.

Hooks, B. (1994). *Teaching to transgress. Education as the practice of freedom*. New York: Routledge.

Hyun, E. (1998). *Making sense of developmentally and culturally appropriate practice (dcap) in early childhood education*. New York: Peter Lang.

Jackson, M. (1992). The treaty and the word: The colonisation of Màori philosophy. In: G. Oddie & R. Perrett (Eds), *Justice, ethics, and New Zealand society* (pp. 1–10). Auckland: Oxford University Press.

Jones, L., & Brown, T. (2001). 'Reading' the nursery classroom: A Foucaldian perspective. *International Journal of Qualitative Studies in Education, 14*(6), 713–725.

Kaomea, J. (2004). *Indigenous studies in the elementary curriculum: A cautionary Hawaiian example*. University of Melbourne.

Kendall, F. (1996). *Diversity in the classroom. New approaches to the education of young children*. New York: Teachers College Press.

King, E., Chipman, M., & Cruz-Janzen, M. (1994). *Educating young children in a diverse society*. Boston: Allyn & Bacon.

Lave, J. (1993). The practice of learning. In: S. Chaiklin & J. Lave (Eds), *Understanding practice: Perspectives on activity and context* (pp. 3–32). New York: Cambridge University Press.

Lincoln, Y. S. (1995). In search of students' voices. *Theory into Practice, 34*(2), 88–93.

MacNaughton, G. (1998). *Respecting difference or recycling racism? A case for reconceptualising curriculum discourses of multiculturalism and gender equity*. Paper presented at the Reconceptualising the Early Years of School Conference, Canberra.

MacNaughton, G. (2004). Exploring critical constructivist perspectives on children's learning. In: A. Anning, J. Cullen & M. Fleer (Eds), *Early childhood education. Society and culture* (pp. 43–56). London: Sage.

Mangione, P. L., Lally, J. R., & Singer, S. (1993). *Essential connections: Ten keys to culturally sensitive child care.* Sacramento, California: Far West Laboratory for Educational Research and Development.

May, H. (2001). *Politics in the playground. The world of early childhood in postwar New Zealand.* Wellington: Bridget Williams Books and New Zealand Council for Educational Research.

May, S. (1999). Critical multiculturalism and cultural difference: Avoiding essentialism. In: S. May (Ed.), *Critical multiculturalism. Rethinking multicultural and antiracist education* (pp. 11–41). London: Falmer.

McLaren, P. (1995). *Critical pedagogy and predatory culture.* London: Routledge.

Meredith, P. (1998). *Hybridity in the third space: Rethinking bi-cultural politics in Aotearoa/New Zealand.* Palmerston North: Massey University.

Metge, J. (1990). *Te kohao o te ngira, culture and learning.* Wellington: Learning Media.

Ministry of Education. (1996). *Te Whàriki. He Whàriki màtauranga màngà mokopuna o Aotearoa Early childhood curriculum.* Wellington: Learning Media.

Ministry of Education. (2004). *Nga haeta matauranga. Annual report on Màori education 2002/2003.* Wellington: Ministry of Education.

Morss, J. R. (1996). *Growing critical. Alternatives to developmental psychology.* London: Routledge.

Noddings, N. (1995). *Philosophy of education.* Boulder, Colorado: Westview Press.

Nuttall, J. (2002). Early childhood curriculum in theory, ideology and practice: Using *Te Whàriki. Delta, 54*(1 and 2), 91–104.

Osborne, B. (1991). Towards an ethnology of culturally responsive pedagogy in small-scale remote communities: Native American and Torres Strait Islander. *Qualitative Studies in Education, 4*(1), 1–17.

Reedy, T. (1995). *Toku rangatiratanga na te mana-matauranga. Knowledge and power set me free.* Paper presented at 6th early childhood convention, Tamaki Makaurau, Auckland.

Ritchie, J. (2001). Reflections on collectivism in early childhood care and education in Aotearoa/New Zealand. In: S. Grieshaber & G. Cannella (Eds), *Embracing identities in early childhood education: Diversity and possibilities* (pp. 133–147). New York: Teachers College Press.

Ritchie, J. (2002). *"It's becoming part of their knowing": A study of bicultural development in an early childhood teacher education setting in Aotearoa/New Zealand.* Unpublished Ph.D., University of Waikato, Hamilton.

Ritchie, J. (2003). Te *Te Whàriki* as a Potential Lever for Bicultural Development. In: J. Nuttall (Ed.), *Weaving Te Whàriki* (pp. 79–109). Wellington: New Zealand Council for Educational Research.

Rosaldo, R. (1989). *Culture and truth: The remaking of social analysis.* Boston: Beacon Press.

Royal Commission on Social Policy. (1987). *The Treaty of Waitangi and social policy. Discussion booklet no 1.* Wellington: Royal Commission on Social Policy.

Schensul, J., & Schensul, S. (1992). Collaborative research: Methods of inquiry for social change. In: M. LeCompte, W. Millroy & J. Preissle (Eds), *The handbook of qualitative research in education* (pp. 161–200). San Diego: Academic Press.

Shotter, J. (1990). Social individuality versus possessive individualism: The sounds of silence. In: I. Parker & J. Shotter (Eds), *Deconstructing social psychology* (pp. 155–169). London: Routledge.

Shotter, J. (1993). *Cultural politics of everyday life. Social constructionism, rhetoric and knowing of the third kind.* Buckingham: Open University Press.

Simon, J. (1996). Good Intentions, but .... In: R. Steele (Ed.), *Whakamana Tangata*, (3rd ed.) (pp. 38–42). Wellington: Quest Rapuara.
Simon, R. I. (1987). Empowerment as a pedagogy of possibility. *Language Arts*, 64(4), 370–382.
Siraj-Blatchford, I., & Siraj-Blatchford, J. (1997). Reflexivity, social justice and educational research. *Cambridge Journal of Education*, 27(2), 235–248.
Skutnabb-Kangas, T. (1991). Bicultural competence and strategies for negotiating ethnic identity. In: R. Phillipson, E. Kellerman, L. Selinker & M. Swain (Eds), *Foreign/second language pedagogy research* (pp. 307–332). Clevedon: Multilingual Matters.
Sleeter, C. (1992). *Keepers of the American dream: A study of staff development and multicultural education*. London: Falmer.
Sleeter, C. (1996). *Multicultural education as social activism*. Albany: State University of Albany Press.
Smith, L. T. (1999). *Decolonizing methodologies. Research and indigenous peoples*. London and Dunedin: Zed Books Ltd and University of Otago Press.
Stonehouse, A. (1991). *Opening the doors. Childcare in a multicultural society*. Watson, ACT: Australian Early Childhood Association.
Wideen, M., Mayer-Smith, J., & Moon, B. (1998). A critical analysis of the research on learning to teach: Making the case for an ecological perspective. *Review of Educational Research, Summer*, 68(2), 130–178.

APPENDIX. BICULTURAL EXPECTATIONS WITHIN TE WHÀRIKI

This appendix provides further examples of some of the bicultural statements within *Te Whàriki*. There is recognition of the need for educators to be actively aware of "bicultural issues" as seen in these statements:

- Particular care should be given to bicultural issues in relation to empowerment. Adults working with children should understand and be willing to discuss bicultural issues, actively seek Màori contributions to decision-making, and ensure that Màori children develop a strong sense of self-worth (Ministry of Education, 1996, p. 40)
- To address bicultural issues, adults working in early childhood education should have an understanding of Màori views on child development and on the role of the family as well as understanding the views of other cultures in the community (Ministry of Education, 1996, p. 41)

Particular Màori content to be included in the program are also suggested, as in these examples:

- Activities, stories, and events that have connections with Màori children's lives are an essential and enriching part of the curriculum for all children in early childhood settings (Ministry of Education, 1996, p. 41)

- There should be a recognition of Màori ways of knowing and making sense of the world and of respecting and appreciating the natural environment (Ministry of Education, 1996, p. 82)

Te Whàriki recognizes that bicultural development in centers should involve local Màori:

- Decisions about the ways in which bicultural goals and practices are developed within each early childhood education setting should be made in consultation with the appropriate tangata whenua (Ministry of Education, 1996, p. 11)
- There should be a commitment to, and opportunities for, a Màori contribution to the program. Adults working in the early childhood setting should recognize the significance of whakapapa, understand and recognize the process of working as a whànau, and demonstrate respect for Màori elders (Ministry of Education, 1996, p. 64)

PART III:
TEACHER EDUCATION AND PROFESSIONAL DEVELOPMENT

POSTCOLONIAL THEORY AND THE PRACTICE OF TEACHER EDUCATION

Radhika Viruru

ABSTRACT

What does a body of work that arose originally from looking at literary works written in formerly colonized societies have to do with the education of those who would teach children? In this chapter I argue that there are several similarities between the concerns that many postcolonial scholars have raised and those of critical teacher educators. After defining postcolonial theory, I explore why this set of ideas is an important theoretical lens for those who prepare teachers of young children. I then explore some of the themes raised by a postcolonial critique of teacher preparation, relating each to my own practices as a teacher educator. In doing so I aim to show how postcolonial scholarship can serve as a vital resource for those engaged in educating educators.

Postcolonial analyses such as those presented in this chapter are particularly relevant in the current context of teacher education and reflect Kincheloe and Steinberg's (1998) call for a new paradigm in teacher education. According to Kincheloe and Steinberg (1998), the culture of "modernist positivism" that has shaped the field of teacher education during most of the 20th century "no longer answers the compelling questions of our time" (p. 3). The rules of such a culture were that all complex phenomena were best understood by reducing them to their smallest parts and then piecing those together according to the laws of cause and effect (Kincheloe & Steinberg, 1998). Thus the study of teaching from a positivist perspective looked at the parts of teaching such as test scores and seating arrangements, in order to eventually understand the whole. Such an approach, however, does not recognize the complex social realities that are part of any classroom as well as the active role that human beings play in creating the environments in which they function. Furthermore, Kincheloe and Steinberg suggest, positivist paradigms focus essentially on the passive nature of teaching, seeing teachers as those who pass knowledge on, not as those who create knowledge. Such a view of teaching not only devalues teachers as meaning-making human beings, but also encourages a "surrender to the given, to view existing institutional arrangements, *authorized* arrangements as objective realities" (Kincheloe & Steinberg, 1998, p. 8).

Within the new paradigm(s) of teacher education proposed by Kincheloe and Steinberg (1998), the focus is what they term "unauthorized methods" (p. 3). Within such paradigms, teachers are encouraged to free themselves from the boundaries within which they have been hitherto fore authorized to function, and to ask the unauthorized questions that the field has ignored. Within such a paradigm, it is assumed that human experience is too complex to be "understood" by reducing it to simplistic categories. The categories themselves are now open for teachers to question. Macedo (1990) emphasized that such critical pedagogies are always antimethod, in that there are no specific roads that have to be followed. Rather, teachers are encouraged to create roads for themselves. As its very name suggests, postcolonial theory is grounded in the dismantling of structures that have placed limits upon groups of people. As such it creates a frame of mind that lends itself easily to asking unauthorized questions. Thus it serves as a vital ally in the effort to create new paradigms of teacher education.

DEFINITIONS OF POSTCOLONIAL THEORY

Postcolonial theory is not a simple concept to define or to limit (Young, 2001). Even though it has been around for some time (at least since the publication of "Orientalism" by Edward Said in 1978), it seems that scholars who use it are asked more than ever to provide definitions of what they mean by it. This in itself seems to illustrate some of the issues that postcolonial theory tries to address: a tolerance for multiplicities and ambiguities, a rejection of simplistic ways of viewing the world that are devoid of complexity, and an unveiling of the will to power that labels such ways 'unintelligible and confusing. However, for the purposes of this chapter an attempt is made to summarize some of the main concerns of postcolonial theory as well as how they relate to the field of teacher education.

Mongia (1996) has asked the question about whether postcolonial theory refers to texts, practices, psychological conditions, or concrete historical processes? According to Dimitriadis and McCarthy (2001), postcolonial theory is a "highly contested terrain" (p. 6) with a peculiar kind of elasticity that makes it hard to define, especially when it is seen as "all kinds of struggles for all kinds of independence against all kinds of domination in and around all parts of the globe" (p. 6). The very broadness of such definitions seems to have led to more and more efforts (Shohat, 1993) to define exactly what is and is not postcolonial. For example, the United States has been seen as contested terrain: both a postcolonial nation in that it was once considered a colony and a colonizer (scholars such as King (2000) have pointed out that it too has engaged, and some would say continues to engage in, colonizing activities). Young (2001) stated that postcolonialism as a body of work embodies recognition of the Western imperialist project and its complicated legacies, such as the appearance of decolonization as nations have attained freedom, juxtaposed with political and economic domination that seeks power over people's identities and intellects. According to Young (2001), an essential part of resistance to this kind of domination is work that focuses on contesting forms of domination, the creation of equal access and the collective generation of political and cultural identities (Cannella & Viruru, 2004; Young, 2001). Therefore, when I write about turning a postcolonial lens on teacher education, the intentions are similar: to look at how forms of domination rule the field and how it can be opened up to diverse forms of knowledge.

As Dimitriadis and McCarthy (2001) have pointed out, getting too involved in questions such as what postcolonialism really means can distract one from some of the real possibilities that have been raised through it. Thus the postcolonial can be "thought of as a site of dialogic encounter that pushes us to examine center/periphery relations and conditions with specificity wherever we can find them" (Dimitriadis & McCarthy, 2001, p. 7). Lopez (2001) defines postcolonialism as a shared condition: that of having been or presently being colonized. As has been explored elsewhere (Cannella & Viruru, 2004), other scholars have emphasized the need to take a broad view of the word colonized, and to view it as any set of conditions where, through the direct or indirect use of power, individuals or groups of people have been constrained to behave in ways that are alien to their cultural ways of being, and that violate and contradict their view of the world.

The postcolonial scholarship of Bhabha (1994) has focused not upon the obvious binaries of colonized and colonizer but on the intermingling of the two. As Lopez (2001) argues, although those who have been subjected to colonization find it impossible to live without the languages and cultural practices of the colonizers, they cannot fully identify with them. Thus, Lopez sees postcolonial studies as having two major tasks: first to reckon with the colonial past, analyzing the ways in which people's lives have been impacted by outside rule, and second, to analyze and articulate postcolonial diasporic identities. Diasporic identities include heterogeneity, diversity and difference that turn accepted truths on their heads and seek to reconceptualize them in forms that tolerate ambiguities, multiplicities, and contradictions. As a teacher educator, two of the most critical elements of my classes are critical reflection on the past, exploring how teachers have been a group that has been denied power on the basis of gender; and exploring ways in which teaching can become a more open field that restructures itself as its populations, knowledge bases, and practices are reconceptualized (Ladson-Billings, 1998).

So far I have outlined some of the main concepts of postcolonial theory and how they are of relevance to the study of teacher education. I now explain some of the tools or key ideas that postcolonial scholars have used in their analyses of different disciplines. These include:

1. Looking at discourse (defined by Loomba (1998) as "a whole field or domain in which language is used in particular ways", p. 38). Postcolonial theory, particularly the work of Said (1978) draws upon the work of Foucault (1980) in recognizing the power of discourse. Said illustrates the power of discourse through the example of the "Orient", a place that had a physical existence, but bore little resemblance to the fantasies created around it and that came to define it.
2. Recognizing the limitations of the concept of voice: Mohanty (1989) has argued that the concept of voice, the idea of allowing people to speak and voice their ideas, but only within the structures of dominant discourses, is at best partial and at worst, a way of reinforcing existing power structures while giving the impression of openness.
3. A focus upon the disciplining of bodies: although the notion of power as operating through discourse is essential to an understanding of postcolonial

theory, it can also be used to analyze situations where power is used to physically repress and subjugate people (Vaughan, 1993).

These concepts are now explored in further detail in relation to teacher education.

TEACHER EDUCATION

The question as to whether or not postcolonial theory belongs in any analysis of a field that seems far removed from nations and colonizers has been addressed by several critical teacher educators (Kincheloe & Steinberg, 1998; McLaren, 1998). As McLaren (1998) explains, postcolonial theory serves as an important way in which pedagogical discourses can be problematized in light of the current trajectory toward global capitalism. McLaren sees postcolonial pedagogies as recreating the field of education in anti-imperial, anti-colonial, anti-racist and anti-homophobic terms, and as the kind of pedagogy that "challenges the very categories through which the history of the colonized has been written" (p. 230).

Echoing similar concerns, Britzman (2003) argues that teacher education has become one of the great concerns of the 20th and 21st centuries, as it grapples with the circumstances of educating masses of diverse populations. According to McWilliam (1995), teacher education is also viewed by many as related to the state of the economy as parallels are often drawn between economic declines and the quality of schools and teachers. Coupled with this is a belief that more governmental intervention in the processes of education is needed, "in the name of greater accountability for diminishing resources" (McWilliam, 1995, p. 8). Hawley (in McWilliam, 1995) has gone so far as to say that reforming teacher education has become a "popular sport in the US" (p. 8). Scholars such as Liston and Zeichner (1987) have argued that as teacher educators tried to incorporate themes such as language, history, and culture into the curricula, many others reacted by defining the problem of teacher quality in increasingly narrower terms (such as vocationalism, differentiating schools). Other teacher education scholars such as Kincheloe (2004) have focused on the need to rebuild teacher education as a discipline that not only helps teachers learn how to transform knowledge disciplines into curriculum but that also engages teachers in the study of students, working within their cultural context. Kincheloe also considers it important for teachers to learn to study their own practice in relation to race, class, and gender oppression. Scholars such as Goodlad (2004) concur that there is nothing more important than making sure that schools that serve young children are committed to democratic goals; however as he points out, little attention to these goals is reflected in most teacher education programs. Thus postcolonial theory and teacher education share a joint commitment to more democratic ways of being, and the opening of fields to new knowledge and to social justice.

Before proceeding I offer a word of caution about my own practice as a teacher educator. As is elaborated in the sections that follow, postcolonial theory cautions one against subscribing mindlessly to binary opposites, and to my way of thinking theory practice is one of the most compelling examples of a binary that is overused. In my case, the practices I use as a teacher educator are very often indistinguishable from how one thinks as a postcolonial scholar. Thus what follows may appear as more of a framework than a set of specific actions. There is another reason for this. One of the things that we often discuss in my classes is the futility of dwelling too long on particular activities, lesson plans, or classroom strategies. As I caution my students, taken out of context these are often meaningless. The practices I describe in this chapter are accounts of the kinds of discussions that we have in classes and the kinds of questions that are raised rather than a recipe for how postcolonial teacher education ought to be done.

LEGITIMACY OF POSTCOLONIALISM AND TEACHER EDUCATION

One of the most striking similarities between these two very different bodies of knowledge has been the extent to which both of them are called into question as being necessary at all. Postcolonialism has been called into question as being little more than "the latest catchall term to dazzle the academic mind" (Jacoby, 1995, p. 2). Postcolonial theory has also been criticized for being situated in too many fields to be useful to any one, for trying to deconstruct something that itself is inevitably part of, and perhaps most damagingly of all, for having collapsed inward on itself as it attempted to bring too many diverse disciplines together (Appiah, 1991; Cannella & Viruru, 2004; Loomba, 1998; Shohat, 1993; Sleman, 1994). However, even when viewed from a numbers perspective, the numbers are staggering: by the 1930s, 84.6% of the globe had experienced colonization in some form or the other and only eight countries worldwide had never been ruled by formal European governments (Fieldhouse, 1989). Given the magnitude of this project, the idea that exploring the legacies of postcolonialism is a wasted

Postcolonial Theory and the Practice of Teacher Education 145

effort seems ludicrous in itself. A more complete discussion of the reasons that postcolonial theory is considered unnecessary is beyond the scope of this chapter, but can be found in the sources referenced above.

Teacher education, especially in the United States, has, like postcolonialism, come to occupy the status of a 'not really necessary' field. In November 2003, for example, the State Board for Educator Certification (SBEC) in Texas approved a new 2-year certification temporary teaching certificate. According to the Texas Association of School Boards (TASB):

> The certification proposal allows those with a bachelor's or advanced degree to teach in grades 8–12 without training in pedagogy if the degree is in the subject taught and if applicants pass two state exams, one covering subject area and the other classroom skills. Districts would be required to provide intensive support, including a mentor, pre-service training, and staff development, which TASB strongly supports... Those given the two-year certification would be eligible for five-year certificates if school districts were satisfied with the teachers' performance in the classroom.

This is the latest in a series of developments that have questioned whether teacher education programs are needed at all. As Kincheloe (2004) has stated, "the first decade of the 21st century is an exciting and frightening time for supporters of a rigorous, practical, socially just and democratic teacher education" (p. 2). According to Kincheloe, teacher education programs graduate only about 100,000 teachers annually whereas approximately 2 million teachers are needed in schools in the next few years. The most common response to this problem is to lower standards for certification, or as Kincheloe comments, to do away the concept of certification altogether and "admit[ting] anyone into the teaching ranks who breathes regularly" (p. 2).

Popkewitz (1993) found that in many parts of the United States alternative certification possibilities have been put together, often to "remedy teacher shortages in the sciences and in urban education" (p. 270). He described the evolution of the "Teach for America" program, which originated in the honors thesis of a student at Princeton University and became a widely organized private effort to meet the needs of school districts that suffered from chronic teacher shortages. According to Popkewitz, Teach for America involves enrolling in an eight-week summer institute and then committing to two years of teaching in urban and rural areas. As Popkewitz puts it, this program represents a unique coming together of both conservative and liberal interests. This program is funded by many major corporations (for example AT&T) and represents the embodiment of the conservative viewpoint that "public services are best accomplished through competition among private interests" (Popkewitz, 1993, p. 271). At the same time, according to Popkewitz, "Teach for America" enables children of affluent America to express their commitment toward a more equitable future. Although the aims of the program may be laudable, the fact remains that such programs call into question the need for colleges of education and their teacher preparation programs.

Postcolonial theory, I often conclude, is challenged because it seems to raise questions that are too uncomfortable to deal with. Similarly, teacher education programs, it appears, do not always fit everyone's agenda. Several of my former students have described how they sometimes encounter a certain amount of hostility to their "pedigree"; they are given the message that their ability to raise questions about existing structures is not always appreciated. In effect they are told not to upset the status quo. Other scholars have also pointed out that alternative certification programs reinforce the idea of teaching as a temporary occupation and that temporary occupations are rarely taken seriously. As they assert, a person who has a 4-year degree in a particular discipline is usually looking for a career, not just a job. One way in which I address the legitimacy of teacher education is through the use of an episode that is part of the Public Broadcasting Service (PBS) education series, "The Merrow Report" (2005). What makes this particularly poignant is that portions of this documentary were actually filmed at our institution and in my classroom a few years ago. The documentary paints our institution in an unflattering way as adhering to outdated ways of teacher education that emphasize theory over practice. The documentary also makes the case that teacher education works as a 'cash cow' for many universities, which is why they insist on keeping the education of teachers within the province of 4-year degree granting institutions rather than opening it to alternatives. As a postcolonial scholar, some of the questions that I often bring to the discussions that ensue are: (1) how do you define theory and practice and how do you think they are different from each other; (2) who does it privilege to constantly focus on practical experience and who does it exclude; (3) how would it change the field of teacher education if it were to move outside 4-year colleges, and who would that include/exclude? As can be expected, the responses are wide-ranging. Some students respond quickly with answers that they would see more of the practice of white middle class females if all they did was spend time in the field. Many of them recognize that they would encounter very few multicultural ideas if they were not at a university. Often too, discussions center on the value of children in contemporary American society, especially when one has to defend the need to have those who work with them to be highly educated.

Legitimacy is a far more complex issue than might appear at first glance. Exposing preservice teachers to issues concerning who should teach and what qualifications and experience constitute quality teaching is a crucial part of re-energizing the field.

WHAT ARE THE BASICS?

Both critical teacher education and postcolonial studies have had to grapple with the question of what constitutes basic knowledge: in the former to answer the question of what all teachers should know, in the latter what constitutes knowledge. Loomba (1998) has shown how processes of colonialism were based upon the need to conquer barbarians and to bring to them the basics of human life. Europeans in late medieval times saw those living outside civilization as equivalent to the 'wild man' of the forest: "hairy, nude, violent, lacking in moral sense and excessively sensual" (Loomba, 1998, p. 57). As Loomba (1998) points out this image is a reflection of "all manner of cultural anxieties" (p. 57) and distorts the fact that precolonial societies possessed multiple knowledges of their own. The disturbing part of this discourse that centers on bringing the benefits of civilization to others is how completely it silences the whole question of the ethics of the colonialist endeavor. By focusing attention on what so-called backward cultures supposedly lacked, the entire ethical question of colonizing another country can be ignored.

Although there are obvious parallels to be drawn between the work of teachers and the task of bringing civilization to backward cultures, I focus on another not so obvious similarity. It appears in many ways that teacher education suffers from a similar malaise of selective attention. Preservice teachers are subjected to course after course about teaching children to read; to much specifically directed coursework on how to teach various subjects such as science and social studies, and to a lesser extent to courses on understanding children, even if from the limited vantage point of child development (Cannella, 1997). All of this is justified as the basics of teacher education, the lore that every teacher must know (Kincheloe & Steinberg, 1998). Britzman (2003) has criticized the kind of utilitarian and practical knowledge that is a staple in many teacher education programs for its "cultivated passivity" (p. 46). As she points out, the term 'teacher training programs' captures the mechanistic essence of this philosophy toward teacher education. Popkewitz (1987) has also shown how overdependence on developmental psychology has further constituted teacher education as a conformist field, as it accepted, unchallenged, the kind of so-called scientific knowledge that psychologists/scientists had 'discovered' about human beings. Yet as scholars such as Apple (1987) cogently ask equally basic but unexplored questions such as who is doing the teaching, and how the construction of teaching as predominantly women's work is linked to the sexual and social division of labor, and patriarchical and class relations.

Kincheloe (2004) has also critiqued what he calls the top-down standards movement, where the role of the teacher is redefined as one who reads from a pre-written script. Teacher education programs have often followed this model, encouraging what Kincheloe calls a technician orientation toward the profession. These models bear close resemblance to colonial conditions of a completely hierarchical situation, where

> a small elite group at the top of the pyramid conduct[s] the scholarly decision-making work while a larger corps of worker bees at the bottom carry out their directives. Such totalitarian organizational models are disturbing as they perpetuate an elitist mode of scientific management that positions teachers as interchangeable cogs in a machine that turns out students as standardized products. (Kincheloe, 2004, p. 5)

For many students, this is the kind of representation of teaching with which they are rarely confronted. They are more commonly exposed to and are more comfortable being exposed to warm and fuzzy images of teaching: to hearing what noble work it is and how the non-monetary rewards are enough to compensate for the inadequate pay, and even that wanting to be paid a decent salary is somehow unethical. Dealing with these kinds of issues is some of the most important work that I do. An example that is often helpful with students, and that draws directly from postcolonial analysis of conditions under colonial rule, is looking at the degree of autonomy that teachers have when compared with other professionals: how many other professionals have restricted access to a phone during working hours? How many other professionals are given written scripts to follow to the letter? Often students relate anecdotes from working in a daycare situation where they have been told precisely how to pat children to put them down for a nap, with no regard for the wishes of the child or the situation, and the dehumanization that they as so-called professionals felt in such a situation. Students often relate stories from field experiences about instructions as to how to help children into their cars when their parents come to pick them up, and how demeaning the insistence on procedures being followed at all times can be. I also share analyses such as that of Agnello (2001), who talks about the five characteristics of semiprofessionals and how teachers often embody those characteristics, even if not intentionally: (1) they are white-collar workers; (2) they provide services; (3) they are subject to supervision; (4) they are salaried bureaucrats; and (5) they lack standards of excellence such as those of the medical and legal professions.

Postcolonial theory has been used to analyze the concept of how those who are colonized can become complicit with their own colonization, where they come to accept colonization as ultimately what is best for them. In such situations, the power of the discourses in which they are engulfed can make people believe that they are incapable of making decisions for themselves (Viruru, 2001). Kincheloe and Steinberg (1998) have referred to this as the "politics of stupidification" (p. 2) of teachers. To counter such stupidification, in my classes I use postcolonial theory to frame discussions about how an emphasis on knowing the basics of teaching, such as how to write an instructional objective correctly, can be viewed as restricting one's access to the kinds of knowledge that changes and empowers the field.

Similarly, I employ postcolonial theory to question many of the accepted realities of teaching young children. For example, we examine why in the State of Texas in the 1998–1999 school year, school districts had to fill over 63,000 teaching positions. The data show that while approximately 5,700 positions were created to accommodate increasing student enrollment, most vacant positions resulted from existing teachers retiring (11,000) or leaving the profession (46,600) (Texas State Board of Educator Certification, 2003). Students find too, that many teachers leave within the first few years of joining the profession. Many students are unused to hearing about these issues and can interpret this as being discouraging or unnecessarily negative. Many would rather hear, it seems, about the latest in decorating learning centers or even more importantly, the one failsafe way to make sure that they can manage the children. The complex and unwieldy realities of employment and resignation that surround the profession that they want to enter do not seem particularly important. Some students seem more likely to look for a reasonable explanation that makes all of these things acceptable than to question the structures that constitute the field of teaching. Despite some initial resistance, the feedback I get from students does indicate that this kind of awareness was something that they felt really helped them understand the field that they would enter as teachers.

In summary, as the above discussion illustrates, it is important not only for scholars of teacher education as well as for preservice teachers to be able to take a critical view of such concepts as the basics of teacher education, but to raise questions about how those basics have been constituted.

Binaries

One of the other "basics" of teacher education seems to be a belief in two things: there is a definite binary (you are either a teacher or not; student teachers are emphatically not teachers) and there is a great belief in the power of practical experience, setting up the other binary of the theoretical versus the practical. Postcolonial theory is particularly useful in examining the effect that binaries have on our ways of functioning, pointing out how this kind of logic denies the multiple states that individuals can inhabit at any one time. It also encourages teachers to separate things into clear categories (you are either a visual or auditory learner) and can cause them to become frustrated with students who do not respond to this kind of categorization.

The first binary, that of having attained the state of teacher, is one that I find postcolonial theory particularly useful in debunking. Just as Said (1978) talked about how colonizing European discourses created the phenomena of Orientalism, it can be said that the myth of the perfect teacher exists and is held up as an ideal toward which students are supposed to strive: someone who knows how to manage the classroom, keep the kids in order and still deliver the state mandated curriculum exactly as scheduled. Said discussed how places that are identified as the Orient do exist, but they bear very little resemblance to the myths that have been constructed around them. Images of the Orient as a place of "romance, exotic beings, haunting memories and landscapes" (p. 21) are critiqued by Said (1996) as being a part of the process by which the Occident created and then managed the corporate institution of the Orient, "dealing with it by making statements about it, authorizing views of it, describing it, by teaching it, settling it, ruling over it" (p. 21). Similarly, preservice teachers are often confronted with images that bear little resemblance to reality. They are told to seek and trust only expert knowledge, not the knowledge that comes from their own life experiences. Many students firmly believe that eventually one does attain a stage where one 'gets it' completely: as teachers, they have the right tools and knowledge to handle any situation and teach any student. In contrast to this state of attainment, postcolonial theory suggests that human beings, including teachers, inhabit multiple and contradictory states at any given time, and that human life (including classroom teaching) is fraught with complex ambiguities that are experienced differently at different times. As can be imagined, the aims of teacher education are quite different when viewed from these opposing angles: in one case one works toward that state where one has the right number of lesson plans, toys, and classroom management techniques to handle any situation. In the other scenario, one recognizes that all knowledge is partial and dependent on the situation in which it is produced, that one can never fully have all the answers, and that such ambiguity itself opens the door to recognizing that the children with whom teachers work should not be fitted into neatly labeled categories. In the latter case, rather than viewing children as bodies to be managed, the focus shifts to creating a classroom environment that is focused on the struggle for equity and justice. An example that I often use has come from my experiences doing research in a classroom in India. One day the teacher had to leave to handle an emergency and left me in charge of the classroom. As she was in a hurry, she did not leave any guidelines as to what to do. Perhaps reflecting many years of Western education, I chose to read the children a story. One of the children did not listen to the story and asked if she could do something else like work on a puzzle. I could immediately come up with two completely different right answers: "yes" and "no". The yes came from training in ideas such as respecting children's rights as individuals and repeated reminders that children only learn when they are interested or motivated to do something. The "no" came partially from my own upbringing and from a knowledge of the school atmosphere, where self indulgence and an overemphasis on personal desires was deeply ingrained. As I emphasize to my students, neither answer would have been really complete in that one rarely knows with certainty what the "right" thing to do is. What is known, however, is that retaining an openness to difference does help in creating equitable relationships with young children.

The second binary that seems to dominate teacher education is the distinction between theory and practice. Across the state in which I live and work, the belief in field-based teacher preparation seems universal as well as deeply embedded. The undergraduate courses that I teach the most often have recently had a fairly extensive field-based component added to them, even though the credit hours that the students receive have remained more or less the same. There has been surprisingly little resistance to this, as students unquestioningly subscribe to the belief that where field experiences are concerned, more is always better. Even when the field experiences turn out to be disappointing, these are accepted with comments such as "I need to learn what not to do as well as what to do". The problem with such an approach, as Kincheloe (2004) argues, is that it creates an artificial divide between theory and practice that ends up giving teacher education students isolated facts without the "conceptual connections that are essential to the development of worldviews, visions of educational purposes and the development of a teacher persona as ethical agent" (p. 20). When theory and practice are seen as separated from one another, many teachers see only the immediacy of their own experiences and do not build sensitivities to forces that are not directly visible.

Britzman (2003) has pointed out that prospective teachers come into teacher education programs with established views about what teaching is about, based mostly on their own experiences of being a student. Such experiences are constructed mainly on classroom performance and are often validated in teacher education programs where the 'how' of classrooms is given primary importance. As Britzman asserts, such an approach denies both the prospective teacher as well as the children s/he works with as creators and experiencers of knowledge. It fixes school as a reality that the preservice teacher must accept. Ginsburg's (in Britzman, 2003) study found that the focus of many teacher education programs was to "insure the maintenance of school structure" (p. 63), illustrated by the coverage of content such as writing instructional objectives and lesson plans. The message that prospective teachers get from such a program is that knowing how to do things like writing elaborate learning plans adequately prepares you to run your own classroom. As Britzman elaborates, reducing such a complex phenomenon as being able to teach down to a binary of prepared/ill-prepared does not do justice to the multiple realities that preservice teachers have to confront. For Britzman, the prepared/ill-prepared binary implies that "everything depends on the teacher" (p. 224). Thus, unless the teacher is in control, no learning will occur. Control, moreover, is located within the individual rather than in a comfortable classroom environment: it rests with the teacher. This is the aspect of the classroom upon which teachers are judged the most harshly, both by themselves and by others. Such a view of control, according to Britzman, impacts the curriculum that is taught, as "pedagogy is reduced to instilling knowledge rather than coming to terms with the practices that construct both knowledge and our relationships to it" (p. 225).

In a similar vein, Stoler and Cooper (1997) have discussed the complex formations of power in colonial regimes, illustrating how an important part of the process of establishing power was the construction of categories that defined those upon whom power was to be established. These categories created boundaries of identity to which the colonized were supposed to conform. As these authors comment, not only did colonial regimes try to define the constituents of a particular society, but they did so based on the assumption that the state was a non-partisan regulator of power. Thus in both cases, power is seen as existing outside the web of social relationships, with one single and neutral source. And in both cases, this turns out to be a myth, as most of these endeavors necessarily fail. Colonial regimes, despite their best efforts, were unable to retain power. Similarly, for many teachers who go into teaching believing not only in their ability but also in the importance of absolute control in the classroom, teaching is a difficult and unrewarding profession (Viruru, 2001).

My efforts in my teacher education classes are to emphasize, once again, the ambiguity and complexity that characterizes all human relationships and to caution students against believing that anything can be as simple as having and keeping power. Rather than looking at classrooms as places where constant binary power struggles are enacted, we try to look from the angle of teaching being about relationships. One of the examples that seems to work well in such situations is talking about the commonly accepted truth about the 'terrible twos'. It is understood that children aged two are prone to throw temper tantrums, especially when they want something and do not get it, and early childhood professionals learn strategies to handle these outbursts (such as ways to hold children so that they can hurt neither themselves or their caregivers). If, however, one thinks of a tantrum not as a phenomenon isolated within children (and more particularly as something that can be attributed to their particular age or developmental stage), but as a disagreement between two people, the ways in which this can be handled change quite dramatically. When caregivers reflect on how they themselves may be contributing to the situation (such as the expectation of a tantrum), other possibilities emerge. If one considers that children also encounter frustration when they are alone, but do not commonly engage in tantrums when by themselves, one is led to consider that a tantrum is part of a social relationship. If a tantrum is considered a "normal" part of growing up, and something that children cannot help doing, it becomes an issue to "manage". However, if it is something that is part of a relationship, the very way in which one approaches it changes. When one focuses on the idea that working with young children is a relationship, then it opens the door to ambiguity and the possibilities of joint solutions.

The structuring of teacher education programs around the binaries of theory/practice and preservice/inservice limits the kinds of thinking in which students can engage and channels their energies toward directions that reify the status quo. Thoughtful consideration of the ways in which binaries have defined the field of education is crucial to a redefined teacher education. When one can challenge the idea that becoming a teacher is a state that one attains, and explore the possibility that teaching is a career where one is constantly creating and furthering relationships with children, new possibilities emerge. Furthermore, when one moves away from the idea that theory and practice or thought and action are separate from one another, spaces are created that allow for more thoughtful actions.

STEREOTYPES: 'AN EASY MAJOR'

If ever there was a field populated by stereotypes, teaching is that field. Britzman (2003) commented on the particularly insidious nature of the stereotypes of teachers: 'bookish', 'brainy', 'like a narc', 'big head', 'old maidish'. Postcolonial theory is a particularly valuable resource in looking at some of the forces behind the creation of stereotypes and the damaging effects that they can have. As Cohn (1996) contends, the classification practices of the British Raj in India, supposedly based on ethnographic surveys, were used to create rigidly fixed categories of existence (such as British and Indian). Once the categories were established people were expected to conform to them. It has even been suggested (Loomba, 1998) that categories commonly used to describe identity such as caste in India and tribe in Africa became much more rigid during colonial times. According to Stoler and Cooper (1997), the creation of stereotypes, by reducing human complexity to a static entity, confuses social and political relations and legitimates control. Furthermore, Loomba (1998) has outlined how specific ways of seeing and representing groups of people are used to establish colonial institutions of control. Classifying people and creating stereotypes about them can be used to create divisions among them and used to justify such stereotypes on the basis of these classifications (such as saying that women are more suited to teaching as they are inherently more nurturing). Therefore a critical examination of teacher education from a postcolonial point of view, as well as teaching teacher education from a postcolonial point of view, must include an examination of the stereotypes that populate the field and an analysis of the forces that both create and maintain those stereotypes.

Female teachers, it has been pointed out, are even more susceptible to being caricatured in well-defined ways, being seen as "self-sacrificing, kind, overworked, underpaid and holding an unlimited reservoir of patience" (Britzman, 2003, p. 220). As Waller (1961) observed, favorable stereotypes about teachers reflect societal ideals about what teachers ought to be and unfavorable ones represent common opinions about what they are really like. Similarly, teacher education students suffer from the stereotype of being there because they have a 'calling'. This, among other things, has led to the fact that universities rarely recruit teacher education candidates, in contrast to other academic programs such as engineering that recruit vigorously (Goodlad, 2004). According to Goodlad, the apparent assumption that students will appear by themselves without any effort on the part of the universities, has led to low percentages of minority students in teacher education programs. Goodlad has documented how large numbers of students may be lured away from teaching due to lack of recruitment efforts, particularly as many programs require students to start taking education coursework in their junior years.

Teacher education programs have also been typecast as an 'easy' major, where all students, especially those in elementary education programs, make things and color (Viruru, 2001). Yet as Goodlad (2004) has commented, this is far from the truth. Goodlad related how charges are often made that most elementary education students major in their particular field. However, as he found, students take as much as 50% of their coursework in their own college in only a few institutions (Goodlad, 2004). Such disdain toward teacher education programs extends beyond popular beliefs as teacher education programs are often among the mostly tightly regulated of university disciplines. For instance, Kincheloe (2004) commented that teacher education programs are commonly threatened with punitive measures unless they meet certain 'standards'. Goodlad also noted how the perception that teaching is an easy major has led to lax requirements as far as the sequence in which courses have to be taken.

Yet what seems the most damaging of all is the fact that many prospective teachers accept the idea that teaching is an easy major as a truth and seem to allow that to limit their own perceptions of themselves as well as their chosen profession. Thus, in my experience, many students come to believe that the salaries of teachers are adequate for the work that they do, as it is genuinely 'easier' than what other professionals do. The postcolonial viewpoint on the concept of voice is useful in understanding this particular kind of logic. According to Spivak (1988), there are limitations on whether the subaltern can speak: subalterns can only speak within the structures of domination in which they function. It is difficult if not impossible for those with little power, and for those who are constantly being given the message that they need instruction and guidance, to truly "speak" outside of the discourses in which they are situated. Thus, preservice teachers may be exposed to teachers who genuinely believe some of the stereotypes about teacher education, for these are the only structures that they know. Exposing students to wider considerations of these issues is one way in which to debunk these myths.

One of my strategies as a teacher educator is to expose students to the work of scholars who can help them consider issues like gender and the status of the profession from other perspectives. The work of Michael Apple (1987) has made it clear that teacher salaries have little to do with the supposed "easiness" of the job, but are closely related to gender. As providing compulsory education to all children became an increasingly expensive endeavor to school districts, due to population growth, hiring women for teaching positions was seen as one way to control those costs, as women were employed for one half or one third of the salaries that men were paid for the same work. The complexity of the job has in many ways deterred men from continuing in the profession (Apple, 1987). According to Strober (1984), when teaching was a relatively casual occupation and one that could be engaged in for short periods of time (such as during winter when the demands of farming eased up), it was fairly attractive to men. However, as both the standards for teacher certification rose (which decreased the autonomy that teachers had over what happened in their classrooms) and the length of the school year increased, the number of men who taught decreased rapidly (Apple, 1987, p. 64). Interestingly too, as Apple further points out, in England, many of the men who enrolled in teacher training colleges did so with a view to gaining entry to the civil service, the branch of the government that administered the colonies. Thus the enterprise of colonialism was one of the factors that contributed to the gendered nature of teaching today, as teaching was seen as a temporary step that led to one's eventual goals, not as a permanent profession. Workers in nonpermanent professions are rarely accorded either respect or equitable pay.

Apple (1987) goes as far as to say that the field of teaching as we know it today is based on deeply rooted stereotypes of what women are like. When women were struggling to gain the right to paid labor, arguments that had kept them out of the workforce in the first place were used to direct them toward teaching. Teaching was seen as closely tied to domesticity as well as good preparation for motherhood. The idea of teaching as some kind of transient occupation was also a way of keeping wages low (Apple, 1987). In later years, the stereotype of women as naturally suited for domestic life expanded to include the idea that women were good at obeying rules, especially when enforced by male administrators. For many women, however, teaching was one of the only respectable ways in which to make a living.

Postcolonial theory provides many examples of how particular kinds of knowledge have been devalued by the dominant culture not because of their level of difficulty, but due to economic and other considerations. Stoler (1997) for example, discussed how in some cultures, practices such as extended breast feeding were frowned upon by Westerners, as during this period sexual relations were not allowed between spouses. Western women saw this as a reason that native men were excessively promiscuous (though this once again seems to represent other anxieties) and aggressively discouraged native women from this practice. Thus one of the greatest benefits of extended breast-feeding, namely contraception, was completely lost. As a result, "native" families began having more and more children, which was seen as proof of their lack of civilization (Stoler, 1997).

Furthermore, as Gilman (in Loomba, 1998) points out, stereotypes involving as they do a "reduction of images and ideas to a simple and manageable form" (p. 60) are useful tools in creating an artificial sense of difference between self and other. Colonialist systems of knowledge that focused upon objectivity of observation reduced complex practices to neatly defined categories which, when taken out of context, lose much of their value. I argue with my students that the reduction of teaching to some of these categories (such as hours actually spent on the job) is one of the reasons that it has been devalued. One of the ways that I have found useful in explaining this point is taking apart the argument of teaching as easy work. We look at what the word easy in itself means, and try to see in what way teaching is easy: physically, socially, and intellectually. Furthermore, we look at who gets to do the defining of what is easy. Many times these discussions lead to the consideration that perhaps teaching is not as intellectually demanding as a discipline such as engineering that requires very specific knowledges. Many students, however, also point out that taking such a stance is to continue to accept that certain ways of thinking are inherently more complicated than others: why for example is it considered more difficult to perform what one might call advanced mathematical operations than to explain simple ones to a group of twenty children in ways that all of them understand? When looked at from these vantage points, the stereotype of teaching as easy work is exposed for what it is: a simplistic reduction.

Analyses of teaching behavior often focus on specifically identifiable categories such as questioning behaviors, classroom management techniques, and classroom arrangement (Good & Brophy, 1994). Each of these when decontextualized may not seem complicated or demanding, but good quality teaching is much more than the sum of its parts (Kincheloe, 2004). By drawing on postcolonial concepts to help students see how stereotypes are created and enacted through particular systems of meaning, students can learn how images of teaching are created through social networks outside the field itself.

CONCLUSIONS

As many scholars of teacher education suggest, teacher education, like postcolonial theory, is a highly contested terrain, with multiple view points existing as to the direction it should take. As a postcolonial scholar and teacher educator, I have found it useful to look not only for similarities in the two fields, but also to use the tools of one to enrich and inform the other. Postcolonial thought enriches the field of teacher education in many ways, with its insistence on questioning accepted realities, its critical examination of discursive practices, and its emphasis on understanding the mechanisms through which power can be wielded over large groups of people. As the other sections of this chapter have indicated, the similarities between the concerns of teacher educators and those of postcolonial theorists make bringing the two together beneficial to audiences both directly (as in teacher education students) and indirectly (as in the children with whom they work).

At a time when the very concept of teacher education is under intense scrutiny, it is helpful to look to outside sources for ways to strengthen its roots that are more respectful of children's lives. As mentioned in the introductory sections of this chapter, positivist ways of structuring teacher education have focused on breaking it down into constituent parts and teaching those to students. Minute details such as how the transition from one activity in a classroom to another have come to occupy a fair amount of the curriculum. This kind of overcategorization of experience (breaking it down and labeling each piece) also lends itself to the development of stereotypes which, as shown above, has had a negative impact on teacher education programs. This is often at the cost of discussing crucial issues that affect both teacher education students and the children they impact. Trivializing the curriculum in this manner can be one of the causes for questioning its legitimacy. Therefore, using insights gained from postcolonial theory and other sources and engaging teacher education students in critical discussions about the nature of the field they are entering, and how it is being impacted by multiple outside influences, is a crucial step in the remaking of teacher education.

REFERENCES

Agnello, M. F. (2001). *A postmodern literacy policy analysis.* New York: Peter Lang.
Appiah, A. (1991). Out of Africa: Topologies of nativism. In: D. LaCapra (Ed.), *The bounds of race: Perspectives on hegemony and resistance* (pp. 134–163). Ithaca, NY: Cornell University Press.
Apple, M. (1987). Gendered teaching, gendered labor. In: T. Popkewitz (Ed.), *Critical studies in teacher education: Its folklore, theory and practice* (pp. 57–84). London and New York: Falmer Press.
Bhabha, H. (1994). *The location of culture.* London and New York: Routledge.

Britzman, D. (2003). *Practice makes practice: A critical study of learning to teach (Rev. ed)*. Albany: State University of New York Press.
Cannella, G. S. (1997). *Deconstructing early childhood education: Social justice and revolution*. New York, NY: Peter Lang.
Cannella, G. S., & Viruru, R. (2004). *Childhood and (postcolonization): Power, education and contemporary practice*. London and New York: Routledge.
Cohn, B. (1996). *Colonialism and its forms of knowledge: The British in India*. Princeton, NJ: Princeton University Press.
Dimitriadis, G., & McCarthy, C. (2001). *Reading and teaching the postcolonial: From Baldwin to Basquiat and beyond*. New York: Teachers College Press.
Fieldhouse, D. K. (1989). *The colonial empires*. London: Macmillan.
Foucault, M. (1980). *Power/knowledge selected interviews and other writings 1972–1977*. Brighton, UK: Harvester.
Good, T., & Brophy, J. (1994). *Looking in classrooms* (6th ed.). New York: Harper Collins.
Goodlad, J. L. (2004). A guiding mission. In: J. I. Goodlad & T. J. McMannon (Eds), *The teaching Career* (pp. 19–47). New York: Teachers College Press.
Jacoby, R. (1995). Marginal returns: the trouble with postcolonial theory. *Lingua Franca*, 5.6(September/October), 32.
Kincheloe, J. L., & Steinberg, S. (1998). Lesson plans from the outer limits: Unauthorized methods. In: J. L. Kincheloe & S. Steinberg (Eds), *Unauthorized methods: Strategies for critical teaching* (pp. 1–27). New York and London: Routledge.
Kincheloe, J. L. (2004). The bizarre, complex and misunderstood world of teacher education. In: J. L. Kincheloe, A. Bursztyn & S. R. Steinberg (Eds), *Teaching teachers: Building a quality school of urban education* (pp. 1–50). New York: Peter Lang.
King, C. R. (2000). Introduction: Dislocating postcoloniality, relocating American empire. In: C. R. King (Ed.), *Postcolonial America* (pp. 1–20). Urbana: University of Illinois Press.
Ladson-Billings, G. (1998). Preparing teachers for diversity: Historical perspectives, current trends and future directions. In: L. Darling-Hammond & G. Sykes (Eds), *Teaching as the learning profession: Handbook of policy and practice* (pp. 86–124). San Francisco: Jossey-Bass.
Liston, P., & Zeichner, K. (1987). Critical pedagogy and teacher education. Paper presented at the Annual Meeting of the American Educational Research Association, New Orleans, LA.
Loomba, A. (1998). *Colonialism/Postcolonialism*. London: Routledge.
Lopez, A. (2001). *Posts and pasts: A theory of postcolonialism*. Albany: SUNY Press.
Macedo, D. (1990). *Literacies of power: What Americans are not allowed to know*. Boulder, CO: Westview Press.
McLaren, P. (1998). *Revolutionary multiculturalism*. Boulder, CO: Westview Press.
McWilliam, E. (1995). *In broken images: Feminist tales for a different teacher education*. New York: Teachers College Press.
Merrow Report, The (2005). Retrieved January 21, 2005 from http://www.pbs.org/merrow/tv/shortage/
Mohanty, C. T. (1989). On race and voice: Challenges for liberal education in the 1990s. *Cultural Critique*, *14*, 179–208.
Mongia, P. (1996). Introduction. In: P. Mongia (Ed.), *Contemporary postcolonial theory: A reader* (pp. 1–25). London: Arnold.
Popkewitz, T. (1987). Ideology and social formation in teacher education. In: T. Popkewitz (Ed.), *Critical studies in teacher education: Its folklore, theory and practice* (pp. 2–34). London and New York: Falmer Press.

Popkewitz, T. (1993). US teacher education reforms: Regulatory practices of the state, university and research. In: T. Popkewitz (Ed.), *Changing patterns of power: Social regulation and teacher education reform* (pp. 263–302). Albany, NY: SUNY Press.
Said, E. (1978). *Orientalism.* London and Henley: Routledge and Kegan Paul.
Said, E. (1996). Orientalism. In: P. Mongia (Ed.), *Contemporary postcolonial theory: A reader* (pp. 20–36). London: Arnold.
Shohat, E. (1993). Notes on the postcolonial. *Social Text, 31/32*, 91–113.
Sleman, S. (1994). The scramble for post-colonialism. In: C. Tiffin & A. Lawson (Eds), *Describing empire: Postcolonialism and textuality* (pp. 15–32). London: Routledge.
Spivak, G. C. (1988). Can the subaltern speak? In: C. Nelson & L. Grossberg (Eds), *Marxism and the interpretation of culture.* Urbana, IL: University of Illinois Press.
Stoler, A. L. (1997). Making empire respectable: The politics of race and sexual morality in twentieth century colonial cultures. In: A. McClintock, A. Mufti & E. Shohat (Eds), *Dangerous liaisons: Gender, nation and postcolonial perspectives* (pp. 344–373). Minneapolis, MN: University of Minnesota Press.
Stoler, A. L., & Cooper, F. (1997). Between metropole and colony: Rethinking a research agenda. In: F. Cooper & A. L. Stoler (Eds), *Tensions of empire: Colonial cultures in a bourgeois world* (pp. 1–58). Berkeley, CA: University of California Press.
Strober, M. (1984). *Segregation by gender in public school teaching: toward a general theory of occupational segregation in the labor market.* Unpublished manuscript, Stanford University.
Vaughan, M. (1993). Madness and colonialism, colonialism as madness. *Paideuma, 39,* 45–55.
Viruru, R. (2001). *Early childhood education: Postcolonial perspectives from India.* New Delhi and London: Sage.
Waller, W. (1961). *The sociology of teaching.* New York: Russell and Russell.
Young, R. J. C. (2001). *Postcolonialism: An historical introduction.* Oxford, UK: Blackwell.

BECOMING EARLY CHILDHOOD TEACHERS: LINKING ACTION RESEARCH AND POSTMODERN THEORY IN A LANGUAGE AND LITERACY COURSE

Celia Genishi, Shin-ying Huang and Tamara Glupczynski

ABSTRACT

In this chapter we describe an action research study on our course "Language and Literacy in the Early Childhood Curriculum." We also explore links between the study and postmodern theory, embedding our analyses in an ongoing accreditation process. This required process positions us to question what authoritative narratives we have accepted and whether, through our action research, we have begun to create our own counternarrative that challenges assumptions underlying the accreditation process.

In this chapter we explore links between postmodern theory and research in a particular early childhood teacher education program. Initiated in the fall of 2002, this program aims to integrate early childhood "general" with early childhood "special" education students and content. Our theoretical, educational, and political workspace is embedded in our college's ongoing national accreditation process. We describe that workspace and our study by presenting:

- our take on postmodern theory and its links to critical theories and the current educational scene in the U.S.;
- a summary of the accreditation process at our institution and the principles or stances underlying that process;
- our positionalities, vis-á-vis this study;
- an overview of the methods of our study;
- findings from our action research on a course called "Language and Literacy in the Early Childhood Curriculum"; and
- a discussion of how the findings are linked to our theoretical framework.

Just as the college's accreditation is "under construction," so is this preliminary analysis of our student participants' coursework in the fall of 2003. We focus here on two contrasting written assignments, which were analyzed from the perspective of social justice, one of the stances underlying the accreditation process. Readers can consider with us the relationship between students' work and the creation of postmodern counternarratives.

POSTMODERN TIMES

Since the term *postmodern* means different things to different people, we begin by presenting a definition that is compatible with our own. What came before postmodern times or postmodernism? In fact what came before, modernism, has not vanished, but is challenged much more now than it has been in the past. In the modern era there were "grand narratives of legitimation" (Lyotard, 1984, pp. 31–37) or broadly accepted explanatory theories of human development, literature, science, technology, and so on. There was a belief that human beings were progressing toward some better condition, following the known and accepted standards of science. For many academics and intellectuals, enlightenment, science, rationality, grand narratives, or widely accepted canons were tightly interwoven and were the foundations of knowledge. From this perspective, knowledge was constructed as an objective reality, which had the authority of history and scholarship within tradition-honored disciplines.

The postmodern era allows for the existence of *counternarratives* that counter not only grand narratives but also official and hegemonic narratives, the "legitimating stories propagated for specific political purposes to manipulate public consciousness by heralding a national set of common cultural ideals" (Peters & Lankshear, 1996, p. 2). Such counternarratives provide legitimacy for what Lyotard (1984) called "little stories" of those marginalized groups, whose voices had been traditionally unheard. In the U.S. these groups are typically different from the creators of official, hegemonic narratives, in terms of race, ethnicity, class, ability, gender, sexual orientation, English language capability, and so on.

In the postmodern era, previously accepted canons and standards are still known (and accepted by many), but they are no longer accepted without challenges. Instead, the current societal context is full of shifting, multiple perspectives. Along with standards, relationships of power have become fluid, as has the standing of modernist theories. Thus a theory of human development that is based on research about males only, or on children in the northern or western hemisphere is questioned, and a view of teachers as unidimensional is no longer viable (Cochran–Smith, 1991; Genishi, 1992, 1997; Grieshaber & Cannella, 2001). For the last 20–25 years, teachers have begun to take on a range of identities that involve them in advocacy for children and families, action research in their own classrooms or centers, and publication that makes their voices audible, no longer private, but increasingly public (e.g., Ballenger, 1999; Brookline Teacher Researcher Seminar, 2004; Gallas, 1994; Paley, 1981, 1997; Stires, 1991). Further disputed is the definition of language as consisting only of grammars and pragmatic rules or rules of use, and of literacy as a set of decontextualized skills (Auerbach, 1995).

Our action research project is an example of an effort to study our own classroom and link research and postmodern theory in the context of teacher education. It centers on a course required for prospective (preservice) teachers titled "Language and Literacy in the Early Childhood Curriculum." As instructors and researchers of this course, we maintain a postmodern perspective toward language and literacy, research, and assessment of the course, the students taking it, and their future students. That is, we reject modernist, scientific definitions of *language, literacy, teaching, research,* or *assessment* that reduce these complex terms to a single group's or institution's definitions.

At present, the institution most heavily influencing the teaching and learning of language and literacy in the U.S. is its Department of Education. Specifically, government-funded research (Report of the National Reading

Panel, 1999) and subsequent legislation (No Child Left Behind Act of 2001) have become the basis of defining *literacy* as a set of skills to be mastered in the English language. According to the report and legislation cited, early literacy instruction must involve the explicit and systematic teaching of phonics. Moreover, the research assessing the effectiveness of instruction must be "scientific," or it must include objective procedures and measures, such as standardized tests. These requirements regarding instruction and research have led to critique and controversy (Allington, 2002; Berliner, 2002; Pressley, 2001); at the same time they have promoted the widespread use of highly structured language and literacy curricula, assessed by standardized tests. The wide-ranging No Child Left Behind (NCLB) Act incorporates these requirements as well, as a way of reforming elementary and secondary education in the U.S. Particularly in urban areas where there is a large population of economically disadvantaged learners enrolled in schools that receive federal funds, teachers are expected to teach children to read through commercial curricula that meet the funders' standards for early reading instruction and research. Embedded in such curricula are assumptions about both urban early childhood teachers' abilities as curriculum makers and urban schoolchildren's capacities as learners of language and literacy.

Thus, here we wish to complicate these reductionist views of language, literacy, teaching, research, and assessment. Along with others in educational research, we accept the postmodern tenet of *multiplicity,* recognizing that there are many definitions, enactments, and interpretations of these five terms and that each participant defines or interprets from a particular stance or position, historically and ideologically. Also in keeping with the spirit of the postmodern, we recognize and accept that our beliefs about the current educational scene do not fit neatly into a single theoretical frame. That is, when we advocate for practices that take into account the specific needs and capabilities of children in urban schools, we slide into a frame of critical theory, "critical of social organization that privileges some at the expense of others" (Bogdan & Biklen, 2003, p. 21).

To further support and theorize our own position regarding current government mandates related to literacy, we look through the lens of critical literacies. Through this lens *literacy* is better termed *literacies*: those who are literate "read" conventional written texts, as well as a broad range of other symbolic forms of expression, including those that are transformed via the media or technology (Tyner, 1998); some use the term *multiliteracies* to refer to this expansive definition (Lo Bianco, 2000; New London Group, 1996). Moreover, through this lens we can examine relationships among languages and literacies, which are intimately related to power and inequality, and foreground the role of language in the making and preservation of power relations (Fairclough, 2001). We understand language to be "a contradictory and unequal set of linguistic varieties" (Cox & Assis-Peterson, 1999, p. 436), the status of which depends upon the political, economic, social, and cultural standing of those who use the language. Thus to use language and to be literate involve the ability to read power relations (Street, 1993).

Further, we accept and include in the content of our course general principles of sociolinguistic theory (Cazden, John, & Hymes, 1972; Genishi, 1979; Heath, 1983; Hull & Schultz, 2002; Moll & Gonzalez, 2001). That is, how able a person looks or sounds depends upon social, cultural, and political factors that are embedded in every instance of use. We therefore keep at the forefront a notion of multiplicity – the assumption that an individual's uses and readings of languages and literacies vary across different contexts and social situations, as a result of different cultural understandings, values, and expectations. This is true for both English language learners and so-called monolingual speakers, who also change their ways of expressing themselves from one situation to another. Moreover, some *choose* to speak variants of English (e.g., African American Vernacular English) or a language other than English (Goldstein, 2003; Valenzuela, 1999), as a way to resist or talk back to traditional grand narratives of power (Delpit, 2001; Ladson-Billings, 2000). Such decisions suggest that language use is a set of sociopolitical acts where language places boundaries around the self and others. Working in a program that strives to educate its graduates to teach in urban public schools where most children speak different variants of English or enter school speaking a language other than English, we believe a sociolinguistic stance underlies our course and fits within a theoretical frame that is both postmodern and critical.

IS THIS A POSTMODERN MOMENT?

We have suggested that there is no clear demarcation between the modern and postmodern eras and that the tenets of postmodern theory overlap with those of other theories. Grand narratives continue to be taught, and official stories of how "all" children learn are common, especially in the current educational and political climate, which privileges narrowly defined, "scientific" ways of teaching language and literacy (Dyson, 1999, 2003; No Child Left Behind Act of 2001; Report of the National Reading Panel, 1999). There are also sites where the modern and postmodern intersect in challenging ways, where official stories from those who regulate, what happens in educational settings overlap with counternarratives.

An example of this kind of intersection is the set of regulations known as National Council for the Accreditation of Teacher Education (NCATE) guidelines. In the U.S. many states, including New York State (NYS), where we work, have changed requirements for teachers to become certified, primarily in the birth through grade 12 range. Most of these requirements have to do with the content of the teacher education curriculum, although some have to do with evaluating the fit between state requirements and each institution's program (e.g., the program in early childhood education). Thus, NYS requires institutions that prepare teachers (many are colleges or schools of education within universities) to be accredited by an association that provides guidelines that evaluate the fit or lack of fit. Some of these institutions, including Teachers College, have chosen NCATE as the association to do this evaluation.

From the perspective of postmodern theory, our institution has bought into the "grand narrative" of NCATE, which embeds evaluative guidelines so that individual institutions are held accountable for the content and outcomes of their teacher education programs. These guidelines are more modernist than postmodern since evaluative measures are to be "objective" or positivist, preferably statistically derived. Thus our institution, Teachers College, has positioned itself to be judged according to guidelines that individual faculty members may accept or resist.

Opinions at our institution vary on whether the language of the regulations is rigid or flexible. There is enough imposed "flexibility" that individual institutions of higher education are required to write their own conceptual framework. This framework could be interpreted as a "local grand narrative" that individual programs (e.g., in early childhood education) must then implement. Members of programs have a complex and layered set of tasks, which are to fit under the umbrella of the conceptual framework: to attend to new state regulations, which require specified content; to align state regulations with NCATE or accrediting requirements; to align both state and NCATE guidelines with the curriculum of the program; and somehow to enact the planned curriculum in ways that are pedagogically and intellectually defensible from the perspective of the program faculty.

THE NCATE CONCEPTUAL FRAMEWORK: THE LOCAL GRAND NARRATIVE

The group of teacher educators at the College responsible for writing the conceptual framework introduce it first as a "mission statement." Within this statement the organizing principles are the three stances that are intended as guides for all teacher education programs at the College. Those philosophical stances follow, with brief explanations that are our takes on the theoretical and/or empirical bases of the stances:

1. *Inquiry stance*: We are an inquiry-based and practice-oriented community. We and our students and graduates challenge assumptions and complacency, and embrace a stance of inquiry toward the interrelated roles of learner, teacher, and leader in P-12 schools.
2. *Curricular stance*: Negotiating among multiple perspectives on culture, content, and context, our graduates strive to meet the needs of diverse learners, both students and other adults, in their school communities.
3. *Social justice stance*: Our graduates choose to collaborate across differences in and beyond their school communities to demonstrate a commitment to social justice and to serving the world while imagining its perspectives (Teachers College NCATE Report, 2003 [hereafter TC], p. 11).

Inquiry Stance

In each stance there is a conceptualization of educators, specifically of prospective teachers at the College. As we elaborate on the above descriptors, we select key points (and citations) from the document itself to provide the gist of several pages of text for each stance, from our own viewpoint. For the inquiry stance, the key terms are *inquirer* and *reflective practitioner*. The inquirer is presented in the theoretical frameworks of Dewey (1933) and Freire (1970), a blend of Dewey's modernist ideals of learning through experience, critical thinking, and scientific inquiry and Freire's postmodern, liberatory notions about teaching as invention and reinvention in social and political worlds. The reflective practitioner (Schon, 1987) seems to be cast somewhere between the modernist and postmodern: her/his reflection is still grounded in scientific inquiry. The practitioner, however, is reconceptualized as an inquirer, not only as a consumer of others' research and theory, but also as a person who can generate research. As further explanation of this stance, the work of Cochran-Smith and Lytle with public school practitioners (1993), teachers (e.g., Paley, 1994), teacher educators (e.g., Feiman-Nemser & Melnick, 1992; Schoonmaker, 2003), and others who feature and thus privilege reflective practitioners as inquirers, is included. (It is notable, though, that most of the researchers cited in this section of the College framework are university teacher educators and not classroom teachers.)

Curricular Stance

This stance is articulated in a way that clearly departs from a traditional representation of curriculum. *Curriculum* is not defined as the conventional content or what is taught in a formal sense; rather it incorporates characteristics of learners who are increasingly diverse socially, ethnically, and racially and who learn in diverse ways. What prospective teachers need to know is, minimally, the content of methods courses, principles of pedagogy, and the complexities of teachers' lives (Zumwalt, 1982). Equally important are ways to learn about learners and the contexts in which they learn (schools, communities), based on knowing "how to use data and data systems" (TC, p. 21) and an appreciation of the traditional disciplines of history, philosophy, economics, and so on (Greene, 1978). (These points link back to the inquiry stance and its modernist underpinnings.) In contrast to that modernist link, however, is an emphasis on culturally relevant practices (Moll & Gonzalez, 2001), which demonstrate that multiple definitions of curriculum are needed as "mainstream" educators acknowledge their need to see beyond their own, sometimes limiting, prior experiences and frames of reference. In short, given the current national trend toward narrowly defined curricula and standards, the College's stance toward curriculum is more postmodern than modernist. Perhaps aspects of the conceptual framework serve simultaneously as a local grand narrative and as counternarratives, as some of its content does not readily fit within NCATE's overarching, evaluative grand narrative.

Social Justice Stance

Because we focus on this stance in our chapter, we consider its meanings within the conceptual framework in a more extended way than we did for the other stances. The explanation of this stance echoes themes embedded in the other two stances (e.g., culturally responsive pedagogy, inquiry as a key to being a curriculum maker) at the same time that it extends and troubles the themes. The philosophy of Dewey (1933) is again invoked to make the point that the purpose of education is more than intellectual, it is also emotional and moral. Morality implies an openness to all learners and the ideal of a democratic society. The key notion, from our point of view, is *all learners*, whom educators must approach as individuals within classrooms and within an increasingly diverse society. The challenge of keeping both the individual and the collective of society in mind is reflected in two principles of educational access included in this section of the framework, based on Banks, Cookson, Gay, and Hawley (2001):

- Every person has the right to develop his or her intellectual, emotional, and physical capacities to the fullest extent, and a good school or school district promotes such development.
- As our society and our schools become dramatically more diverse, education leaders play pivotal roles in meeting new and different learning needs, in anticipating and addressing potential tensions, in ensuring that all students reap the educational and social benefits of diversity, and in promoting the mutual understanding and respect among students, staff, and communities on which our pluralistic society depends (TC, p. 26).

A position is then developed in the conceptual framework about the difficulties of ensuring access and of changing inequities in education and society, acknowledging that efforts at school reform must rely on collaboration and the building of community.

The ideal of educating all learners, then, depends on a collective vision of transformative action. The necessary actions (collaborating across social divides, learning about diverse learners, changing curricula, reducing inequities in schools and society, etc.) have been presented throughout the framework as the content of the college's teacher education programs. Further, in the section on social justice, the focus is eventually on "preparing change agents (transformational educators) for social justice" (TC, p. 28), and programmatic content is described in this way:

- The issues of race, class, gender, language, and ability are explicitly emphasized in professional preparation curriculum. Our graduates understand how students' particular life contexts influence their willingness and propensity to learn in schools.
- They are prepared to act sensitively and effectively with students whose life experiences are most often very unlike their own. We do not just talk about this aspect of being an educator but we provide opportunities to learn about it in life situations (TC, p. 29).

This paragraph contains a striking challenge to everyone working in teacher education programs at the college and begs some challenging questions that we attempt to answer in the remainder of this chapter. In their work in the language and literacy course, to what extent do our students demonstrate an understanding of issues of race, class, gender, language, and ability? To what extent are we preparing our students "to act sensitively and effectively with students whose life experiences are most often very unlike their own?"

POSITIONALITIES

As we begin to report on our ongoing research project, we acknowledge the influence of our own experiences in education and teacher education as they relate to the stance of social justice. As an Asian-American who spoke Japanese as her first language and as a former preschool and secondary Spanish teacher, Genishi has long been aware of the need for teachers to be responsive to children of diverse races, socioeconomic and cultural backgrounds, and abilities. While participating in this study, she seemed to position herself somewhere between her professor/researcher identity and her classroom teacher identity, though in the world of action research those two identities are assumed to merge. Genishi's professor/researcher identity was concerned with infusing NCATE stances into the course, especially the social justice stance, whereas the classroom teacher in her continually wondered about individual students' experiences in the course and whether they were "learning enough" about language and literacy – as if those purposes were separable from each other.

Huang, a Taiwanese who grew up for the most part in Taiwan, learned English as a second/foreign language as a child and taught English as a foreign language in Taiwan for 2 years before coming to TC. Learning English as a second/foreign language during a nearly 3-year stay in England from age 9 was a positive experience that taught her how knowledge of an additional language can be most empowering, especially for those that have the privilege and resources to ensure that addition. However, it was reflections on her teaching while at TC that stimulated her interest and belief in the need for a social justice stance in language and literacy education. Teaching for social justice not only provides meaning for the process of language learning, but also demonstrates the need for language *teachers*, rather than ever more advanced instructional software. As a researcher, she continues to ponder what it means for a teacher educator to take a social justice stance, how action research can aid that development, and how teaching and learning language and literacy can be linked to becoming agents of change in society.

As an African-American who grew up in a major American city, Glupczynski vividly recalls childhood events that shaped the ways that she saw societal inequities occurring within schools. Therefore, the possibility of social activism through education drew her to the teaching profession. As a preservice teacher, her understandings of curriculum incorporated the social and ideological factors that had an impact on the lives of urban children. However, in her earliest years of teaching, Glupczynski learned to negotiate the mandated use of a scripted curriculum, pushing her to recognize the challenges practitioners face, despite their own pedagogical stances and beliefs. As an instructor of early childhood preservice students, she continues to maintain a commitment to teachers being curriculum makers, while considering the day-to-day realities that young children and teachers face in urban schools.

An Action Research Project

As teachers and researchers, working in a particular early childhood education course, we take a postmodern perspective toward teacher education by viewing teachers as persons with multiple identities and abilities. Like us, they take their own positions on the curriculum we present and on issues such as social justice, which may or may not be compatible with the "local grand narrative" of the TC conceptual framework. In keeping with postmodern theory and also like us, our students may hold contradictory positions about specific aspects of that narrative. For example, students may agree that social justice is vital, but disagree that it matters as much as the curriculum-making stance. Our eventual goal is to develop teachers/educators who are not only knowledgeable about children, families, and multiple ways of learning and teaching, but are also reflective practitioners and critical inquirers. Further, within the frame of critical theory, we see the students as potentially able to change the educational world they are preparing to enter, because they see that any set of practices can privilege one group at the expense of others (Lubeck, 1994). We aim to foster students' sense of themselves as change agents who contribute to social justice and transformation through work with children, their families, and other peers and educators.

Thus we considered ourselves and students to be potential change agents as they participated in one course, "Language and Literacy in the Early Childhood Curriculum," a requirement in an early childhood teacher education program that was initiated in the 2002–2003 academic year. Genishi taught the course for the first time in the fall of 2002, and she and Glupczynski cotaught the course in the fall of 2003. To provide background for our preliminary study of two aspects of that course, we present its broad goals here, which are excerpts from the course syllabus:

> This course is an introduction to early communication and spoken and written language in the early childhood curriculum (infancy through grade two). It provides a) an overview of how young learners communicate and learn language, including English

language learners; b) a focus on practices that promote communication, talk, and literacy in educational settings for children with a range of abilities; and c) a sociocultural framework that highlights the importance of the multiple contexts that influence how children learn. (This course offers 3 credits toward the New York State Early Childhood certification requirement of 6 credits in language acquisition and literacy.)

Course Objectives:

- To understand the importance of communication and language in culture and the learning of literacy practices.
- To appreciate and build on the strengths of all learners to use a variety of communicative means to establish relationships with others and learn with them.
- To begin to build our own individual interpretations of both language and literacy.
- To understand the influence of individual experiences and beliefs and sociocultural and political contexts on literacy learning and its assessment – to act upon that understanding and begin to be an *"advocate for social justice."*
- To learn about a range of approaches to learning and teaching in early communication and literacy, partly through observation and participation in a classroom or center.
- To learn about language and literacy curricula for young learners, as well as modifications to curricula for children with delays or disabilities.
- To observe a learner and plan appropriate experiences for her/him that promote communication and literacy learning – to begin to be a *"curriculum maker."*

As you work toward all these broad objectives, we will all take on the role of a professional *"inquirer"* or teacher researcher.

METHODS

Site and Participants

Teachers College is a large graduate school in New York City that is affiliated with Columbia University. The enrollment in 2004 is about 5,000, and the students participate in programs that cover a range from kinesiology to sociology to teacher education. Students in teacher education programs account for about a third of credits taken in the college. We authors are part of the Department of Curriculum and Teaching, which offers certification through the early childhood and elementary education preservice programs, along with dual certifications in those two programs with each other (i.e., early childhood/elementary) and with early childhood special education, learning disabilities, deaf education, and mental retardation. Master's degrees are also offered for those not seeking certification, including an advanced master's degree (Ed.M.). In addition the Department has a doctoral program (Ed.D.), offering a range of concentrations, including early childhood and early childhood special education.

The program of interest here is the early childhood preservice program, which offers a Master of Arts degree and three state certifications, early childhood education ("general"), early childhood special education, and dual certification in early childhood general and special education. Faculty integrate content related to both general and special early childhood education within the same courses; thus it is officially called the Integrated Program in Early Childhood Education (referred to here for convenience as the "early childhood program.") Field placements, such as student teaching, cover the infancy through grade 2 range in public and privately sponsored sites in New York City. Depending on a student's certification goal, these may be self-contained special education sites, general education centers or classrooms, or inclusive settings.

In the Spring of 2004, there were 33 students (preservice) seeking certification in the early childhood program. Of the 33, 17 were enrolled in the 28-member class we were studying. Of those 17, nine were of Asian or Latino/a heritage, and 8 were White. All students, faculty, graduate instructors, and staff in the program and the class were women. Because the tuition at TC is currently over $800 per credit, the majority of College students are not economically disadvantaged, but there is great variation in this regard within any group. At the beginning of the fall semester, we explained to the language and literacy class the three NCATE stances and the purpose of our study (see the appendix for the description of research), assuring students that there was no obligation to participate and that there would be no additional work involved for participants. (The three NCATE stances had also been presented at a program orientation meeting and in its core curriculum class, of which the 17 early childhood program students are a part. This course, then, is not alone in its efforts to incorporate the three stances.) We said that there would be requests after the course ended for volunteers for focus groups and member checks as data were being analyzed. (At the time we wrote this chapter, we had conducted two focus group sessions. These included questions about participants' views of the course, but not member checks or questions related to our data analyses.) Of the 17 students in the early childhood program, 14 consented to be in the study.

In addition two preservice students seeking dual certification through another department and two students not in preservice programs gave their consent. For this preliminary analysis we include data only from the 14 students in our department's preservice program.

Data Sources

When we planned the study, we decided that the main sources of data would be the students' work in the course. This included an integrative exercise that functioned as a midterm and had a visual or nonverbal component; a group critique of a literacy curriculum; a child study; and an issue-related letter. All of these assignments were graded, as was each student's oral telling of a story. Supplementary sources were to be occasional reflective notes, resembling short journal entries; audiotapes; videotapes of discussions or activities in class; and focus group interviews held after the course ended. Ultimately, we used neither audio- nor videotape in part because not all students were participants in the study. We did, however, take still photographs of the students, which they said could be shown at presentations about the study.

Data Analysis

In this chapter we present a preliminary analysis of two contrasting written assignments. One was the *integrated exercise* (IE) that functioned as a take-home midterm and the other, a position statement or *letter* (LE) in which each student was to articulate her stance toward an issue of her choosing, related to language and literacy. We saw the IE as an assignment that would focus on "what was learned" in the first half of the course; thus participants might or might not foreground social justice. The LE, on the other hand, was to focus on a public issue related to language and literacy. By its nature this assignment would foreground social justice.

We shared the analytic tasks in the following way: Huang did the bulk of the analysis of the IE; Glupczynski did the bulk of the analysis of the LE; and the three of us looked for thematic commonalities within each assignment and across the two assignments. Genishi also took responsibility for weaving the coauthors' analyses and discussions into the chapter. We did not do a reliability check since we were not doing a positivist study in which an accurate "measure" is sought; rather, we were pragmatically dividing the labor and being friendly critics or question raisers as we reviewed each others' identification of themes or codes.

In the first phase of analysis, the IE and LE were read a number of times by Huang and Glupczynski, respectively. The process was similar for both researchers. Each began by identifying topics in each participant's assignment. Most participants' IE contained between eight and ten topics, such as "importance of observation," "contextual influences," or "infant's smile." Most LE contained between three to seven topics, such as "standardized testing," "No Child Left Behind," or "Head Start." Glupczynski coded topics that were explicitly named and thus brought to the reader's attention.

In the second phase, topics were combined into themes, for example, topics related to the use of sign language and its cultural contexts were combined into "deaf culture," or topics related to school funding and legislation like the NCLB Act were combined into "national/ federal issues." If implied or stated, the three NCATE stances were also identified in this phase in the LE. The number of occurrences for the different themes across the 14 participants was tallied for both sources. In the third phase themes were combined again and sought across both data sources (see Fig. 1). In the fourth "reporting" phase, Huang and Glupczynski created narratives around the themes they identified, which initiated a discussion of the findings.

FINDINGS AND DISCUSSION

In analyzing the data, we considered all three of the stances foregrounded in the College's conceptual framework, but in our presentation of findings we focus primarily on advocating for social justice. This is not only a way of narrowing our analytic tasks, but also of focusing on the stance that we judged to be most challenging since it is not woven into conventional definitions of "methods." That is, traditional methods courses are about ways of teaching particular content, with little attention to sociocultural issues such as race or gender.

The two assignments differed in terms of purpose, content, length, and grading. These are the guidelines for both assignments from the syllabus:

> 3b. Due Oct. 14 – draft of *integrated exercise*. This exercise should show how and what you have been learning in this course and will be a combination of written and visual presentation.
>
> For this assignment we assume that (1) *you* are best able to sum up your learning and (2) awareness of your own and your colleagues' learning processes helps you to become aware of children's varied learning processes.

Integrated Exercise (IE)	Letters (LE)
Concern with ELLs	ELL, ESL, dual language, language diversity
(similar topic of ELLs, but different emphasis and focus)	
Validation of personal experiences	Personal experiences—ELL
Deaf culture	

Inquiry (stance)
    Teachers' knowledge of self
    Observation
	Inquiry/observation

Understanding of young children
    Concepts of development
    Infants' smile	

Attitudes towards language/literacy
    Different paths to language/literacy
    Language vs. dialect
	Stance: multiple approaches to literacy needed

Teachers' attitudes
    Respect differences
    Social interaction
    Children's experiences/background
    Contextual influences	

Methods of teaching
    Benefits of signing
    Dramatic play
    Story-telling
    Phonics instruction	

	Stances (all against the status quo except for one)

	Literacy
	    Curriculum making
	    Literacy programs
	    Reading/writing workshop

	National/federal issues
(two students mentioned teachers as advocates of social justice for young children)	Social justice as topic
	Parent involvement, families
	Topics: standardized testing

Fig. 1. Analytic Themes in Integrated Exercises and Letters.

Written part: Keep a journal or "log" of notes, ideas, and questions about readings and other content, such as class discussion, which will remind you of how and what you are learning. Keep in mind the course objectives (listed above) as possible categories or topics to organize your thoughts. These topics might help you see themes and patterns that reflect your own interests and questions. On Oct. 14, hand in at least your notes and a draft of the *written* part of the assignment. Please also post the draft on the ClassWeb (as a file), so people can learn from/respond to what you have written.

Visual part: You will also be asked to enhance what you write with visuals that you create (computer-based or drawn by hand, sculpted, painted, or photographed, etc.). This visual enhancement/form of literacy should encourage you to experiment with media or skills you have or want to develop. If you have experimented with something by Oct. 14, feel free to hand it in. Otherwise, keep developing it until Nov. 4. Remember that the children you teach will benefit from your experiences with non-verbal or non-print sources of information. (What you hand in on Oct. 14 will be non-graded – it's an opportunity for feedback.)

3b. Due Nov. 4 – the completed integrated exercise. This should build on feedback received in October, from us and from your colleagues. (graded, 25%)

Due by Dec. 1 – Letter. Throughout the semester it is expected that you and your classmates will be sharing news, including stories about upcoming events, teaching, politics, kids, etc.; newspaper clippings, informative websites, etc. One place we can exchange such information is on the ClassWeb. At one point, please write a formal letter responding to an article, publication, commentary, etc. published in a newspaper, magazine, online source, etc. on language or literacy. Your letter should take a stance on some issue related to language and literacy. That is, your letter (no more than one double-spaced page long) should persuasively agree or disagree with the theories and issues in language/literacy that are publicly presented. For models, see the editorial page of various newspapers, such as the *New York Times* or a local paper that is accessible to you in hard copy or online. The *Times* is online at www.nytimes.com. While it is not mandatory, you are encouraged to mail your letter to the editor or writer of the publication that you are responding to. For our purposes, you should post your letter on ClassWeb in the folder titled, Letters to Editors. You can post your letter at anytime, however, all letters should be posted by *Monday, December 1, 2003*. In addition, please attach or provide the reference for the article, website, etc. that you are responding to. (graded, 15% for letter, 5% for participation)

Not surprisingly, we found after analyzing the written part of the IE and the LE that the most frequently identified themes overlapped but also differed. The three themes that appeared in both the IE and LE were "personal experiences of English language learners," "inquiry/ observation," and "need for multiple approaches to literacy." The IE contained other more specific themes as well, combined into "deaf culture," "understanding of young children," "attitudes toward language and literacy," "teachers' attitudes," and "methods of teaching." In contrast, themes in the letters, not present in the integrated exercise, were "literacy" and subthemes related to specific programs, "national/federal issues," "family involvement," and "standardized testing." An infrequent, explicitly named theme was "social justice," which was named twice in the IE. In the next sections we discuss the two assignments separately.

Integrated Exercise (IE)

Students were instructed in follow-up, more detailed guidelines for the IE to choose two topics (weekly themes) from the syllabus in order to organize their IE, which were to demonstrate what and how they were learning in the course. Alternatively, some students created their own organizing themes. The three syllabus topics chosen most often were: "born to communicate," "ways of communicating without speech," and "born to be curious: children as question-askers and meaning-makers."

Here we discuss a "cross-theme" analysis, based on the broad themes in Fig. 1. Looking across what participants wrote related to "understanding of young children," "attitudes toward language and literacy," and "teachers' attitudes," we found a common thread: an elaboration of a sociocultural understanding of child development. Participants took care to demonstrate their understanding of individual development, including the varied meanings and development of the infant's smile. They also emphasized the impact of individual differences and contextual – including family and cultural – influences on learning. One participant made reference to "context" as including not only cultural, but also social, economic, and political influences upon language and literacy learning. In short, a point repeatedly brought up was that there is "no one prescriptive way" to the acquisition of language and literacy, and no one best method of teaching all children, because "[e]ach child is an individual with different needs, coming from different backgrounds." Implied in this often-made point, within our framework, is the responsibility of teachers as social justice advocates not to cast a normalizing gaze on students but to understand differences between individuals to be the norm, and that such differences need to be taken into account in the teacher's day-to-day interactions with students.

Only two of the participants explicitly mentioned the role of teachers as advocates of social justice for their students, in terms of "equal access to education, inclusion, diversity, parent involvement, curriculum ... ." There was no explicit mention of teachers as social justice advocates within the field of language and literacy or early childhood education or within the teaching profession as a whole, nor any mention of teachers who teach children to be social justice advocates for themselves. (It should be noted that although we talked about the importance of advocating for social justice regularly in class, there was no specific "requirement" for the IE assignment to include those aspects of advocacy.) The study participants instead wrote in terms of what they as individual teachers could do for the students. This could be interpreted as teacher-to-child advocacy or advocacy within the classroom.

Although we are focusing on the social justice stance, the stance of teacher as inquirer overlapped with social justice through the common thread of observation. Teachers' abilities to observe linked the broad themes of "concern with English language learners (ELLs)," "validation of personal experience," "deaf culture," and "inquiry." In particular, observation of ELLs or children not from an European-American background was emphasized. One participant saw teachers as "inquirers who must inquire about the contexts of our children, as well as our own contexts as teachers"; *context* for her was each person's personal and sociocultural history, what she or he brought into the classroom. A few of the participants also reflected on their own learning of English as part of their understanding of language and literacy development, an important dimension of being an inquiring practitioner.

The last broad theme in the IE was "methods of teaching," which overlapped with both the curriculum-making and social justice stances. There was a concern with general methods of teaching, including experience-based phonics instruction and the use of story-telling as a possible way of incorporating children's own cultures. Signing and the inclusion of gestures and body language were thought to be useful for all young children, especially for ELLs. Non-oral communication was also thought to "link those children who are nonverbal, preverbal, and non-English speaking" and could also "help social development in children." Participants showed that their definitions of communication were broadening and that they understood how power relations underlie different forms of language. Several students noted that in most communities spoken English, for example, was associated with higher status than signing or speaking another language. In contrast, however, one student mentioned that sign language is not so "class oriented."

The same student, on the other hand, pointed out how "literacy equals success" in some cultures, and that language "can also determine your place in society." Through personal experience outside the U.S., she became acutely aware of how certain languages or dialects determine the status and power of speakers. She did not, however, explicitly connect this realization to the classroom and her future responsibilities as a teacher. Nevertheless, what this student wrote in her IE does reveal a critical perspective on her understanding of how power relations underlie languages and literacies. Explicitly discussing links to classroom practice could be an activity for us to emphasize in the next version of our language and literacy course.

Respecting and valuing children with special needs, especially ELLs, was also mentioned frequently as something that teachers need to bear in mind. In the course readings, ELLs were represented not as needy, but rather as resourceful. Nevertheless, one participant described ELLs as having "handicapped ability with the English language" and speaking a "broken version" of a new language. In contrast, another participant quoted Audre Lord: "even if you do believe...stereotypes, begin to practice acting like you don't believe them." It seemed that participants could articulate the need for teachers to respect differences of all kinds as advocates for social justice in the classroom, but some might still be coming to terms with ways of re-conceptualizing those differences in theoretically consistent ways.

Letters (LE)

Students were asked to keep each other abreast of topics of interest outside the classroom such as meetings related to education, politics, kids, and relevant websites. Time was provided in class to exchange information, which could also be exchanged online through e-mail and the college's ClassWeb. The students' task was to articulate their position or stance toward the issue. The main guideline was that it was to be about one-page long, and the format could vary. We offered news articles and websites that they might respond to, but did not provide written examples of our own, as we did not want to influence the style, format, or position that students might choose. Students posted this assignment, as well as the others, on the ClassWeb so that they had access to each other's thoughts and perspectives.

Unlike the IE, the LE were explicitly presented within a social justice framework. Even if we did not always use the term "social justice," we talked about the assignment in terms of current events or news articles that focused on inequities, lack of access, or specific groups lacking the power to effect educational changes, for example, to resist mandated curricula.

As with the IE, we discuss the broad themes that resulted from combining the initial set of coded topics, with the exception of the themes that appeared in both data sources, which were presented earlier (see also Fig. 1). In almost all of the LE, participants took a stance that was committed to social justice. While there was some variation in the ways that the students interpreted social justice, they generally talked back to current policies affecting young children. Related to the theme of "national/federal issues," many participants wrote about concerns over the federal government's interventionist role in early childhood education. Some students discussed the NCLB Act of 2001 in terms of policy makers' gap in understanding the needs of early childhood educators and young children. The letters repeatedly expressed concern over government intervention, using words ranging from "disagreement" to "enrage." In particular, participants disagreed with defining accountability in preschools in terms of another frequent theme, "standardized testing." One student wrote, "Showing little trust in the thousands of early childhood practitioners, who work intimately with children each day, they [supporters of NCLB] insist that the government must ensure that children are being academically prepared for kindergarten." A number of others responded to an article about standardized testing in Head Start centers, for example, one participant wrote, "At age 4, children still don't have the capacity to understand the true significance a test can have." Another, who was completing a field experience in a preschool, wrote, "The child's intended education through Head Start will be compromised, as will the benefits that they and their families hope for as the child prepares for further education." The embedded theme of "families and parent involvement" was expanded upon in other LE. Still others cited observation, as an alternative assessment method a practitioner could incorporate into daily practice. Indeed, such a recommendation reflects a growing understanding of how the stance of teacher as inquirer can overlap with a social justice stance.

Regarding the theme of "language and literacy," several students referred to the local context of New York City as a site for concern. Recent dramatic policy decisions in New York City (Goodnough, 2003) have led to the mandating of uniform curricula and assessments in reading and math for K-12 students. One participant, doing her field experience in a public first-grade classroom, knew what such mandates could mean. Addressing both the themes of literacy and testing, she wrote that "our children cannot afford to have so much of the teachers' time spent doing paperwork." Implicit in such a statement is a sophisticated understanding of the responsibilities teachers assume and often juggle in their work. Other students noted that a pitfall of mandated curricula is the challenge it presents to meeting the unique needs of each child. In particular, several students expressed concern over unmet needs of ELLs. Another participant sent her LE to a local newspaper, *which published it*, demonstrating that a course assignment can have an impact well beyond the classroom. She responded to an article published in that paper, congratulating them for publicizing a particular literacy program that used a variety of methods to teach children successfully with a range of abilities and knowledge of multiple languages. She closed by saying, "We should then repeat these achievements [teaching language and literacy] over and over in every city school until each child is literate." Although most participants pointed out how policies or practices needed to change in order to work toward social justice, this writer focused on an exemplary program.

Personal narratives from classrooms and autobiographical accounts were at times used to illustrate a particular stance. One student used her story, that of a mid-life career changer entering the teaching profession, to position herself in her letter to the Chancellor of the New York City schools, another businessperson turned educator. The participant was objecting to inappropriate tests, particularly for ELLs. Another student described her own experience as an ELL in U.S. schools, as a positioning point to articulate her belief that dual language programs should continue. Implicit in such letters is an overall belief that personal histories and experiences are valid and interconnected with the work of early childhood educators.

In sum, through the LE participants demonstrated an understanding of a range of contemporary issues, related mainly to testing and literacy curricula, both aspects of early childhood education affected by federal policies. Although we provided most of the articles or letters to which students responded, they elaborated on their stances in a range of concise and effective ways. Thus through their LE they appeared to raise the level of their understanding in an educational and political context that went well beyond the boundaries of course content and the classrooms in which they worked. From our point of view they were stepping on to a path toward liberatory practice (Freire, 1970), although in their discourse they were not regularly naming factors like race and gender as central to social justice or what hooks (1994) calls transgressive teaching. The participants were beginning to position themselves as change agents, involved in transformative action (Lieberman & McLaughlin, 1982), in a small and public way.

REFLECTIONS ON WHAT WE ARE LEARNING: FROM PRACTICE TO THEORY

Drawing on the College's NCATE conceptual framework, we began to address these questions through the action research described in this chapter:

- In their work in the language and literacy course, to what extent did our students demonstrate an understanding of "issues of race, class, gender, language, and ability?"
- To what extent are we preparing our students "to act sensitively and effectively with students whose life experiences are most often very unlike their own?"

In addition, in our efforts to link practice with postmodern theory, we asked:

- To what extent did we and the students in this course construct "counternarratives," little stories that talked back to grand narratives, either local or national?

We have analyzed a narrow wedge of what the study participants have done and learned in this single course. And although individual words of the conceptual framework, such as *race, class, gender, life experiences* seldom appeared in the writing of the students, the words they did choose certainly corresponded to the implicit and explicit theoretical framework we provided.

In the IE, for example, the themes outlined in Fig. 1 convey the meaning of many of our course objectives, aimed at understanding "the importance of communication and language in culture" and "the influence of individual experiences and beliefs and sociocultural and political contexts on literacy learning and its assessment." The latter influence was explicitly tied in the objectives to becoming an advocate for social justice. Thus we can feel gratified that the participants were at least partially learning what we hoped they would learn. (Indeed if grades are an indication of learning, most students in the course earned an A or A- for the semester.) However, as we said, there was hardly any explicit mention of social justice in the IE. Since the content of the first half of the course might have been characterized as focusing on individual development within sociocultural contexts, perhaps we should have expected that lack of explicitness.

Many students demonstrated an appreciation of the politics of language and literacy acquisition; they knew that certain forms of both languages and literacies, associated with working class or ethnic/racial "minority" groups, are stereotyped and other forms are more powerful. Students' awareness of this type of privilege seemed to be presented in their IE along with their often-articulated acceptance – supported by referring to a number of assigned materials – of the different routes that individual children take to development and learning. Thus children may or may not learn the discourses of power outside the classroom. Juxtaposed with this political knowledge were participants' expressed concerns about pedagogical knowledge, about how to teach "all" children, especially ELLs and those with special needs. Yet these two streams of knowledge were seldom linked or addressed in the same IE. As this was the first semester in the program for many of the participants, this is not surprising. Moreover, because we recommended that students organize their IE according to specific themes, we may actually have discouraged the blending of the political and critical with the world of pedagogical methods. In attempting to make easier the task of synthesizing complex material into a concise format (we recommended no more than 8 pages), we may have encouraged rather compartmentalized thinking and presentation. Still according to their IE, the study participants can articulate well their desire to "to act sensitively and effectively with students whose life experiences are most often very unlike their own." Field-based courses would provide direct information about their actions with young children.

The LE, in contrast, required students to articulate stances within the social justice framework. So not only did the assignment place them within an advocacy discourse, it also came later in the semester when the topics under discussion were linked clearly to language and literacy policies imposed by out-of-school/classroom agencies. Thus the link between the political and pedagogical was an easy one to make; participants read about those links, and we discussed them in class. Federal mandates for particular phonics-based approaches to literacy instruction and for standardized testing of Head Start children made the intersection of power relations and teaching clear. We discussed the contradiction between the conception of "curriculum-making" presented in the course and the federal government's imposed conception. Like most prospective teachers, they wanted to know how to teach language and literacy, but they wanted to make their own choices as to what methods to use. Most of them expressed the view that reading is not simply a set of decontextualized skills (Auerbach, 1995) and that children need to be presented with multiple options as they learn to read and write.

Although government intervention into schooling was the dominant theme in the LE, several participants focused on language and how languages other than English should be given equal status in the classroom, demonstrating that they understood the inequality among different linguistic varieties in society (Cox & Assis-Peterson, 1999; Goldstein, 2003; Valenzuela, 1999). The discontinuation of dual language programs in New York City provided the context for taking this stance. The participants did not use the academic terminology of critical literacies or sociolinguistic theorists, but they were able to position themselves within the discourse of complex issues, sometimes drawing on personal experiences to develop their stances.

REFLECTING ON THE CONSTRUCTION OF COUNTERNARRATIVES AND THEIR PURPOSES

To what extent did we and the students in this course construct "counternarratives," little stories that talked back to grand narratives, either local or national? Because it is the nature of narratives to weave themselves into other narratives, this question has a complex and multilayered response. In retrospect we see that we wove aspects of the local grand narrative of the College's conceptual framework into our syllabus, especially in terms of the three stances of inquiry, curriculum making, and advocacy for social justice.[1] Thus our course could be the "most local" grand narrative, in which we as teachers and researchers respond to the requirements of NCATE. On the other hand, because the social, educational, and political issues we presented originate in grand narratives of federal and local agency mandates, counternarratives that we or our students created cannot be directly or exclusively linked to NCATE accreditation.

For example, if we look first at the participants' two assignments, we would say that they have created counternarratives in the face of current educational policies that homogenize children and pedagogical practices (No Child Left Behind Act of 2001). Thus what seemed to be the mantra in their IE, elaborated upon in a range of ways – that every child develops and learns along a particular path influenced by social and cultural contexts and, thus, no single method works for all children – is a brief counternarrative to one-size-fits-all views of pedagogy. Further, the stances that the participants took in their LE often built upon this counternarrative. The policies they were objecting to often made flawed assumptions about "all" children, and it was these assumptions that the students critiqued in their role of advocates for social justice.

On another level, though, the students were not creating a counternarrative to the most local grand narrative that we instructors presented in the first part of the course. There were aspects of the IE that clearly countered traditional assessment, as specified in NCLB and mandated literacy curricula: students chose themes to focus on, they shared their work online, and they could receive in-progress feedback from instructors and peers. Still we thought that the content of the course was being mirrored, not in a rote-like way but with consistent themes, including the mantra we referred to above. Again in retrospect and in the spirit of self-critique, we wonder whether counternarratives to our grand narrative were possible. The assignment could be interpreted as a take-home midterm and accounted for 25% of the students' grade. In this situation the power relation students were most aware of may have been between instructor/grader and student. Thus although the participants may have been theoretically in tune with our preferred theories and practices, students could be tempted to generate "what the teacher wants," and we would be naïve not to acknowledge the politics of "doing school." Indeed at the same time that we appreciated the students' lack of a normalizing gaze at children, we wondered if we instructors cast our own normalizing gaze. To what extent did we want our students to perform in uniform ways? There was room for individuality and variation in our assignments, but the consistent themes in the IE did raise the question about our normalizing a supposedly open-ended exercise. Or in terms of postmodern and critical theories, through the structure of the IE and the use of conventional grading, we may have constrained the students' ability to create counternarratives and instead encouraged the reproduction of our course's local grand narrative.

Within the framework of NCATE, there is another complex weaving together of narratives. We conclude that the study participants are moving in the direction of becoming advocates for social justice, as well as curriculum makers and inquirers. Interestingly, the principles they referred to in both assignments reflected an aspect of the explanation of the social justice stance in the college's conceptual framework. That is, all learners must be approached as individuals with particular capacities. It is the task of a democratic society to provide a school that will promote individual learning in a society that is extremely diverse. Although the participants did not emphasize aspects of schooling in the IE, they did address issues of choice in the face of government intervention in the LE. Thus, neither we as instructors nor they as students created counternarratives to those principles of the NCATE framework. Still, because the NCATE framework is multifaceted, there is a way in which this study constitutes a counternarrative. Through the qualitative and descriptive methodology of this study, we created our own assessment, a self-study, that is not replicable since it is unlikely that the course will be taught in exactly the same way again or assessed in exactly the same way. In order to be reviewed and approved by NCATE, each program within the institution being reviewed must have an "assessment system." This system is to be reliable and objective and will be based in part on the development of rubrics, or scoring systems that create hierarchies of quality or achievement. Our method of searching for themes and assuming that each participant would differ in multiple ways from every other participant is a methodological counternarrative to the establishment of scoring systems. Eventually, we are expected to develop these systems for selected assignments in a range of students' courses over time, and it remains to be seen whether "counterrubrics" will be allowed. Of course since most programs have maintained a hierarchical way of evaluating work (grading), rubrics might not be so counter to our practices. So again the narratives and counternarratives weave together as we admit that a postmodern and critical way of looking at language and literacy clashes with a traditional, modernist way of evaluating students – grading them.

Thus, perhaps the most significant counternarrative we have created is the study itself. In designing an *action research* project, we join teachers who adopt an alternative definition of research, which is designed and implemented – controlled – by teachers themselves (e.g., Brookline Teacher Researcher Seminar, 2004; for other examples see Genishi, Ryan, Ochsner, & Yarnall, 2001). Our context is different from many teacher researchers': we are in a college classroom, but we too are working against the time-honored and current grand narrative of research as "science" (Cochran-Smith, 2004; Whitehurst, 2002) and assessment as testing. In a "scientific" study teachers who are deeply invested in the success of their students and their teaching would not be the researchers or assessors, as teachers could not be objective.

We acknowledge our subjectivity at the same time that we believe that our analyses and interpretations can be part of a counternarrative whose purpose is to lead to deeper understanding of practice and theory. We study ourselves not to claim that ours are "best practices," but to understand – from multiple stances – something about what students and we as instructors/researchers can take from an evolving and complex course. We agree with Feldman (2003) that valid self-study is explicitly described political work that ultimately aims to improve teaching and learning. Thus we make our own work public (accountable) not by doing a scientific experiment, but by being as clear as possible about our questions, methods, and findings to date. In this chapter we have attempted to communicate the contexts of our work and our processes in the beginning phases of analysis. Moreover, we plan to continue our counternarrative by analyzing in depth the work of individual students and analyzing other sources of data, including less conventional work, such as the visual representations that complemented students' written work. Finally, as we complete this chapter, we begin to plan the next – we hope improved – version of our language and literacy course.

NOTES

1. The insights and questions of two anonymous reviewers helped us articulate the nature of this interweaving.

REFERENCES

Allington, R. L. (2002). *Big brother and the national reading curriculum: How ideology trumped evidence*. Portsmouth, NH: Heinemann.
Auerbach, E. R. (1995). The politics of the ESL classroom: Issues of power in pedagogical choices. In: J. W. Tollefson (Ed.), *Power and inequality in language education* (pp. 9–33). New York: Cambridge University Press.
Ballenger, C. (1999). *Teaching other people's children: Literacy and learning in a bilingual classroom*. New York: Teachers College Press.
Banks, J. A., Cookson, P., Gay, G., & Hawley, W. (2001). Diversity within unity: Essential principles for teaching and learning in a multicultural society. *Phi Delta Kappan, 83*(3), 196–202.
Berliner, D. C. (2002). Educational research: The hardest science of all. *Educational Researcher, 31*(8), 18–20.
Bogdan, R. C., & Biklen, S. K. (2003). *Qualitative research for education: An introduction to theories and methods* (4th ed.). New York: Allyn & Bacon.
Brookline Teacher Researcher Seminar. (2004). *Regarding children's words: Teacher research on language and literacy*. New York: Teachers College Press.
Cazden, C. B., John, V. P., & Hymes, D. (Eds) (1972). *Functions of language in the classroom*. New York: Teachers College Press.
Cochran-Smith, M. (1991). Learning to teach against the grain. *Harvard Educational Review, 61*, 279–310.
Cochran-Smith, M. (2004). Taking stock in 2004: Teacher education in dangerous times. *Journal of Teacher Education, 55*(1), 3–7.
Cochran-Smith, M., & Lytle, S. L. (1993). *Inside/outside: Teacher research and knowledge*. New York: Teachers College Press.
Cox, M. P., & Assis-Peterson, M. A. (1999). Critical pedagogy in ELT: Images of Brazilian teachers of English. *TESOL Quarterly, 33*(3), 433–451.
Delpit, L. (2001). The politics of teaching literature discourse. In: E. Cushman, E. E. Kintgen, B. M. Kroll & M. Rose (Eds), *Literacy: A critical sourcebook* (pp. 545–554). Boston: Bedford/St. Martins.
Dewey, J. (1933). *How we think: A restatement of the relations of reflective thinking to the educative process*. Boston: DC Heath.
Dyson, A. H. (1999). Transforming transfer: Unruly children, contrary texts, and the persistence of the pedagogical order. In: A. Iran-Nejad & P. D. Pearson (Eds), *Review of research in education*, (Vol. 24, pp. 143–173). Washington, DC: American Educational Research Association.
Dyson, A. H. (2003). Popular literacies and the "all" children: Rethinking literacy development for contemporary childhoods. *Language Arts, 81*(2), 100–109.

Fairclough, N. (2001). *Language and power*. Harlow, England: Pearson Education Limited.
Feiman-Nemser, S., & Melnick, S. (1992). Introducing teaching. In: S. Feiman-Nemser & H. Featherstone (Eds), *Exploring teaching: Reinventing an introductory course* (pp. 1–17). New York: Teachers College Press.
Feldman, A. (2003). Validity and quality in self-study. *Educational Researcher, 32*(3), 26–28.
Freire, P. (1970). *The pedagogy of the oppressed*. New York: Seabury Press.
Gallas, K. (1994). *The languages of learning: How children talk, write, dance, draw, and sing their understanding of the world*. New York: Teachers College Press.
Genishi, C. (1979). Young children communicating in the classroom. *Theory into Practice, 18*, 244–250.
Genishi, C. (Ed.) (1992). *Ways of assessing children and curriculum: Stories of early childhood practice*. New York: Teachers College Press.
Genishi, C. (1997). Assessing against the grain: A conceptual framework for alternative assessments. In: A. L. Goodwin (Ed.), *Assessment for equity and inclusion: Embracing all our children* (pp. 35–50). New York: Routledge.
Genishi, C., Ryan, S., Ochsner, M., & Yarnall, M. M. (2001). Teaching in early childhood education: Understanding practices through research and theory. In: V. Richardson (Ed.), *Handbook of research on teaching*, (4th ed.) (pp. 1175–1210). Washington, DC: American Educational Research Association.
Goldstein, T. (2003). *Teaching and learning in a multilingual school: Choices, risks and dilemmas*. Mahwah, NJ: Erlbaum.
Goodnough, A. (2003). All schools doing poorly would get one curriculum. *New York Times*, January 15, p. B-3.
Greene, M. (1978). *Landscapes of learning*. New York: Teachers College Press.
Grieshaber, S., & Cannella, G. S. (Eds) (2001). *Embracing identities in early childhood education: Diversity and possibilities*. New York: Teachers College Press.
Heath, S. B. (1983). *Ways with words: Language, life, and work in communities and classrooms*. New York: Cambridge University Press.
hooks, b. (1994). *Teaching to transgress: Education as the practice of freedom*. New York: Routledge.
Hull, G. A., & Schultz, K. (2002). *School's out: Bridging out-of-school literacies with classroom practice*. New York: Teachers College Press.
Ladson-Billings, G. (2000). Racialized discourses and ethnic epistemologies. In: N. K. Denzin & Y. S. Lincoln (Eds), *Handbook of qualitative research*, (2nd ed.) (pp. 257–277). London: Sage.
Lieberman, A., & McLaughlin, M. (Eds) (1982). *Policy making in education: Eighty-first yearbook of the National Society for the study of education*. Chicago: University of Chicago Press.
Lo Bianco, J. (2000). Multiliteracies and multilingualism. In: M. Kalantizis & B. Cope (Eds), *Multiliteracies: Literacy learning and the design of social futures* (pp. 92–105). New York: Routledge.
Lubeck, S. (1994). The politics of developmentally appropriate practice: Exploring issues of culture, class, and curriculum. In: B. L. Mallory & R. S. New (Eds), *Diversity and developmentally appropriate practices: Challenges for early childhood education* (pp. 17–43). New York: Teachers College Press.
Lyotard, J.-F. (1984). In: G. Bennington & B. Massumi (Trans.), *The postmodern condition: A report on knowledge*. Manchester: Manchester University Press.

Moll, L., & Gonzalez, N. (2001). Lessons from research with language-minority children. In: E. Cushman, E. E. Kintgen, B. M. Kroll & M. Rose (Eds), *Literacy: A critical sourcebook* (pp. 156–171). Boston: Bedford/St. Martin's.

New London Group. (1996). A pedagogy of multiliteracies: Designing social futures. *Harvard Educational Review*, 66(1), 60–92.

No Child Left Behind Act of 2001. (PL 107–110). www.ed.gov/nclb/landing.jhtml

Paley, V. G. (1981). *Wally's stories*. Cambridge, MA: Harvard University Press.

Paley, V. G. (1994). *The kindness of children*. Cambridge, MA: Harvard University Press.

Paley, V. G. (1997). *The girl with the brown crayon*. Cambridge, MA: Harvard University Press.

Peters, M., & Lankshear, C. (1996). Postmodern counternarratives. In: H. Giroux, C. Lankshear, P. McLaren & M. Peters (Eds), *Counternarratives: Cultural studies and critical pedagogies in postmodern spaces* (pp. 1–39). New York: Routledge.

Pressley, M. (2001). Effective beginning reading instruction. *Executive summary and paper commissioned by the National Reading Conference*. Chicago, IL: National Reading Conference.

Report of the National Reading Panel. (1999). *Teaching children to read. Report of the Subgroups*. Washington, DC: National Institute of Child Health and Human Development.

Schon, D. (1987). *Educating the reflective practitioner*. San Francisco: Jossey-Bass.

Schoonmaker, F. (2003). *"Growing up" teaching: From personal knowledge to professional practice*. New York: Teachers College Press.

Stires, S. (1991). *With promise: Redefining reading and writing for "special" students*. Portsmouth, NH: Heinemann.

Street, B. (1993). Introduction: The new literacy studies. In: B. Street (Ed.), *Cross-cultural approaches to literacy* (pp. 1–22). New York: Cambridge University Press.

Teachers College National Council for the Accreditation of Teacher Education (NCATE) Report. (2003). www.tc.edu/administration/ncate/ConceptualFramework

Tyner, K. (1998). *Literacy in a digital world: Teaching and learning in the age of information*. Mahwah, NJ: Erlbaum.

Valenzuela, A. (1999). *Subtractive schooling: U.S. Mexican youth and the politics of caring*. Albany: State University of New York Press.

Whitehurst, G. (2002). *Scientifically based research on teacher quality: Research on teacher preparation and professional development*. Paper presented at the White House Conference on preparing tomorrow's teachers, Washington, DC.

Zumwalt, K. K. (1982). Research on teaching: Policy implications for teacher education. In: A. Lieberman & M. McLaughlin (Eds), *Policy making in education: Eighty-first yearbook of the National Society for the study of education* (pp. 215–248). Chicago: University of Chicago Press.

APPENDIX

Research Description

Description of the Research

You are invited to participate in a research study on how you, as prospective teachers, begin to take on three roles that Teachers College has decided are primary for all preservice students: inquirer, curriculum maker, and advocate for social justice. As we on the faculty developed syllabi for our teacher education programs in Early Childhood and Early Childhood Special Education, we have kept these roles in mind. In this study we plan to describe how this course on Language and Literacy in the Early Childhood Curriculum is enacted and to assess it in terms of these three aspects of teachers' roles. Our purpose is to carry out a self-study or "action research project" that asks, *how and to what extent are students in this course demonstrating that they are inquirers, curriculum makers, and advocates for social justice?*

You will not be asked to do anything different while you are enrolled in the course, although at times we may audiotape a discussion for later transcription and analysis. One of us might also take notes during segments of the class that focus on one or more of the three stances. Once the data analysis has been completed (which will occur once the course is over), we will discard the tapes. The research will be conducted at Teachers College by Celia Genishi, professor; Shin-ying Huang, research assistant, and Tamara Glupczynski, instructor.

Risks and Benefits
The research has the same amount of risk students will encounter in discussions in a typical class. It is possible that some students will find discussion of inequities in education uncomfortable or will find it challenging to think of themselves as less politically aware than they had thought. We expect to discuss the challenges to all students, and ourselves as well, so that this discomfort or challenge should not be damaging. The benefits should be those of taking the course. Participants who agree to participate in "member checks" or focus groups might benefit from additional reflection on the impact of the course once it has ended.

Data Storage to Protect Confidentiality
Once data analysis begins, a numerical code will be given to each participant to keep her identity confidential. Data, including transcripts from segments of class and written work, will be kept in a locked file in 302 Main Hall.

Time Involvement
Your participation will last until the course ends. If you agree to participate in member checks, this would take approximately 20–30 min sometime in the Spring semester. If you agree to participate in follow-up focus groups, these would take approximately 1 h.

How Will Results be Used
The results of the study will be used (a) to document student (your) and faculty performance in this course, with regard to the three teacher roles, (b) to meet requirements for NCATE assessment of our programs, (c) to make presentations at professional meetings, and (d) to provide the basis of publications in journals or chapters in books.

PUTTING POSTMODERN THEORIES INTO PRACTICE IN EARLY CHILDHOOD TEACHER EDUCATION

Jennifer Sumsion

ABSTRACT

In this chapter, I describe how postmodern perspectives assist me in negotiating my multiple roles and responsibilities as an early childhood teacher educator in an increasingly complex pedagogical and workplace context. In particular, I focus on how postmodern understandings support me in theorizing my practice and envisioning productive possibilities for change. Underpinning the chapter are three interconnecting motifs that imbue my work as teacher educator – reflexivity, hope, and a commitment to transformative change. The chapter concludes with reflections about the potential of postmodern perspectives to enhance the agency of teacher educators and preservice teachers alike.

INTRODUCTION

An invitation to write about how I am using postmodern perspectives in my practice as an early childhood teacher educator was a daunting but enticing prospect. Daunting because it reinforced the complexities of postmodernism and the challenges of coming to understand its possibilities, but enticing because it enabled me to name the directions in which I have been moving in my work with preservice teachers. For increasingly, I have become convinced that an appreciation of postmodern perspectives can assist prospective teachers to develop and sustain the agency to engage productively and optimistically with the uncertainties and ambiguities they will inevitably encounter in their practice as early childhood educators. This conviction stems, in part, from my own experience of how postmodern understandings enable me to respond with some sense of agency to the challenges I face as a teacher educator. In this chapter, I describe some of these challenges to illustrate how postmodern perspectives can assist in negotiating passages through increasingly complex pedagogical contexts (Martusewicz, 2001).

The chapter begins with an overview of those aspects of postmodern perspectives that have been especially helpful in theorizing and guiding my practice and in envisaging possibilities for change. I then introduce three interconnected motifs that imbue my work as teacher educator – reflexivity, hope, and a commitment to transformative change. After describing my work context, I draw on three examples to illuminate how postmodern perspectives, in conjunction with my belief in reflexivity, hope, and transformative change, shape and enrich my practice: first as a member of the broader university community with responsibilities for interpreting and implementing its policies; second, as coordinator of the practicum component our preservice program; and third, as convener of a compulsory semester-long *Reflective Practice* seminar within the preservice program. The chapter concludes with reflections about the potential of postmodern perspectives to enhance the agency of teacher educators and preservice teachers alike.

POSTMODERN PERSPECTIVES

Many writers caution that the term 'postmodern' defies definition or simplistic explanation. Indeed, they argue that trying to define postmodern subjects it to a modernist or 'scientific' way of thinking that is incompatible with postmodern understandings (Usher & Edwards, 1994). Hence, rather than attempt to define postmodern, I focus on those aspects of postmodern perspectives that have been most salient in navigating my passage as teacher educator: questioning certainty, the politics of representation, the interrelationship of discourse, knowledge and power, multiple identities, and agency.

Questioning Certainty

Usher and Edwards (1994) describe postmodern as 'state of mind' (p. 2) that is characterized by a commitment to questioning the certainty of truths that have underpinned modernist thinking. Postmodern perspectives reject the possibility of systematic explanation and thus problematize and challenge "existing concepts, structures, and hierarchies of knowledge" (p. 3). Adopting a postmodern stance, therefore, requires us to forgo the reassurance or security of "fixed referents and traditional anchoring points" (p. 10). Yet, as Usher and Edwards go on to point out, postmodern theories and approaches compensate for this lack of certainty by providing a rich array of "conceptual resources for thinking anew...at both the personal and structural level" (p. 3).

Politics of Representation

A further premise of postmodern thought is that language constructs meaning rather than reflecting reality. Language and meaning are not fixed or stable but shift according to different social, cultural, and philosophical contexts (St Pierre, 2000; Weedon, 1997). Hence they are subject to multiple, often disputed, interpretations, and forms of representation. As Weedon (1997) notes, "once language is understood in terms of competing discourses, competing ways of giving meaning to the world...then language becomes an important site of political struggle" (p. 23). These struggles result in some discourses becoming dominant and others marginalized. Here, discourse refers to language, texts, and artefacts that signify particular ways of "thinking, feeling, believing, valuing, and acting" (Gee, 1996, p. 131). Discourses, then, are inherent in the exercise of power, for "once a discourse becomes 'normal' or 'natural', it is difficult to think and act outside it" (St Pierre, 2000, p. 485). In this sense, discourses regulate how we know and engage with the world; "they shape our understanding of what is possible and what is desirable" (Dahlberg, Moss, & Pence, 1999, p. 31). For this reason, as Foucault (1980) argues, discourse, knowledge, and power are inextricably related.

Discourse, Knowledge, and Power

In Foucault's terms, power is not fixed, nor possessed, nor necessarily repressive. Rather, he conceptualizes power as fluid and unstable, circulating through a network-like capillary of relationships, sometimes relatively unimpeded and sometimes resisted. Power, or more specifically power relations, can be productive, not just constraining, especially when thought of as *power to* and not *power over* (Zournazi & Massumi, 2002). Power can also be dangerous, however, especially if directed to "a compulsive quest for foundationalist certainties and guarantees" (Faubion, 1994, p. xix) and employed in ways that fail to recognize knowledge as "always partial and perspectival" (Usher, Bryant, & Johnstone, 1997, p. 205). Power operates through discourses, knowledge, and disciplinary practices that regulate by normalizing, categorizing, and measuring (Usher et al., 1997). These disciplinary practices or technologies of power are double-edged; they can help us to know ourselves more fully but they can also govern us by turning us into compliant, self-policing identities (Usher et al., 1997).

Multiple Identities and Agency

In contrast to modernist notions of identity as singular, stable and coherent, postmodern perspectives see identities, or subjectivities, as multiple, complex, and constituted through discourse, sometimes precarious and contradictory and "always becoming and never quite fixed" (Foley, 2002, p. 473). When we recognise that we construct our subjectivities and the world as we see it through the discourses we perceive available to us, then we can also deconstruct and reconstruct these discourses. Realizing that many of the structures and practices we take for granted "are not essential or absolute but are created and maintained everyday...through the exercise of power" (St Pierre, 2000, p. 483) can be liberating and energizing. Deconstructing and reconstructing these structures and practices "can help us rewrite the world and ourselves again and again and again" (St Pierre, 2000, p. 483) and in doing so, to cultivate hope. These postmodern perspectives on language, discourse, power, and subjectivities affirm our agency as cultural actors who choose sometimes to enact and perpetuate, sometimes to contest, and sometimes to improvise on normative structures and discourses (Foley, 2002). Like Davies (2004), I refer to agency as the capacity to recognize how one is constituted through discourses; the capacity to "resist, subvert, and change" these discourses; and the capacity to "recognize multiple readings such that no discursive practice, or positioning within it by powerful others, can capture and control one's identity" (p. 4).

Some critics contend that in challenging the certainty of taken-for-granted 'truths' or a stable identity, postmodernist perspectives undermine confidence and agency and induce a kind of paralysis. In contrast, I believe that by contesting previously unchallenged constraints, postmodern perspectives can expand our margins of manoeuvrability, or our perceptions of "where we might be able to go and what we might be able to do" (Zournazi & Massumi, 2002, p. 212). As I set out to show in this chapter, postmodern perspectives have expanded and enriched my understandings of reflexivity, hope, and transformative change and how I might work these into practice.

REFLEXIVITY, HOPE, AND TRANSFORMATIVE CHANGE

A commitment to reflexivity, a belief in the power of hope, and confidence that, in synergy, these can contribute to transformative change are integral to my work as a teacher educator. To set the scene for the remainder of the chapter, I briefly explain what I mean by these terms.

Reflexivity

As a teacher educator, I believe I have an ethical responsibility, like all educators, to be critically reflexive. In other words, as educators, we have an obligation to continually ask searching questions about "what our work means" (Martusewicz, 2001, p. 20) and what "our work...should be" (Luke, Luke, & Mayer, 2000, p. 5). This responsibility means scrutinizing the categories and structures we have established; examining their impact, both intended and unintended; acknowledging our investments in them; and recognizing that while we may shape these categories and structures, they also shape us (St Pierre, 2000). It also means challenging our assumptions and engaging in ongoing internal dialogue and conversations with others about how to respond imaginatively, courageously, and with integrity to the troubling questions that arise when we unsettle the status quo. In requiring a continual rereading and rewriting of our selves and our practices, reflexivity keeps alive the possibility of seeing and acting differently.

Hope

Imagining new ways of seeing and acting creates hope. By 'hope', I refer to the energy mobilized by "a convergence of new agendas, conversations and possibilities" (Zournazi, 2002, p. 17). Hope generates momentum for change by encouraging us "to keep asking what risks need to be taken", and what habits, thoughts, practices, and structures need to be changed (Zournazi, 2002, p. 19). In this way, hope stretches the boundaries of the present and of what is considered possible (hooks, 2003, p. xiv). In so doing, it enables spaces for new possibilities to emerge and new visions to be created. Like Giroux (2002), I see hope as a mix of the personal, the political, and the pedagogical or, in his words, an 'educated hope' where individual experiences, dreams and desires contribute to collective imagination, responsibility, and agency through political engagement. The nature of these contributions is mediated by pedagogical contexts, the questions and problems emphasized in these spaces, and the power relations that characterize them. Hope, grounded in reflexivity, can give rise to transformative change.

Transformative Change

Through their openness to and capacity to imagine new alternatives, reflexivity, and hope generate synergies that can rupture the bonds that tie us to old, ingrained habits and taken for granted practices and dislodge previously accepted certainties. In destabilizing 'truths', they make possible new interpretations, new meanings and new configurations of practice and power relations. Although conceptualized variously, for many theorists (e.g., Giroux, 2002; Sachs, 2003) transformative change is characterized by inquiry, ethical practice, participation, public dialogue, and debate that acknowledge diverse perspectives, democratization, activism, a concern for social justice and the fostering of capacities, skills, and knowledge that support these.

Reflexivity, hope, and a commitment to transformative change seem fundamental to sustaining the commitment and capacity to respond productively to the challenges, complexities, and uncertainties educators inevitably encounter throughout their professional lives. One reason they are so important is that they have the potential to expand the 'margins of maneuverability' or sense of what is possible (Zournazi & Massumi, 2002). Before I explain why I hold these beliefs and why I find them sustaining, I describe the context of my work and journey as a teacher educator.

CONTEXTUALIZING MY WORK AND JOURNEY

Practice is inevitably located in context and each context has its own complexities and subtleties. While I focus on here on the political, institutional, pedagogical, and personal-professional particularities of my particular context, the broader discursive landscape may well be familiar to those involved in early childhood teacher education elsewhere.

The Political Context

Following a decade or more of neo-liberal government policies, the Australian university sector remains embroiled in a climate of competition, managerialism, and performativity. Judgements, comparisons, and detailed accountability measures are rife. So, too, are initiatives intended to 'reform', control, and confer strategic market advantage. Power (1994), citing Cohen (no date) sums up the scene well when he refers to "a series of conjuring tricks in which agencies are shuffled, new games invented, incantations recited, commissions, committees, laws, programmes, and campaigns announced" (preface).

The Institutional Context

In this context of competition and marketization, Macquarie University management expressed concern that, in recent national surveys, Macquarie graduates had not rated their acquisition of generic skills[1] as highly as those of some other universities. To address this perceived competitive weakness, all faculties and departments throughout the University were invited to apply for curriculum development grants to foster students' generic skills and their awareness of these skills. A team of faculty from the Institute of

Early Childhood a department of the University, was awarded one of these grants, in part to develop a generic skills self-evaluation document for student use. The awarding of this grant was not unexpected for within the University, the Institute of Early Childhood, has developed a reputation for responding adroitly to such policy initiatives.

The Pedagogical Context

The Institute of Early Childhood offers a highly regarded four year undergraduate Bachelor of Education (Early Childhood) program that qualifies its graduates to work with children aged from 6 weeks to 8 years of age, primarily in long day-care care services, preschools,[2] and the first 3 years of school. Like many preservice programs of this kind, it is predicated on modernist principles with a strong continuing commitment to developmental psychology as its main theoretical underpinning. The dominance of child development theory has only recently begun to be challenged within small fragmented pockets of the preservice program. The preservice program is also characterized by a commitment to child-centered philosophies as evidenced, for example, through a commitment to emergent curriculum that takes children's interests as its starting point.

The practicum component emphasizes reflective practice, mostly of a technical or personal, rather than critical nature (Zeichner & Tabachnick, 1991). Preservice teachers tend to focus on the effectiveness or otherwise of their practice in enabling them to achieve their goals for children's learning or on the resonance, or lack thereof, between their practices and their philosophical beliefs about teaching. Rarely do they appear to examine social and political factors that respectively advantage and marginalize children and their families or ways in which taken-for-granted practices in early childhood education may or may not contribute to socially progressive outcomes.

Perhaps this focus is not surprising as up to half of the Institute's students enter the preservice program as high-school leavers, mostly from white, English speaking, socially conservative, middle class backgrounds. The remaining students are 'mature age'.[3] Some are upgrading a 2-year TAFE (community college) qualification in child care; others have gained university entry under schemes that enable usual academic entry requirements to be bypassed; and a smattering are university graduates from other disciplines. The mature-age students are more likely than their younger counterparts to be from diverse sociocultural backgrounds.

The Personal-Professional Context

In my doctoral research, I worked closely with 18 preservice teachers to explore their reflexivity as they progressed through the preservice program (Sumsion, 1997). Overall, these preservice teachers spoke highly of their preservice program and their teacher educators. Yet, their perceptions that their teacher educators' passion, ideals, and constructions of exemplary practice precluded preservice teachers from exploring alternative constructions of early childhood teaching was a strong and persistent theme. I was disturbed and saddened to find this same theme evident in a recent investigation of new graduates from the preservice program (Britt, 2002; Britt & Sumsion, 2003). One of the participants in this study, Belle, likened her preservice program to a forced journey dragged behind a moving truck, "swept along in pursuit of the one true ideal" (Britt, 2002, p. 68). Her representation of her lack of manoeuvrability to negotiate alternative discourses to the dominant discourses taken up by her teacher educators is graphically portrayed in Fig. 1.

The absence of agency in these accounts has been instrumental in prompting my gradual and continuing shift, as a teacher educator, from a primarily liberal humanist perspective to a postmodern stance. One of the

> Educational philosophy is a truck going down the highway
> And I'm tied to the back of it.
> Every so often it stops and I get a lovely view,
> and we're driving past all this beautiful scenery
> but all the time
> **I'M BANGING my HEAD**
> against the CONCRETE and the METAL.
> and I'm getting grit and gravel embedded in my skin.
> I'm at a point now where I've just got to untie myself.

Fig 1. Belle – Educational Philosophy is a Truck.

many challenges involved in this shift has involved learning to become much more self-conscious about how I negotiate multiple and frequently competing discourses. In the reminder of the chapter, I describe my efforts to negotiate some of these discourses. As foreshadowed, I focus on three aspects of my role that highlight the challenges involved: as project leader of a University generic skills policy initiative, as practicum coordinator, and as convener of a *Reflective Practice* seminar. Implicit in my account is the importance of postmodern perspectives, reflexivity, hope, and a commitment to transformative change in helping me to conceptualize and make sense of what were often tentative steps and unpredicted outcomes.

NEGOTIATING THE DISCOURSES OF UNIVERSITY POLICY IN RELATION TO GENERIC SKILLS

When our project team was awarded a grant to foster the development of preservice teachers' generic skills, we harbored grave concerns that the University's rhetoric set the scene for a continuation of the dominant instrumentalist discourses and agendas underpinning the "current obsession with skills" (Bolton & Hyland, 2003, p. 16). These agendas are characterized by discourses of productivity and self-sufficiency. They aim to enhance prospective employees' economic capital and to fashion citizens who can provide for and regulate themselves and thus make minimal demands on the economic resources of the state (Barnett, 1997; Edwards, 2002). Although these instrumentalist discourses did not fit comfortably with our values, purposes, and subjectivities as teacher educators, we were hopeful that we could disrupt these discourses and resist and circumvent any imposition by the University of instrumentalist approaches to the generic skills agenda that might have unwelcome implications for our preservice program.

Resistance as Reflexive Conversations

As Foucault (1981) notes, the power of a dominant discourse, "also undermines and exposes it, renders it fragile and makes it possible to thwart it" (p. 101). Here he is referring to resistance, which can operate in a myriad of ways, including groups of individuals mobilizing around issues about which they feel strongly. As a group, we mobilized against instrumentalist discourses and agendas by establishing spaces in which they could be debated, reconceptualized, and reshaped.

These spaces were characterized by reflexive conversations. At their heart lay the challenge of identifying what we meant by generic skills and what they might look like in practice. Because we recognized that language has no fixed meaning and because we valued multiple perspectives, we sought the views of diverse groups of people. We talked at length among ourselves in focus groups of teacher educators and preservice teachers. We also engaged in conversations with the wider University community, including faculty from other disciplines and departments, and staff from the library and the career development office. Beyond the University, we spoke with major employers of our graduates, managers of job recruitment agencies, and chief executive officers of large corporations that employed graduates from diverse disciplines.

Here, I focus on the conversations amongst teacher educators and preservice teachers because they perhaps best illustrate how our grappling with possibilities was informed and enriched by postmodern understandings, as well as by hope and a commitment to reflexivity and transformative change. Because we wanted to work with a broad, rather than constraining, notion of generic skills we adopted Stephenson's (1998) notion of capability. *Capability* involves integrating and drawing on our personal qualities, understandings, knowledge, and skills in ways that enable us to make a valued contribution, not only when faced with familiar problems in familiar contexts, but also when we encounter new challenges in "unfamiliar and changing circumstances" (Stephenson, 1998, p. 3). We readily agreed that *capability* embraced the capacities prospective teachers are likely to need if they are to live rich, fulfilling, hopeful, and critically aware lives in an increasingly complex, fragmented, and uncertain world.

When we tried to identify what particular capabilities, such as creativity, critical analysis, or problem-solving might look like in practice, our task became much more difficult. We rapidly became aware of the multiple and shifting meanings of language underpinning what we had assumed to be our shared culture, beliefs, values, and expectations. We also realized how culturally bound our conversations were and that, inevitably, any list of capabilities or their characteristics would reflect our particular cultural bias. We were mindful, too, of the dangers of reductionism and the pointlessness of developing lengthy but essentially meaningless lists of capabilities and what they might look like in practice. Despite our reservations, we eventually drew up lists of possibilities that we hoped had the potential to form the basis of a generic skills self-evaluation document.

POWER AND THE POLITICS OF REPRESENTATION

When we took these lists of capabilities to our preservice teachers and asked for their feedback and assistance in further developing and refining the lists, many of the same issues about the cultural boundedness and slipperiness of language that had arisen in our focus groups with colleagues re-emerged. In addition, many preservice teachers raised concerns about surveillance and power. How would the document be used? Who would have access to it? Would they be pressured to conform to particular values or norms? From our more powerful position as teacher educators, we had assumed naively that our preservice teachers would have been reassured by our intention that they use the document as a reflexive tool. Although we emphasized that our purpose was not to attempt to 'measure' or assess their capabilities, they equated the document as yet another in "a whole mass of documents that capture and fix them" (Foucault, 1979, p. 189).

As they named their concerns and contested some of our assumptions about how the self-evaluation documents might be used and stored, rich debates and reflexive discussions unfolded. Some focused on the categories we had used and how and why, in our society, certain qualities and skills had come to be valued. Others focused on performativity, or as the preservice teachers put it, the process of 'going through the motions' (for instance, in appearing to appreciate cultural diversity without demonstrating a real commitment to it). Other conversations centered on monitoring and control, either by self or those in more powerful positions. Barnett (1997) synthesizes the essence of many of these issues and understandings. For the most part, teacher educators and preservice teachers eventually managed to agree that:

> Self-monitoring can be read in essentially two ways. It can indicate an internalization of others' agendas. Here, self-monitoring is self-censorship. Or it can stand for powers of self-control *and* self-agency. Here, self-monitoring can have emancipatory overtones: through self-reflection, we put new possibilities to ourselves and so extend ourselves and our potential range of actions. (p. 42)

A preservice teacher conveyed these ideas more simply: "I'm not here to learn what you want. I'm here to grow in ways that are important to me. That's why I like the process. It gives me an opportunity to ask, 'What do I expect of myself'?"

Although some preservice teachers remained dubious about the implied monitoring function of the document, the focus group conversations enabled them to negotiate changes to the document and to our expectations about how it might be used. They insisted, for example, on the rewording of the document to distinguish between performance and commitment and to highlight the importance of personal agency. They were adamant, as well, about retaining their copy of their self-evaluation document; they did not want it kept on file with their practicum records as we had originally intended. These negotiated changes addressed many of the preservice teachers' initial concerns.

The self-evaluation document that emerged from these in-depth discussions and extensive consultative processes was extremely lengthy, despite our attempts to keep it to a manageable size. Our joint commitment as teacher educators and preservice teachers to conveying the complexity and nuances of these capabilities as we had conceptualized them highlighted for all of us the problems of representation, an understanding that is central to postmodern perspectives. Moreover, we were acutely aware that, to outsiders, the document might appear a modernist and reductionist attempt to impose order on complexity. We recognized, too, that in many respects it was yet another manifestation of what Foucault (1994/1978) would see as governmentality, that is, a concerted attempt to constitute preservice teachers in a particular way by subjecting them to "an all-encompassing gaze" and having them "keep a watchful eye" on themselves (Usher et al., 1997, p. 58).

The Beginnings of Transformative Change

Yet for those of us engaged in producing the text, the experience also involved a rich exploration of a multiplicity of discourses, possibilities, and positionings. Our experiences in trying to adequately represent this richness and diversity reinforced what Usher et al. (1997) call the postmodern lesson: "that there is no one story to end all others, no grand narrative of all-encompassing explanation, and no final theory of everything" (p. 224). We learnt that it is possible to interrupt, resist, and counter dominant instrumentalist discourses, in our case, with discourses of collegiality, critique, and reflexivity. And it gave us the opportunity to begin to explore how an understanding of processes associated with power, resistance, surveillance, and self-formation can help us negotiate possibilities that offer hope of some degree of freedom, autonomy, and agency and thus potentially transformative change.

So far, I have tried to convey how postmodern understandings about discourse, power and resistance, overlaid with reflexivity and hope, assisted me as project leader in responding to the challenges inherent in negotiating different perspectives and agendas of the generic skills initiative. In the following section, I explain how postmodern perspectives are also beginning to influence my practice as coordinator of the practicum component of the preservice program. I focus especially on how these perspectives have heightened my awareness of the structures or "grids of regularity and normalcy" (St Pierre, 2000, p. 479) we have put in place; my growing concerns about their limitations; and my tentative efforts to dismantle them. First, though, I supplement the earlier brief contextual overview by describing the practicum, its structures, and the discourses underpinning them.

NEGOTIATING THE DISCOURSES OF THE PRACTICUM

The practicum component of our preservice program is embedded in a sequence of five compulsory, and one optional, 13-week, and semester-long *Reflective Practice* seminars. Each of these seminars involves 3 h of weekly class contact time with preservice teachers and has embedded within it a carefully structured and sequenced 10 or 15-day block teaching practicum. *Reflective Practice* seminars are taught by small teams of faculty. Our commitment to team teaching has led to a strong collegial ethos. We value this ethos highly and draw frequently on our colleagues' support and wisdom when dealing with the many complexities, tensions, and dilemmas so often associated with practicum.

Over the years, we have put in place many regulations and structures that are intended to provide a clear, coherent, and consistent framework for the practicum. The most fundamental is the requirement that preservice teachers achieve a passing grade in the practical and theoretical components of each *Reflective Practice* seminar before proceeding to the next in the sequence. We also have rules about mode of enrolment, locations in which preservice teachers are able to undertake practicum, and the ages of the children with whom they must work. Likewise, we have numerous protocols stipulating the tasks preservice teachers must undertake during their practicum, the written records they must keep, and the ways in which they are to make use of these records. To evaluate their progress, we follow tightly defined procedures that involve closely monitoring students' work within the six dimensions of competence we have defined as central to professional practice. Within each of these areas, we have identified what we consider to be a developmental sequence that governs our expectations of student capabilities at each stage of the program. We have long considered these regulations and structures essential in supporting preservice teachers, their cooperating teachers and their university advisers, and we rely heavily on them to guide our decision-making. In brief, we have a considerable investment in these regulatory structures for they convey an enticing picture of intrinsic order and readily measurable progression, and reassure us that we are fulfilling our gate-keeping responsibilities to the early childhood teaching profession.

Superimposed on these regulatory structures are the convictions and passions of respective members of the different teaching teams. These variously include a strong attachment to a singular, tightly orchestrated planning format, an unwavering faith in child development theory, and a fervent commitment to documentation processes similar to those used in the preschools of Reggio Emilia in Northern Italy. Each of these convictions and passions is steeped in its own set of discourses, expectations, and requirements that are intended to govern preservice teachers' thinking and practices.

Questioning Normative Frameworks

In many respects, the cultural framework underpinning the practicum component of our preservice program has served us well. For the most part, it has reflected our collective constructions of our roles as teacher educators, and our views about learning and professional development and practice. As my philosophical shift to postmodern perspectives continues, however, my confidence in its essentially modernist "fixed reference points" (Usher et al., 1997, p. 5) is rapidly eroding.

My concerns are of three kinds. First, we argue that our practicum framework is based on a sound understanding of preservice teacher development. Yet, we are inclined to overlook that it reflects our normative views constructed within the limits of our cultural experience. Second, in serving to categorize, normalize, measure, and control, the cultural framework of the practicum embodies what Foucault refers to as disciplinary power (Usher et al., 1997). In other words, it seeks to perpetuate the knowledge base and views traditionally valued within early childhood teacher education programs and to actively discipline or mould preservice teachers into becoming 'subjects' or upholders of that knowledge base and those views rather than encouraging them to imagine new possibilities. Third, the structures we have put in place serve to keep our preservice teachers under close surveillance that, in turn, tends to generate an uneasy and frequently unproductive mix of compliance and resistance.

Like Segall (2002), I am discomforted by the 'tip of the tongue' facility with which many preservice teachers invoke the discourses of their teacher educators. Segall concluded that these discourses can be taken up "not so much in order to engage in a serious debate about teaching, but as...a way of speaking about teaching that no longer required...critical engagement" (p. 60). Reluctance to engage critically with the complexities of teaching seems to go hand in hand with a performativity that has as its primary goal a determination to be seen to conform to the expectations and regulations governing the practicum. This tendency can be exacerbated if preservice teachers perceive they need to strategically juggle the sometimes conflicting expectations of their teacher educators and cooperating teachers in their practicum settings.

If we want to achieve more than the production of preservice teachers characterized by seemingly "docile bodies and obedient souls" (Foucault, 1981; in Leach, Neutze & Zepke, 2001, p. 296), we may need to dismantle some of these structures and inject a fluidity into our ways of thinking about practicum. That fluidity that is evident informally, for I suspect that all of us on the practicum team have knowingly made decisions that do not conform with the structures we have set in place. But we have yet to acknowledge collectively and openly that "what may seem necessary or set in stone hardly ever is" (St Pierre, 2000, p. 493).

Courage, Hope, and Change

In questioning the rigidity of the structures of the practicum we will need to find the courage to ask disturbing questions: Have we spent too much time trying to distill and document the essence of professional practice, rather than investing our energies in pushing the boundaries of what professional practice might mean? Do we use these structures to exclude those who don't meet our normative constructions of "a particular kind of early childhood teacher with particular kinds of knowledge" (Novinger & O' Brien, 2003, p. 12)? Rather than focusing on structures, should we be asking new and different questions if we are to assist our preservice teachers to grow in more productive ways? If so, what questions might these be?

Our experience from the generic skills project discussed earlier in this chapter highlighted the value of inviting preservice teachers to contribute to such discussions and to identifying the questions that need to be asked. I have begun to draw on this experience when working individually with preservice teachers whose 'performance' during practicum is causing concern. Instead of automatically invoking the regulations of the practicum and making decisions according to these regulations, I try to engage preservice teachers in critical reflection not only about the issues of concern in relation to their practice, but also about the impact of the practicum structures in which they are expected to operate.

This means that I no longer ask questions primarily of a technical-rational nature (e.g., "How might you go about this differently so that the outcome is more effective?") or those designed to prompt reflection of a personal-humanist kind (e.g., "Do you see any conflict between your practices and your beliefs?"). Frequently, such questions are designed to encourage preservice teachers to conform to accepted practices and to work within predetermined structures. Rather, I am trying to acknowledge explicitly in my conversations with preservice teachers the multiplicity of possibilities that may have contributed to them having been identified as being 'at-risk' of failing the practicum. I now routinely ask myself two questions: "How am I reading this situation, and are there alternative readings available?" (Usher et al., 1997, p. 230); and "Are the rules and structures of the practicum limiting what this preservice teacher is able to achieve and contribute in this early childhood setting and if so how might they be changed to enable a more productive outcome?" I also encourage preservice teachers to ask these questions of themselves. We then jointly negotiate possible courses of action that may or may not accord with existing practicum structures.

Although I am hopeful that this approach has the potential to bring about transformative change with respect to how faculty conceptualize and preservice students experience the practicum, it is not without risks. These questions seem to provide useful reflexive "hooks" that may assist preservice teachers, and indeed teacher educators, "to think more critically and productively about their practice" (Usher et al., 1997, p. 232). But there is no guarantee that in considering these questions, preservice teachers will not be driven by short term, perhaps not particularly well informed, perceptions of self-interest. Nor is it easy to balance reservations about normative, narrow views of what constitutes good professional practice and reluctance to exclude versions of professional practice simply because they are not mainstream, with our moral obligations to perform some kind of gate-keeper role. Further, if my decision-making processes differ substantially from my colleagues', equity considerations may arise for preservice teachers that could have far-reaching implications for their progress in the program.

Our highly valued collegiality as a practicum team could also conceivably be threatened. These are potentially "troubling dimensions" (Novinger & O'Brien, 2003, p. 17) of my shift towards a postmodern stance.

In the third example of how postmodern perspectives are influencing my practices, I turn to my role as convener of one of five compulsory, semester-long *Reflective Practice* seminars in the practicum sequence of the preservice program. Here, I continue to explore the themes of creating conversational spaces in which to negotiate new possibilities, and the importance of reflexivity and critique in attempting to bring about transformational change. To illustrate how I am trying to work explicitly with preservice teachers to highlight the potential of postmodern perspectives, I focus specifically on assessment practices.

NEGOTIATING THE DISCOURSES OF ASSESSMENT IN THE REFLECTIVE PRACTICE SEMINAR

The *Reflective Practice* seminar on which I focus here is the third in the sequence of five compulsory practicum seminars and is typically undertaken by preservice teachers in the fifth semester of the preservice program. The two previous seminars in the sequence place a heavy emphasis on observation and planning skills grounded in a strong allegiance to child development theory and developmentally and culturally appropriate practice (Bredekamp & Copple, 1997). Consequently, preservice teachers tend to enter the third *Reflective Practice* seminar with confidence in their developing skills and an unquestioning acceptance of the knowledge base on which these skills are based. By this stage of the preservice program, they are also well versed in the discourses, structures, and expectations of the practicum, as well as in the writing of academic essays that have constituted the majority of their assessment tasks to date. One of my goals in this seminar is to unsettle my students' assumptions about themselves as learners and teachers and to create spaces in which these assumptions can be challenged. A major focus of this *Reflective Practice* seminar, therefore, is to encourage preservice teachers to adopt a "constructively critical" approach (Usher et al., 1997, p. 229) in considering how they might recognize, name, question, and mediate the processes in their constructions of their identities as university students and prospective early childhood teachers.

One of the ways I have tried to assist preservice teachers to take a critically reflexive approach has been by changing my assessment practices and making explicit the reasons for these changes. In this section, I describe two such changes: involving preservice teachers in decisions about assessment and departing from the traditional academic essay as a major assessment task. In my discussions with preservice teachers, I frame these changes in terms of my commitment to continually questioning and critiquing my practice. In doing so, I try to illustrate the influence of postmodern perspectives on my thinking. To this end, I talk with preservice teachers about the discourses of assessment and the tensions inherent in them. Together, we then attempt to deconstruct these discourses and to consider some of the implications for ourselves as teachers and learners. Issues that invariably arise include the valuing of some types of knowledge and texts more highly than others, especially the privileging of theoretical knowledge over practical knowledge, and the dominance of academic essays as the main mode of assessment in their preservice program. I explain to preservice teachers, how I am attempting to disrupt this hierarchy and invite them to join me in what are still relatively small, but nevertheless hopeful, acts of resistance.

Expanding the Margins of Manoeuvrability: Self and Peer Evaluation

One such act has been to acknowledge their mounting dissatisfaction about their practicum folders not being assessed beyond a pass/fail basis. Many of our preservice teachers argue that their detailed recording in their folders should be recognized more explicitly by attracting marks that contribute to their grade for the seminar. Traditionally, the practicum team's justification for not acceding to these requests for a more detailed assessment revolved around potential inequities, given the widely differing circumstances in which preservice teachers undertake their practicum and the differing degrees of support they receive. Pragmatic reasons also played a part – we simply do not have the resources to closely examine hundreds of practicum folders. A further, but unspoken, concern was that by including the practicum folder as an assessment item, preservice teachers whom we perceived to be academically weak and likely to otherwise fail the seminar may gain sufficient marks to pass.

Because I wanted to continue dismantling some of the inflexible structures associated with the practicum, I suggested a compromise to preservice teachers. Those who wished could submit their practicum folder for assessment, but the marks awarded would be decided by a combination of self and peer evaluation. The teaching team would step in as final arbitrators only when the preservice teachers could not reach agreement. Those preservice teachers who chose to take up this option took a major role in devising the assessment criteria and the processes to be adopted. While the criteria and processes will benefit from continuing refinement, valuable learning has already emerged. Preservice teachers have gained a heightened appreciation of the complexity of the evaluation process and of the difficulties of comparison given the contextual embeddedness of practice. They have also come to recognize the multiple possibilities for representation, even within the strict guidelines of the practicum structure within which they were working, and they seem to have developed some understanding of the shallowness that can be associated with performativity. Particularly important has been the sense of agency that seems to have emerged amongst these preservice teachers following their successful negotiation of changes to assessment practices.

Exploring Alternative Forms of Representation

The second change involved departing from the traditional essay as a major assessment component. In this *Reflective Practice* seminar, preservice teachers are asked to identify, articulate, reflect on, and critique their developing philosophies of practice as emerging early childhood teachers. Rather than writing a formal essay, they are encouraged to use alternative forms of representation. Mind-mapping, photography, poetry, drawings, collage, and three dimensional constructions are common choices. This expectation induces considerable anxiety for some preservice teachers but seems to unsettle dominant and routine ways of thinking, and encourage playfulness, creativity, and reflexivity. It also gives rise to fundamental questions such as: *What is known? How do we know? Whose knowledge counts? Whose voices get to be heard?* Ensuing conversations range from what might be lost through routine adherence to normalizing processes and structures, to power, resistance, discourses, and the practices and strategies we adopt in living in the world.

The visual representations of preservice teachers who have preceded them through the program (see, for example, Sarah's representations in Sumsion, 2002) or those of recent graduates (such as Belle's portrayal of being dragged behind the truck in Fig. 1) also generate much discussion. While it is difficult for most of our preservice teachers to move beyond their accustomed frames of reference, the opportunity to critique discourses and practices in their preservice program seems to at least open the possibility of revisiting and critiquing aspects of their own practice and their constructions of self as teacher. To this end, the final component of the "philosophy assignment" asks preservice teachers to reflect on and critique their constructions and in doing so, to respond to several questions from a question bank that they have generated in collaboration with their peers. This year, their questions included:

> To what extent does your philosophy reflect your own sociocultural background and experiences? How might your philosophy expand and/or limit options and possibilities open to you as a teacher? Can you see any tensions/possible contradictions in your philosophy, and if so, do you see these primarily as a strength/limitation?

The "loss of certainty in ways of knowing and what is known" (Usher et al., 1997, p. 201) troubles some preservice teachers. Others find the realization that they can question assumptions and challenge orthodoxies what they have previously not thought to question exhilarating and liberating. The response of these preservice teachers encourages me to continue to explore, with considerable hope, ways that this *Reflective Practice* seminar might provide a forum that welcomes and supports this sort of questioning and critique. In particular, my hope is that it will enable us collectively and individually to develop a sense of confidence and agency in our ability to negotiate the many and often competing discourses and challenges that we encounter in negotiating and transforming our roles as learners and teachers.

REFLECTIONS

Writing about our hopes and our practices requires courage (Martusewicz, 2001). In my case, it has involved challenging many of the truths adhered to by colleagues whom I respect, admire and regard with great affection, and the processes and structures we have collectively put in place to uphold these truths. It has also highlighted the smallness of the steps that I have taken and the tensions inherent within them. But even small, imperfect steps can help to instigate change because they sustain the imaginings, hopes, and ways of seeing and doing things differently that can lead ultimately to transformation. For transformation "begins with an act of imagination that elevates a...dream of change above the intimidating presence of things as they are" (Washington, 1996, p. 32). If we are to transform early childhood education we need to create spaces in which we can critique constructively and challenge what we may have previously taken for granted. In this chapter, I have described how I am trying to work with preservice teachers in ways that contribute to creating such spaces.

Underpinning the chapter is the premise that teacher educators are implicated in the 'production' of early childhood teachers and that preservice teachers' experiences of 'being produced' may shape the ways in which they take up, resist, or negotiate the dominant discourses about teaching, learning, and being an early childhood educator. It is crucial, then, that the production process engenders agency and hope. For as St Pierre (2000) notes, "the space of freedom available to us is not at all insignificant, and we have the ability to analyze, contest, and change practices that are being used to construct ourselves and the world" (p. 493). Postmodern perspectives, in my experience, can provide rich conceptual tools to guide us in using this space well.

My intention is selecting these examples of how postmodern perspectives are influencing my practice is to highlight the many parallels between the discursive contexts and challenges of teacher education and early childhood education. As Novinger and O'Brien (2003) argue, educators in both sectors need to negotiate competing discourses associated with skills, standards, curriculum, assessment, surveillance, and regulation. It is essential, therefore, that we recognize the discourses that are shaping the spaces in which we are operating, and ways in which we can make these discourses visible (Horsfall, Byrne-Amstrong, & Rothwell, 2001, p. 95). We also need the reflexive and conceptual tools to be able to "explain the working of power on behalf of specific interests and to analyze the opportunities for resistance to it" (Weedon, 1997, p. 40). We will then be well positioned to "formulate tactics" (Danaher, Schirato, & Webb, 2000, p. 131) that enable us to negotiate productively for change.

By being explicit with preservice teachers about how postmodern perspectives are influencing my practice, I believe that I have been able to create opportunities that have encouraged them to engage in reflexive inquiry, critique, and explorations of previously unconsidered alternatives. Their experiences seem to have generated a sense of agency and flexibility that has enabled them to expand their 'margins of manoeuvrability' as preservice teachers. The challenge now, is to build on this agency to explore more specifically ways in which they might draw on these experiences to continue to expand their 'margins of manoeuvrability' in their future work as early childhood educators, and thus keep alive the hope of transformative change.

NOTES

1. Also known as transferable/key/core/life-long learning skills. Designated by Macquarie University to include literacy, numeracy, and information technology

skills; self-awareness and interpersonal skills, including self-management, collaboration, and leadership; communication, critical analysis, and problem-solving skills; and cultural understanding and creativity.

2. In New South Wales, preschools generally cater for children aged 3–5 years, from 9 am to 3 pm in four, 10-week terms. In contrast, long day care services open for a minimum of 8 h per day usually for at least 48 weeks of the year. Many long day care services accept children aged from 6 weeks to 5 years.

3. 'Mature-age' refers to students who enter their program of study at 21 years of age or older.

REFERENCES

Barnett, R. (1997). *Higher education: A critical business.* Buckingham: The Society for Research into Higher Education & Open University Press.

Bolton, T., & Hyland, T. (2003). Implementing key skills in further education: Perceptions and issues. *Journal of Further and Higher Education, 27*(1), 15–26.

Bredekamp, S., & Copple, C. (Eds) (1997). *Developmentally appropriate practice in early childhood programs* (REV. ed.). Washington, DC: National Association for the Education of Young Children.

Britt, C. (2002). *Within the borderlands: An anthology of beginning early childhood teachers in primary schools.* Unpublished Bachelor of Education (Early Childhood) (Honors) thesis, Macquarie University.

Britt, C., & Sumsion, J. (2003). Within the borderlands: An anthology of beginning early childhood teachers in primary schools. *Contemporary Issues in Early Childhood, 4*(2), 115–136.

Dahlberg, G., Moss, P., & Pence, A. (1999). *Beyond quality in early childhood education and care: Postmodern perspectives.* London: Falmer Press.

Danaher, G., Schirato, T., & Webb, J. (2000). *Understanding Foucault.* St Leonards, NSW: Allen & Unwin.

Davies, B. (2004). Introduction: Poststructuralist lines of flight in Australia. *International Journal of Qualitative Studies in Education, 17*(1), 3–9.

Edwards, R. (2002). Mobilizing lifelong learning: Governmentality in educational practices. *Journal of Education Policy, 17*(3), 353–365.

Faubion, J. D. (1994). Introduction. In: J. D. Faubion (Ed.), *Power: Essential works of Foucault 1954–1984,* Vol. 3. London: Penguin xi–xliii.

Foley, D. E. (2002). Critical ethnography: The reflexive turn. *International Journal of Qualitative Studies in Education, 15*(5), 469–490.

Foucault, M. (1979). *Discipline and punish: The birth of the prison.* Hammondsworth: Penguin.

Foucault, M. (1980). *Power/Knowledge: Selected interviews and other writings 1972–1977 Pantheon Books.* New York: Pantheon Book.

Foucault, M. (1981). *The history of sexuality: An introduction,* Vol. 1. Hammondsworth: Pelican.

Foucault, M. (19941978). Governmentality. In: J. D. Faubion (Ed.), *Power: Essential works of Foucault 1954-1984,* (Vol. 3, pp. 201–222). London: Penguin.

Gee, J. P. (1996). *Social linguistics and literacies: Ideology in discourses.* London: Routledge/Falmer.

Giroux, H. A. (2002). Educated hope in an age of private visions. *Cultural Studies Critical Methodologies*, 2(1), 93–112.
Hooks, B. (2003). *Teaching community: A pedagogy of hope*. New York: Routledge.
Horsfall, D., Byrne-Armstrong, H., & Rothwell, R. (2001). Embodying knowledges: Challenging the theory/practice divide. In: J. Higgs & A. Titchen (Eds), *Professional practice in health, education, and the creative arts* (pp. 90–102). Oxford: Blackwell Science.
Leach, L., Neutze, G., & Zepke, N. (2001). Assessment and empowerment: Some critical questions. *Assessment & Evaluation in Higher Education*, 26(4), 293–305.
Luke, A., Luke, C., & Mayer, D. (2000). Redesigning teacher education. *Teaching Education*, 11(1), 5–11.
Martusewicz, R. A. (2001). *Seeking passage: Post-structuralism, pedagogy, ethics*. New York: Teachers College Press.
Novinger, S., & O'Brien, L. (2003). Beyond "boring meaningless shit" in the academy: Early childhood teacher educators under the regulatory gaze. *Contemporary Issues in Early Childhood*, 4(1), 3–31.
Power, M. (1994). *The audit explosion*. London: White Dove Press.
Sachs, J. (2003). *The activist teaching profession*. Buckingham: Open University Press.
Segall, A. (2002). *Disturbing practice: Reading teacher education as text*. New York: Peter Lang.
St Pierre, E. A. (2000). Poststructural feminism in education: An overview. *International Journal of Qualitative Studies in Education*, 3(5), 477–515.
Stephenson, J. (1998). The concept of capability and its importance in higher education. In: J. Stephenson & M. Yorke (Eds), *Capability and quality in higher education* (pp. 1–13). London: Kogan Page.
Sumsion, J. (1997). *Early childhood student teachers' reflection on their professional development and practice: A longitudinal study*. Unpublished Ph.D. thesis, University of Sydney.
Sumsion, J. (2002). Becoming being, and unbecoming an early childhood educator: A phenomenological case study of teacher attrition. *Teaching and Teacher Education*, 18(7), 869–885.
Usher, R., Bryant, I., & Johnstone, R. (1997). *Adult education and the postmodern challenge: Learning beyond the limits*. London: Routledge.
Usher, R., & Edwards, R. (1994). *Postmodernism and education*. London: Routledge.
Washington, V. (1996). Professional development in context: Leadership at the borders of our democratic, pluralistic society. *Young Children*, 51(6), 30–34.
Weedon, C. (1997). *Feminist practices and poststructuralist theory* (2nd ed.). Oxford: Blackwell.
Zeichner, K. M., & Tabachnick, B. R. (1991). Reflections on reflective teaching. In: B. R. Tabachnick & K. M. Zeichner (Eds), *Issues and practices in inquiry-oriented teacher education* (pp. 1–19). London: The Falmer Press.
Zournazi, M. (2002). *Hope: New philosophies for change*. Sydney: Pluto Press.
Zournazi, M., & Massumi, B. (2002). Navigating moments. In: M. Zournazi (Ed.), *Hope: New philosophies for change* (pp. 210–242). Sydney: Pluto Press.

CHALLENGING THE CULTURE OF EXPERTISE: MOVING BEYOND TRAINING THE ALWAYS, ALREADY FAILING EARLY CHILDHOOD EDUCATOR

Sue Novinger, Leigh O'Brien and Lou Sweigman

ABSTRACT

In this chapter, we look critically at the discourses of expertise as a lens for examining our experiences as teacher educators. We explain why we think that current notions of early childhood teacher training contradict the ideals of equity, liberation, and the development of human potential – our goals for education – and use two of the authors' stories of their work with teachers of young children to provide a window into some of the contradictions, challenges, and borders we perceive. Building on the stories and our analyses of them, we posit some possible avenues to help us cross borders.

INTRODUCTION

We have been concerned for some time about the multiple forces that perpetuate a culture of expertise in early childhood education: in the U.S., these include the notion of Developmentally Appropriate Practice (DAP) (Bredekamp & Copple, 1997), the National Association for the Education of Young Children's *Guidelines for Early Childhood Teacher Preparation* (1996), the discourses in U.S. journals such as *Young Children*, and so on. We see expertise as a power relation in which some early childhood educators, typically those nearer the apex of the hierarchy, are seen by the profession as having more valued skills and more desirable knowledge; these skills and knowledge – as well as these people – are thus privileged in early childhood education (ECE) discourses. Because of our concerns, we want to look critically at the discourses of expertise as a lens for examining our experiences as teacher educators. As we undertake this examination, we attempt to make our struggles, discomfort, confusion, and ambiguity transparent. We also try to be clear about our stances, the extant power differentials between teacher educators and preschool teachers, and how we came to be where we are as we explore the contradictions embedded in notions such as expert versus novice or training versus education.

We argue that our positioning within the dominant discourse of expertise as teacher educators frequently places us in the role of experts training novices when we work with pre- and in-service preschool teachers. With this position comes power; as persons perceived as having expertise, we also have a fair amount of agency. Conversely, classroom teachers, especially those working in preschool settings, typically have limited power and hence limited agency. They are positioned, then, as recipients of our disseminated wisdom and socially sanctioned knowledge about how to "best" work with young children. Of course, this is a rather simplistic description of the situation. We are all positioned multiply, and classroom teachers can – and do – assert their power and agency in a number of ways as our stories will show. While acknowledging that power is relational, it seems to us that the mainstream discourse of ECE maintains a power hierarchy and thus we believe it is important to explain why we think that dominant notions of early childhood teacher training contradict the ideals of equity, liberation, and the full development of human potential – frequently touted as cherished goals for education. Last, we look at ways we have tried to move beyond this hierarchal and inequitable model by metaphorically crossing the border into a place where preschool teachers have more power and can more readily utilize agency. We discuss some of the ways we have tried to interrupt the culture of expertise and work as allies sharing power and agency, as well as identifying our struggles and tentative ideas for continuing to move in this direction – for we have just begun this journey.

Ultimately we argue for a deep and lasting critique of the culture of expertise – indeed we trouble the very notion of "expert" – and a move toward a participatory, inclusive model, wherein power is shared and knowledge is co-constructed and continually reassessed. As Dahlberg, Moss, and Pence (1999) have argued regarding children, we contend that preschool teachers, too, ought to be viewed as strong and rich in possibilities – and actualities. However, taking this view is not possible unless we resist the discourse of expertise.

THEORETICAL GROUNDING

Our thinking is informed by the theoretical perspective that the discourses in which we are situated shape and also constrain the meanings we construct. Discourses can be thought of as "socially accepted association[s] among ways of using language, of thinking, and of acting" (Gee, 1992, p. 21). As such, discourses are semiotic domains, wherein meanings are constructed differently than in other, competing discourses (Barthes, 1972; Hicks, 1996; Ryan, 1999). What is considered valid knowledge, valid ways of knowing, and valid ways of being in the world varies within discourses. For example, what counts as legitimate teaching knowledge and practice varies widely between the discourse of DAP and feminist, postmodern discourses of teaching and learning. To cite one core difference, DAP posits a (externally defined) dichotomy for thinking about and judging teaching practice: it is either "appropriate" or "inappropriate." In contrast, postmodern theorists argue that multiple perspectives must always be considered and that dichotomous thinking is necessarily simplistic and exclusionary. As we are socialized into particular discourse communities, then, we learn the ways of seeing and being in the world made possible by the various discursive practices of those communities (Davies, 2000). And, we learn who is allowed to own and wield expert knowledge within those discourse communities.

Professional development interactions are among the many places where such multiple, often contradictory, discourses come together. Importantly to our discussion, a discourse may gain a dominant position over alternative discourses in the way it is strengthened and supported by credentialed individuals and prominent organizations (Pacini-Ketchabaw & Schecter, 2002). This privileging of certain kinds of expertise makes perfect sense in an education system that sees the world in categorical binaries such as ability and disability; that uses grading and tracking to identify "winners" and "losers;" that values competition over cooperation; and that glorifies and rewards individual success in the education and economic hierarchy, rather than the building of community. The school, as a formal vehicle of education, exists largely as an instrument that reinforces social and economic power for the most influential elite groups (Karier, 1973); this conception of education is one of narrow, technical rationality focused on efficacy and efficiency. And thus, as Ware (2001) puts it, educators are bound by a constraining and impoverished system that extinguishes imagination.

Bakhtin's (1981) notion that there are two types of (conflicting) discourses, authoritative and internally persuasive, is also relevant here. He saw authoritative discourse as being "indissolubly fused with its authority – with political power, an institution, a person – and it stands and falls together with that authority" (pp. 342–343). In contrast, internally persuasive discourse is "denied all privilege, backed up by no authority at all, and is frequently not even acknowledged in society" (p. 342). Discourse that is authoritative must be embraced without question, whereas discourse that is internally persuasive invites the mutual construction of knowledge. The latter form is dialogic – it enables people to go beyond internalizing dogma to infuse the message into their own understanding, and hence to collaborate in the construction of potentially liberatory communication. The tension between the two types of discourse is seen again and again in professional development sites.

Given our experiences within such a system, within what we have come to think of as the "professional development machine," we read the differential positioning of "professional development" providers (*us*) and the teachers who are recipients of such "development" (*them*) as follows:

Providers: "Us"	*Receivers: "Them"*
choice about topic	topic chosen for them
choice about process	process foisted upon them
knowledge producers	consumers of knowledge
competent	needy
evaluated by self, peers	evaluated by powerful others
inquiry	training
individual	group
providers	products
understanding	improved practice

While we recognize these categories as always shifting, muddied, and contextualized, we nonetheless believe the dominant discourse of expertise supports these kinds of dichotomies. These positions are not neutral or static, but are instead constructed and reconstructed through multiple interactions immersed within the discourses of expertise (see, e.g., Lubeck, 1998).

To be positioned, to take up a position, is to be located and to locate ourselves in relation to others within a particular discourse. Discursively constructed positions shape our perspectives and the meanings we make. Unlike the static notion of role, subject positions are understood to be fluid and dynamic. Thus, we take up different positions within different discourses (Davies, 2000). Further, because multiple discourses overlap in given contexts, multiple positionings are available within those contexts (Berghoff, 1997). How the participants in a particular situation interpret that situation determines, in large part, the discursive practices that are enacted, and thus the positionings that the participants might take up. Here, then, is a possible space for resistance, as we discuss later.

Discourses embody relations of power (Foucault, 1977) and so the right to position others (and oneself) is not equally distributed within discourses (Harré & van Langenhove, 1999). Certain individuals are privileged to take up powerful subject positions, with the right to position others in particular ways (Davies, 2000). Within the dominant discursive practices of early childhood professional development, for example, experts typically (but not always) take up positions of power, and their right to position teachers in particular ways is legitimated by their own positioning. Thus the positions available to teachers are shaped and constrained, although not necessarily determined by the experts. Of course, we "experts" are positioned in particular ways by the discourse, too: While we may have more agency than most classroom teachers, others, including regulating agencies and institutions of higher learning (Novinger & O'Brien, 2003) and our own students, also position us. The stories we tell in this chapter give ample proof of the latter. Once more, we are all ascribed and take up multiple positions in our work as educators.

Even when we try to resist or interrupt this model, many preschool teachers are so steeped in what Foucault labeled "expert discourses" (1980) that generate particular kinds of public policies regarding teaching and learning that they resist our attempts at interruption. They – and we – are used to ways that 'providers' and 'receivers' are positioned within discourses of expertise. Such positionings are always created within relationships of power and knowledge, and that of early childhood educators in relation to early childhood teacher educators is no different. However, as Harré and van Langenhove (1999) remind us, we (all) can choose to accept or resist particular positionings; we (all) are active agents in the construction of our subjectivity (Ryan, 1999) although our choices are always circumscribed by who we are and the experiences we have had.

Ellsworth's (1997) explanation of "mode of address," borrowed from film studies, provides us with a theoretical tool to examine this process. Mode of address includes both the content of what we wish to communicate, and also *how* we communicate that content. The modes of address we employ are grounded in our discursive positionings and are among the ways we enact such positionings. As Ellsworth explains, "Each time we address someone we take up a position within knowledge, power, and desire in relation to them and assign them to a position in relation to ourselves and a context" (p. 54). The modes of address we use in our teaching, Ellsworth argues, "are aimed precisely at shaping, anticipating, meeting, or changing who a student thinks she is" (p. 7). Thus, the modes of address we use, what we say and how we say it, are aimed at constructing a particular kind of teacher, with particular kinds of knowledge, skills, and beliefs.

We have some choice about the modes of address we choose to employ, and those choices, at both conscious and unconscious levels, are shaped by our interpretations of our own and others' positionings – of who we think we are, and who we think our audience is (Bakhtin, 1986). We aim our address at those perceived positionings. As Ellsworth (1997) explains, however, our audiences are never quite who we imagine them to be. For instance, we do not know, can *never* fully know, the multiple positionings our students have taken up. Nor can we fully know the ways that our students' positionings are constantly shifting across and among the discourses that inhabit their lives.

Because of this fundamental unknowability of the multiple and shifting ways in which others are positioned, our modes of address always "miss their audience in some way or another" (Ellsworth, 1997, p. 37). Thus, our audiences can choose, whether consciously or unconsciously, to meet and return our address from a different subject position than the one we anticipated. This creates what Ellsworth calls "slippage" or "spaces of difference" (1997, p. 42). These spaces of difference, these slippages, then create the critical space for agency, for individuals to resist attempts to position them in particular ways. It is within these spaces of difference that meanings are constantly being contested and negotiated.

The notion of spaces of difference, or slippage, helps us imagine how we might cross the boundaries among the multiple, often contradictory discourses in which we are immersed, to navigate the borderlands in ways that allow us to resist positionings such as expert and novice. Working in such discursive borderlands creates the possibility for acting with agency; for making choices about which discourses to enact, which positions to resist, and which positions to take up. And although "discourse is encompassing" (Berghoff, 1997, p. 9), the more critically aware we are of the discourses in which we are immersed, and the points of slippage among those discourses, the more able we are to make conscious choices about how we seek to position ourselves and others. Such "intentional positioning" (p. 17) is about being the subject of one's life, rather than an object. We have come to believe it is this process of intentional positioning that might provide meaningful spaces for reconceiving expertise.

RECONCEIVING EXPERTISE

Perhaps the most fertile ground for the de-construction of existing power dynamics is the border that crosses over into the inner landscape of the ones positioned as expert: *us*. The dialectic of resistance requires us to recognize our privilege and acknowledge our power without flinching or re-naming it. This dialectic – the inner conflict of antagonistic themes that wage war for our allegiance: the desire to be an authentic ally to the learner and the desire to preserve our position of power and privilege as sanctioned and "experts" with a certain status – calls upon us to engage in a genuine struggle, fought at close quarters, with weapons of irony and integrity, consciousness and compassion, humility, courage, and faith. In Freire's (1986) terms, we are both drawn to and afraid of freedom. In our attempts to enact meaningful dialogic pedagogy, we encounter the resistance of both our internalized sense of privilege and our received image of the learner as "needing" our expertise in order to achieve liberation. Short of moving outside the structure of the sanctioning/regulating bodies and co-creating circles of teacher/learner/teacher/learner, this sort of inner work may be a valid and effective means of sabotaging some parts of the machinery even as we collect our monetary rewards from a different part of the same machine. For us the contradiction, and its resulting tension, makes for a very interesting borderland indeed.

Can we re-conceive expertise as being developed in dialogic, collaborative work, rather than something a select few bring to the table? To do so, we have to believe that knowledge is distributed in the early childhood community and does not reside solely in the heads of the "experts." Even the teacher who experiences her/himself as struggling must have the knowledge, skills, and disposition to be able to balance a myriad of responsibilities. For instance, teachers must know how to manage specific groups of children; they must be sensitive to and able to work with diverse children and families; they must educate in an externally controlled and constrained context in which various mandates are often in conflict; and they must meet both the pressing needs of the classroom, as well as deal with standards, short- and long-term planning, and seemingly endless reams of paperwork.

If we are to challenge the culture of expertise, we who have been designated as experts need to acknowledge that our own beliefs are only one of many realities – all of which are valid. Further, we have to accept that some (much?) "expert knowledge" is flawed, impractical, or imperfect. If the core of such belief is solid, the professional development/teacher education experience that flows there from will have a much better chance of leaving spaces for teachers to move forward, creating their *own* pedagogical paths.

We present two of our stories here, chosen because they represent different angles into doing "professional development" at very different sites, as one possible point of entry into that site of struggle. Although the stories differ in terms of settings and our positionings as "experts," the problems we encountered highlight the fact that power relations are always at play between teacher educators and teachers. We need to be aware of, and work to reconceive, the culture of expertise wherever we do our work.

Lou's Story

In the fall of 1999, I was hired by the Rochester (New York) City School District as an Instructor for two courses: Child Development Associate (CDA) I and II. The subject matter of these courses was aligned with the Thirteen Functional Areas that have been identified by The Council for Early Childhood Professional Recognition as fundamental to achieving a baseline of competency in the field of ECE. Candidates seeking the CDA credential had to successfully complete the 120 classroom hours of these courses.

By signing the contract, I was immersing myself in a system with borders designed to reinforce separation and maintain positions of power (Foucault, 1980). The nomenclature used (Workforce Preparation, Council for Professional Preparation) was intentional and significant. These borders were, for the most part, visible, but unacknowledged: the gates and fences erected within the mind, but not imaginary; the guards and checkpoints disguised as teachers, texts, and tests.

The CDA candidates were also immersed in this system. Working in the field of early childhood – some for less than a year, others for decades – they had received the message from those empowered to affect their paychecks that in order to move from the foothills of the nonprofessional to the summits of professionalism, they needed this credential. The CDA was a passport that permitted a border to be crossed. They were on a journey upward. I was a guide. That was the best of possible learning scenarios I could envision given the structure of the CDA system. I had optimism, enthusiasm, and a desire to help facilitate the genuine construction of meaningful knowledge in an atmosphere of safety, respect, and equity.

I was, to be kind to myself, naïve. I failed to understand certain social and positional realities that altered the scenario and pushed the process into an even more distorted version of a learning experience than the constrained vision I had entertained at the outset. What were these realities?

I was male. I was white. I was middle class and credentialed. English was my first language. In my career I was positioned within a hierarchical system as a supervisor. I earned more money and had more perceived social standing than the CDA candidates. I was the beneficiary of linguistic, gender, race, and class privilege.

The learners were female. They were predominantly African-American and Latina. They were working-class and for some, English was a second language. They were members of an underpaid, undervalued workforce who were used to being positioned as supervisees. Employers who used the carrot of a pay increase and the stick of unemployment to cajole/coerce attendance sent the learners to the class. I know this because I asked. Without the prod of a supervisor, there would have been no class.

They experienced little, if any agency at their worksites. The socially constructed system that privileged me victimized them. The unspoken barriers erected by that system heavily influenced our ability to form a community of learning.

The message these women received about the learning experience told them, in part, that they were powerless and unimportant. The disrespect they experienced in their work life (Spanish-speaking employees forbidden to speak Spanish; preschool teachers seeking a Preschool CDA switched, mid-course, into Toddler classrooms; Assistant Teachers working in the role of, and with the responsibilities of, Lead Teachers, but receiving Assistant Teacher pay; and so on) extended to their professional development life.

The learning environment spoke loudly and reinforced the sense of disrespect. The class was held in an austere building in a poor section of the city. There was a sentry on duty when we entered and when we left. Students were required to sign in. Instructors were not. The classroom was on the 3rd floor. Often, the elevator did not work. Others used the room during the day, and it was clear that we were in borrowed space. I had the use of two drawers in someone else's desk. The candidates had no space or place to store anything. Tables were long and filled the room. Chairs faced front where the source of knowledge held forth. It was difficult, sometimes impossible, to re-configure the furniture. The lighting was harsh. The ventilation/heating system was inefficient and so loud at times that conversation became difficult. Layered onto these messages of disrespect for the learner was the time of the class: Tuesdays from 4:00 to 8:00 p.m., which meant that these women had to spend 4 hours in an uninviting environment after already putting a 6 to 8-h work day. Further, for some, there were children at home requiring varying levels of care. Many of the candidates took time during our dinner break to phone home to check on their children. Worry, distraction, and fatigue were in attendance at each class.

Harsh realities. Added to which was the reality that long ago these learners had internalized a model of schooling, based on experience, that positioned the teacher as expert, and that accepted that attaining knowledge was a matter of learning the answers to questions posed by others. Further, answers were right or wrong; therefore practice was either appropriate or inappropriate, and someone (certainly not the learner) was positioned to decide and define what was right, what was appropriate, and what must be learned so that the credential could be earned, allowing the learner to pass through the guarded gates leading to the next level (entry level) of professionalism.

If I had been aware of all these realities at the outset I might have never tried, but as I said before, I was naïve. And so, try I did, to co-create a community of learning, constructing knowledge and making meaning from individual and shared experience. I rejected the role of expert because to accept it meant reinforcing and increasing the already substantial distance between the candidates and myself. The barriers in place on the first day of class were formidable enough. I did not want to make them more impenetrable by adding another layer of separation. I wanted to explode the concept that knowledge resides "out there" and is knowable by being told what "it" is. I wanted to de-mystify the process of becoming a professional, demonstrate respect for what the learners already knew, and co-construct concepts based on exploration of theory and experimentation with practice.

So I provided lots of class time for talk about personal experience and how that experience related to the text's notion of best practice. I talked openly about issues of racism, classism, and sexism as they impacted the lives of children and as they related to the lives of all of us in the class. We read articles that presented alternative voices. We talked about their worksites and actual working conditions. We generated lists of attributes of good teachers and formulated a vision of good teaching. We explored ideal learning environments for children. We discussed issues of respect for children, parents, and ourselves.

The tensions that arose around these discussions were palpable. I was trying to open a door and show them the broader social context in which their personal struggles were embedded. I was trying to help them locate the lack of respect afforded to them by our culture as residing in that culture, and not in the work or the women. I was trying to make explicit the contradictions between the purported premise of the CDA class's purpose (to "make" them into better teachers) and the reality of the experience as an edict, mandated by their employers. I was trying to make their oppression by social forces clearly visible.

What I was not trying to do, however (because I did not know how to do it), was to connect any new awarenesses of their location in a web of oppressive positioning to a strategy or strategies that would be effectively liberatory. I did not have answers for the questions that began to emerge; questions about how to change their positioning. In that regard, my teaching was incomplete. And to their credit, these women stopped me from doing any further damage by refusing to go past a certain point in our exploration of these issues.

Once it began to be clear that I was only able to bring forward reasons for the oppressive conditions of their working lives without generating strategies for overcoming those conditions, they shut the conversation down. They did so by dis-engaging, by not responding, by taking the conversation down what seemed to me to be side-roads. For them, however, these "tangents" were the path back to control of a situation that had begun to become disturbing, if not dangerous. I believe they used the power of their position as learners to re-claim the agenda of the class and bring its focus back to the one thing it was advertised to bring them: a credential. They were being practical. I was being unrealistic.

From the vantage point of reflective distance I can say now that I failed, not so much because I was unable to help them in the way I perceived them to need my help (who did I think I was addressing?), but because of the way I positioned myself. I was not only positioned by the Professional Development machine as an "expert," I also saw myself as an agent of liberation; self appointed and self anointed. I was enacting the arrogance of my privileged position. In my well-intentioned attempt at facilitating a liberating experience, I merely reified the power relationships I was trying to dismantle. It is clearer to me now that if teaching is to be genuinely liberatory, the teacher cannot in any way be positioned above the learner nor can the curriculum be imposed. It does not matter if that curriculum purports to liberate. Given the constraints of most teaching situations within the Professional Development Machine, it is only through acts of resistance that we can deliberately create a more authentic form of teaching. If the goal of our teaching is to help learners be more fully human, to find and use their voices, then we must resist the way we are positioned by our employers and our culture.

What could I have done differently? How could I have enacted a border pedagogy within the context of that CDA class? My first act of resistance could have been to resist my own arrogant assumptions about who these women were (Bakhtin, 1986; Ellsworth, 1997). My second act could have been to resist my equally arrogant assumption that I could liberate them – or that they needed or wanted to be liberated. Instead, I could have listened and learned more about who was sharing that classroom space with me. I could have learned more about the multiplicity of their various positionings (Davies, 2000). I could have listened more respectfully to what they were telling me they wanted from the time, energy, and effort they were investing. If, as Bakhtin (1986) asserts, meaning emerges only within the dialogue, I could have made our class discussions more truly dialogic. I could have made sure they had enough concrete and contextually familiar curricular content to ensure their success in obtaining the credential. I could have allowed space for any exploration of their oppression to be generated *by* them, in unity *with* them. I could have explored ways of overcoming those oppressions in the same way. When your job hangs in the balance and your paycheck barely keeps you above the poverty line, there is precious little room for flights of intellectual fancy, abstract theories of learning, or even examinations of your own oppression. Those who engage in these pursuits are free to do so, because they (we) are in positions of power and privilege, benefiting from the same system that oppresses the CDA candidate. In some measure, our status derives from their debasement. Nothing short of revolutionary action will dismantle that most harsh reality. We, at least, have the power to choose. If we are not part of the solution...

Sue's Story

Several years ago I spent a semester working with a small group of preschool teachers from our campus child care center, and through that work I came to understand that even when we think we *are* resisting the expert-novice discourse, it is not so easy to step outside the power-knowledge relationships at the heart of that discourse.

I attended a Center staff meeting and invited teachers to join me for a teacher study group, and eight of them (four teaching teams) took me up on the offer. The Center program director arranged staff schedules so that all eight teachers were free for the study group sessions for 90 minutes following lunch every other week. My intention was to work with the participating teachers to create a group where teachers' inquiry was at the heart of the work. Ayers' (1992) notion of "Teacher Talk" was an important influence, as was the work of many teacher-researchers (e.g., Ballenger, 1999; Compton-Lilly, 2002; Gallas, 1995) and teacher educators who work alongside teachers in inquiry (e.g., Cochran-Smith & Lytle, 1993; Lubeck & Post, 2000). Although ways of working may vary, the conviction that teachers are active inquirers and meaning makers is at the center of such work. The power of dialogue to support such active meaning making is also typically seen as essential for this work (Bakhtin, 1986; Ballenger, 1999; Gallas, 1995).

The task (determined by me) at our first meeting was to share questions and tensions around teaching practice, and to decide on the overarching topic for our first study. As we shared, I recorded teachers' questions and tensions on a chart, and we spent time talking about what led them to those questions. In this dialogic process, teachers added to and elaborated on each other's ideas. Our list included stress management for teachers; dealing with "non-responsive" children; early literacy; dealing with parents'/guardians' unrealistic expectations; communication with parents/guardians; and working with children with behavior difficulties (chosen as our first topic).

In my field notes I wrote that, with the exception of the early literacy topic, the participants located their questions/tensions as problems within others: children, families, and others at the Center. I was, I'll admit, disappointed in the group's choice of behavior guidance as the topic for our first study. I was secretly hoping they would choose emergent literacy: after all, I'm considered an 'expert' in that. I also thought their choice somehow showed a preoccupation with controlling children. Here's an excerpt from my 9/20/01 notes that illustrates my response to our first meeting and *my* agenda for *their* work:

> I want to complicate their notions of behavior guidance. They seem to be locating the problem within children – and I want them to begin to look at themselves, at their expectations, at classroom environments ... I'm thinking that we'll want to try to examine, early on, our own beliefs about behavior, guidance, our goals for children,

development, etc. This part will be rocky, I think. The notion that adults ought to oversee and control children is so ingrained. "How do we get kids to comply with what we want them to do?" I think I'll ask teachers to do some focused observations in their classrooms, and some initial analyses. In our discussion, we might try to read their narratives differently – to disrupt the readings of "behavior problem children".

Lubeck, Jessup, deVries, and Post (2001) ask if "those who assist and evaluate programs [are] open to local interpretation and invention and prepared to engage dialogically with local actors?" (p. 520). I thought I was – but my notes tell a different story. Instead, I took up – quite readily – the position of outside expert, making judgments about the teachers' topic choice, the way they interpreted their situations, and the goals they had for their work. Reading these notes now through the lens of modes of address, I have to ask myself, who did I think these teachers were? I saw them, it now seems clear, as needy, as recipients of my expert guidance, not as active inquirers and meaning makers. I thought I knew who they were, and failed to acknowledge the ways they might be positioned in multiple, overlapping discourses. And so, in my judgments and in my plans for the coming sessions, I enacted modes of address that reproduced and perpetuated our unequal positionings within power relationships.

Early on we decided (at my suggestion) that each teaching team would observe "problem" situations in their classroom, and then present an informal case at the next session. Our (my) goal would be to talk about the issues, try to understand the situation from multiple perspectives, and then brainstorm possible courses of action. The following excerpts from my 10/10/01 notes give a glimpse of my reflection on the teachers' talk and thinking.

> First, Sally and Melissa talked about a two year-old little girl who started in their room this past August ... The problem is that she cries throughout the day, especially, they say, when she thinks about nap. As we talked, it seemed to me that the teachers did a nice job of thinking about several possibilities around what might be behind her problems ... It seemed like this was new for them ... I encouraged others to ask them questions about what was going on ... They're drawing on the articles we've been reading, but also on their own experiences ... Don and Anna talked about John, who is physically aggressive and defiant ... I was impressed at how they didn't just seem to position him as 'the bad kid.' However, in both cases, the teachers DID seem to position the parents as 'bad parents': the little girl's parents spoil her; John's mom vents her anger about the dad who abandoned them before John was born ... Toward the end of the discussions, Sally and several other teachers asked me to tell them what I thought they should do. I was disappointed...

I cringe as I revisit these field notes, and realize that I was locating what I perceived to be problems within the teachers – in exactly the same way that

I thought the teachers were locating problems in children and teachers! And yet, on reflection, I'm not at all surprised. Even though I professed to be committed to supporting teacher inquiry and agency, it was my own vision, my own agenda, which I put into motion. As Cochran-Smith (2004) points out, for teachers there is a huge difference between taking part in an inquiry project as a strategy for staff development and taking an inquiry stance toward one's work. "Taking an inquiry stance," she writes, "means new and experienced teachers and teacher educators working within communities to generate local knowledge, envision and theorize their practice, and interpret and interrogate the theory and research of others" (p. 14). Cochran-Smith argues that the notion of stance "describes the positions that teachers and others who work together in inquiry communities take toward knowledge, its relationships to practice, and the purposes of schooling" (p. 14). In such inquiry communities, teachers and teacher educators position themselves as co-learners and co-creators of knowledge, rather than as providers and/or receivers of expert knowledge.

In contrast, analysis of my field notes shows that in our group teachers were positioned quite differently. I remained viewed as the expert and the teachers continued to see themselves more as receivers of knowledge and less as co-creators of knowledge. My field notes reveal that I continued to pose many of the questions during our discussions, rather than listening for and supporting the group members in pursuing their own questions. I wrote on 11/14/01, for instance, that "they still look to me as a discussion leader" and on 12/12/01 that "even now, the teachers still seem to want me to tell them what I think is the best approach, even after the group has analyzed situations and generated several possible courses of action." My knowledge, it seemed, was still more valued by the teachers (and by me?) than their own; apparently we were all steeped in expert discourses (Foucault, 1980).

Why did not we achieve significant shifts in the power relationships in our group? The easy – and difficult – answer is that I was as immersed in the discourses of teacher training as were the teachers. Instead of coming together as a teacher-initiated inquiry group, the preschool teachers joined *my* group. In the teacher inquiry groups of which Cochran-Smith (2004) writes, the participating teachers occupied positions of relatively equal power. In contrast, as the college professor/professional development provider I occupied a position of far greater power than the preschool teachers in our group. As a matter of fact, their biweekly discussions would not even have met the state training criteria if I had not been in the room. This further highlights the ways that teachers working with very young children, especially in childcare centers, are positioned much lower in the hierarchy than are teachers working with older children in primary and elementary settings. Within the discursive practices of the Professional Development Machine, childcare teachers are not seen as competent enough to position themselves as co-learners and co-creators of knowledge.

Although I tried to put a liberatory structure into practice in our group, I do not think I had interrogated deeply enough the ways that my practices reproduced and perpetuated the dominant professional development discourses. For example, like other teachers who seek to enact liberatory pedagogy, I had faith in the power of dialogue as a democratic, egalitarian pedagogical structure for participants, and me to talk our way into understanding. Ellsworth (1997) complicates this notion, though, writing that we only imagine that "when we enter into dialogue, we agree to be open-minded and open to being changed by the process of hearing and coming to understand another's arguments, experiences, viewpoints, and knowledge" (p. 82). What we (usually) fail to acknowledge, Ellsworth argues, is that

> ... dialogue is not a neutral vehicle that simply carries those subjects' ideas and understandings back and forth, unmediated, between student and teacher ... Dialogue is not a transparent window on its participants' realities, meanings, intentions. When someone initiates a dialogue with me, s/he calls me into dialogue's structure of relations. When I enter into a dialogic structure of discussion, or learning, I am constituted as a subject of dialogue. (1997, p. 83)

How were the teachers and I constituted as subjects of dialogue? An analysis of my field notes of 11/14/01 help shed light on this question. I wrote,

> I asked the teachers to spend 5 or 10 minutes talking with their teaching partners about the patterns they notice in their analyses of problem behavior situations. During the large group discussion Mandy suddenly blurted, "We blame everything and everybody but ourselves!" While I'm not sure that's always the case, I had noticed that pattern, too. Dan and Sally agreed with Mandy, giving examples of this in their own analyses. But then Melissa spoke of her continuing frustration with asking children to do something again and again. She said, "I do blame the children. They're intelligent. They know what we're asking them to do. They choose to misbehave!" Shaking her head in agreement, Chandra added, "I may be quick to blame parents, but I do think that lots of the children's misbehavior is the fault of the parents!" No one said anything for a moment. Several teachers offered their agreement, citing examples from their own experiences... .
> I acknowledged that while some problems are located in children and parents, it's still important for us to look beyond individual children and their parents in our analyses and actions.

Ellsworth (1997) writes that as teachers our typical goal for engaging students in dialogue is to create an opportunity for students to construct understanding. In particular, we want them to develop understandings of expert knowledge. What we desire is continuity – continuity of the knowledges that we value and continuity of our positioning as experts (Ellsworth, 1997). Rather than using dialogue for students to construct their own new understandings, we use dialogue to regulate the understandings they might construct, as well as the positions they might take up.

In the example above, this was certainly the case. Over the two preceding months, the teachers and I had spent much time analyzing children's behavioral difficulties from multiple perspectives. In particular, I had pushed teachers to consider how their own practices might create or exacerbate such difficulties. I wanted to persuade the teachers that they needed to move past locating all problems in individual children and families. When Melissa and Chandra returned my address in a way I did not expect or desire, I heard this difference as their lack of understanding, as a deficit. Their responses disrupted the consensus that I desired in our group. The modes of address I enacted in my response to them sought to reassert our positions as expert and students in the group. In effect, I dismissed what they said, their grounded knowledge, and reasserted the primacy of expert knowledge. As happens so often in such situations, the professional voice determines the discourse, supporting Foucault's contention that power creates truth.

I also reasserted their positioning in power relationships with the parents of the children in their classrooms. At our first session several teachers proposed problems between teachers and parents as possible topics for our work together. They spoke about many parents' negative attitudes toward teachers, unrealistic parental demands for attention for individual children, discontinuities between homes and the center, parents' unwillingness to hear the truth about their children, and lack of honesty on the part of some parents. This list of concerns, like Melissa and Chandra's comments in the above example, seem to give voice to the ways that child care teachers are often positioned as less-than-professional in their relationships with parents.

As we wrote earlier, the most fertile ground for the de-construction of existing power dynamics may well be the borderlands that cross over into the inner landscape of the one positioned as expert. For me, entering those borderlands was prompted by my disappointment that the teachers in the group did not take up an inquiry stance. In asking why 'they' had not embraced 'my' agenda, I had to move beyond blame, beyond locating the problem in the teachers or in myself, and to instead more thoughtfully interrogate how we were *all* positioned within professional development discourses. And so I ask myself, what might I have done differently?

I needed, I think, to complicate my understandings of the multiple ways that we were all positioned within a range of discourses. In particular, I needed to listen differently to what teachers said in dialogue with each other and with me. In an earlier draft of this chapter, I wrote that I didn't think I had made space for the teachers and me to talk about their expectations, their desires, their thoughts and feelings about shared inquiry and joint meaning making. But re-reading my field notes and listening again to tapes of our discussions I'm struck by what I did not seem to hear – or at least value – at the time. These teachers made themselves vulnerable by sharing the tensions they were experiencing in their teaching. They took each other's problems and ideas seriously, and engaged in an ongoing dialogue that drew on their own funds of knowledge, and their subjective experiences as teachers in this center (Lubeck & Post, 2000). Internally persuasive discourse (Bakhtin, 1986) was dominant in their discussions. They began to challenge deficit discourses, and began to consider multiple possibilities. Their talk was messy and indeterminate, but also rich and challenging.

Who gets to say what counts as understanding? As meaningful dialogue? All too often, it is we 'experts' who make such determinations. Rather than reject the authority that comes with the expert position, we can use that authority to redefine what counts as understanding and as meaningful dialogue in professional development settings. In Heshusius's (1994) terms, we can embrace a "participatory mode of consciousness" wherein there is a deeper level of kinship between the knower and the known. Ellsworth (1997) has helped me understand that by working to change the goals and structure of dialogue we can begin to make changes in how teachers are positioned within the Professional Development Machine. I could have acknowledged the "impossibility of full understanding" (Ellsworth, 1997, p. 115), the impossibility and undesirability of transferring expert knowledge to others. Instead, I could have taken as my goal participants' construction of local, contextually situated knowledge. I could have grounded my work in the notions that teaching and learning are always unfinished, that understanding is always partial (Ellsworth, 1997).

Even as I sought to develop relationships wherein the teachers and I might come to know each other better, I could have acknowledged and accepted that I could never fully know the multiple discourses in which those teachers were immersed, nor could I know the positions they had taken up within those discourses. This understanding might have created a space for me to try to enact a different kind of dialogue in our sessions, dialogue that allowed for what Ellsworth calls a "return of a difference" (1997, p. 140). Such dialogue might be characterized as permeable, in that possibilities are created for participants to choose to respond from a range of subject positions. I could have valued the viability, credibility, and usefulness of knowledge constructed through such discourse, instead of continuing to privilege the validity of my own expert knowledge (Bakhtin, 1986; Ellsworth, 1997). To do so, I could have enacted different modes of address in our sessions. Instead of judging teachers' responses through the lens of my own expert knowledge, I could have valued differences as opportunities for us all to challenge our current understandings. Rather than viewing the return of a difference as a disruption (Ellsworth, 1997), I could have sought to understand from what discursive positioning those differences came. For instance, instead of evaluating Chandra's judgments about parents' responsibility for children's misbehavior, I could have respected her statements as reflecting her positioning in parent—teacher relationships. To do so might have opened up spaces for members of our group to draw on their knowledges embedded in a range of discourses, and to have those knowledges respected and honored in our dialogue. Such a pedagogical practice might go far in creating possibilities for teachers to be differently positioned within the Professional Development Machine.

REACTIONS TO OUR STORIES/INNER WORK/ CONTRADICTIONS

As noted earlier, the circumstances of and auspices in these stories differ. The populations and professional positionings are not the same. Still, there is a common critical thread that weaves its way from story to story. This thread is spun from the same spool. In all of the settings in which we work the tension between our impulse to be egalitarian co-creators of learning while at the same time being positioned outside of and above the learner speaks to the same basic contradiction that is the focus of this chapter. For instance:

- We were uninvited guests, at least from the teachers' perspectives;
- The agency's or professional developer's agenda was the focus, not the teachers';
- There were clearly power differences between 'us' and 'them,' although they went (largely?) unacknowledged;
- Upon reflection, we felt that we had arrogantly, without questioning, used our privilege; and
- We were distressed because we had not lived up to our internal idealized images of ourselves as egalitarian, liberatory, and concerned with the full development of human potential.

The central problem with the expert discourse model is that teaching is seen as a role, a composite of functions that teachers fulfil on behalf of others, rather than an identity that speaks to who the teacher is: her or his own investments, beliefs, commitments, and desires. When a teacher merely fulfils a role, his/her identity/ies and integrity are challenged in that who s/he is does not matter to the fulfilment of the job. The teacher becomes a technician, the neutral provider of the experts' notions of "best practice" (Giroux, 1988; Palmer, 1998). In this model, teacher educators unilaterally fashion education in a "generically" narrow mold, rather than co-creating expansive learning opportunities based on what students bring to the table. The professionals, positioned as experts, thereby engage in a process of governing subjectivity, or regulating the very being of teachers (Gore & Morrison, 2001). Ultimately, when this view of teaching is sanctioned, teacher education (or training or consultation or professional development) simply reinforces the type of knowing and being already in place. Thereby teacher education functions to maintain and accommodate the status quo, as is intended by the power elite (see, e.g., Garrison, 2000; Karier, 1973; Mills, 1956).

The three of us are opposed to "the notion of knowledge given antecedently and independently of knowers" (Regenspan, 2002, p. 72), what Heshusius calls an "alienated consciousness" (1994, p. 15), and believe, in fact, that the very concept of privileging certain kinds of knowing must be challenged. In this Western, rational male model, the mind is severed from the body, and theory is privileged over "practice" (McWilliam & Taylor, 1998). This model has a long history in the U.S. and is rarely challenged; from at least the early 1900s, the culture has valued and rewarded those considered to be experts in their fields, dismissing grounded knowing as being "folklore" or worse (Miller, 1997). For example, the current DAP text states, "experts serving on NAEYC's Panel on Revisions to Developmentally Appropriate Practice worked for more than two years advising on the proposed revisions to the position statement" (Bredekamp & Copple, 1997, p. vi). Those experts included many well-known names in ECE – Lilian Katz, Barbara Bowman, and Carol Brunson Phillips, to name a few – and it is these folks, not classroom teachers, who are determining "current *best understanding* of theory and research regarding how children learn as well as *shared beliefs* about what practices are most supportive and respectful of children's healthy development" (p. vi) [italics ours]. Our own stories also speak to what is valued in early childhood professional development ... and it is not the wisdom of practice. This well-entrenched and seldom questioned model valorizing authoritative discourse will be extremely difficult to dislodge, requiring a paradigm shift wherein we begin to imagine a more equitable world where many kinds of knowing are valued, and theory and practice stand together.

If we reject the discourse of expertise, if we are opposed to the necrophilic, banking model of education (Freire, 1986), how might we frame teacher education as a dialogic process, wherein teachers begin to construct and reconstruct themselves as subjects? Even if we create sites where learners can take a stance that provides them with agency, even if the intention of the designated expert is to empower the learner to create his or her own truth, the very superstructure that houses and regulates professional development (college or university, state governing body, accrediting agency, and so on) reconstructs discourses of expertise thereby undermining such efforts. How might this dynamic be re-thought and re-constructed?

CREATING BORDER PEDAGOGIES

We believe there are some sites where slippage might occur *now*, "third spaces" (Bhabha, 1994; Soja, 1996) where we may be able to cross borders ... where

- Binaries and dichotomies can be dismantled
- Boundaries can be blurred
- Doors can be opened a crack
- Vistas can be widened

With a postmodern view of pedagogy, the aim is not to substitute one model of professional development for another, but to think about daily actions in local settings that may challenge and disrupt the power relations enacted by the discourse of expertise. We therefore offer the following suggestions as sites where this work might begin.

First, if we really want the teachers with whom we work to "read their worlds," we should think more deeply about how to be in dialogic relationship with them, teacher as student and students as teachers (Freire, 1986). This position argues for long-term support being provided as needed in areas that *teachers* find most important. The three of us are now trying to bridge the gap between the "ivory tower" and preschool settings by crossing the border from the land of expertise to a place where all are valued for what they bring. This means we who have been designated as experts need to work alongside teachers, as allies, as they take ownership of their teaching (Lewis, 2002).

But shifting the location of our work will not be effective unless teacher educators also pay attention to the modes of address they are using. Teacher educators need to constantly ask themselves, who do we think we are addressing in our work with teachers (Ellsworth, 1997)? Why? Who is responding? Why? How have we (all) been positioned? Why? Can we resist such positioning? If we can, how do we do so? We need to attend to how we name ourselves, and how others are named; how physical environments are structured and who structures them; how learning is assessed, and by whom; and how success or failure are defined, and by whom. Examining and changing our modes of address and our literal and figurative locations is a concrete strategy for being part of the solution, for acting as saboteurs from within a system that disempowers not just preschool teachers, but *all* of us in education.

Along with altering our modes of address, teacher educators can also try to enact approaches to professional development that view teaching as a complex, challenging, social and intellectual task. The work we do, for example, might help "... teachers to be observers and documenters of children and researchers of learning, rather than consumers of dicta for practice" (Darling-Hammond, 1996, p. 12), and should challenge us to ask not what is 'true', but rather what best fits the situation (Lubeck, 1996, p. 159). Although not a cure-all, a view of teacher as learner by way of collaborative and action-oriented classroom research, for example, positions teachers very differently than the expert discourse does: it puts them in charge of their own learning, and most of us recognize that we learn by engaging with something we want to learn.

Furthermore, the ways in which we make sense of our worlds cannot be separated from the contexts in which we operate, context always matters. Any attempts at change have to consider local conditions, norms, and goals and the discourses shaping them. If teacher educators try to diminish status differentials and see knowledge as jointly created in dynamic interaction – with others and with specific environments – it may be possible to move from judgement and prescription to helping teachers to address concrete and practical dilemmas they see as important (Lubeck, 1998; Lubeck & Post, 2000; McGhan, 2002). How can we become and stay aware of the shifting power relations in such situations – and what would this awareness mean for our work? In order to work in this way, we who are teacher educators might ask teachers, "Which discourses do *you* find authoritative and difficult to reject? Why? What are the discourses that are internally persuasive to *you*, and why? We might ask (and really mean it), *what do you need*? What do you want me to do – if anything?" The tricky part seems to be how one leads or guides without imposing or disempowering. This requires, we think, continually asking ourselves what discourses we find persuasive, and why. We could ask, for instance, "What, in fact, makes *me* the leader? Do we really even need a 'leader?' Has my privileged position of professional dominance led to a dogmatic discourse? Has the power of authoritative discourse negated the possibility of authentic collaboration? Can power be shared more equitably? What will I have to give up in order for this to happen?"

We are not suggesting that reconstructing our work as teacher educators is a choice between being seen as experts or giving up all pretense of having some knowledge about ECE. Rather, we are arguing that teacher educators ought to take multiple perspectives into consideration whenever we consider teaching practices. We can become more aware of and responsive to the dialogic tension between unequal social languages, the "prestige languages" that seek to "close the world in system" while the "subordinated languages" battle "completeness in order to keep the world open to becoming" (Clark & Holquist, 1984, pp. 79–80). We can accept and embrace the incompleteness, messiness, and unpredictability of teaching and learning. We can learn to value ambiguity and conflict over enforced consensus.

Of course, when we open that door a crack, allow for some slippage, try to create spaces for meaningful dialogue, we risk losing some of our power. But we think that's okay. We are willing to do both the inner and outer work of resisting the current model of expertise. If those of us positioned as experts can challenge ourselves to be honest and acknowledge the contradictions of the culture (cult?) of expertise, maybe we can stop training the always, already "failing" early childhood educator. Maybe together we can create a climate where early childhood teachers (and teacher educators) are seen as always, already "becoming," rather than always, already failing.

ACKNOWLEDGMENTS

We thank Catherine Compton-Lilly for her comments on an earlier draft of this chapter, and two anonymous reviewers who provided very helpful feedback.

REFERENCES

Ayers, W. (1992). Disturbances from the field: Recovering the voice of the early childhood educator. In: S. Kessler & B. Swadener (Eds), *Reconceptualizing the early childhood curriculum* (pp. 256–266). New York: Teachers College Press.

Bakhtin, M. M. (1981). Discourse in the novel. In: M. Holquist, C. Emerson & M. Holquist (Eds), *The dialogic imagination: Four essays by M. M. Bakhtin* (pp. 259–422). Austin, TX: University of Texas Press.

Bakhtin, M. M. (1986). *Speech genres and other late essays*. Austin, TX: University of Texas Press.

Ballenger, C. (1999). *Teaching other people's children: Literacy and learning in a bilingual classroom*. New York: Teachers College Press.

Barthes, R. (1972). *Mythologies*. London: Paladin.

Berghoff, B. (1997). Stance and teacher education: Understanding the relational nature of teaching. ERIC document ED 424218.

Bhabha, H. (1994). *The location of culture*. London: Routledge.

Bredekamp, S., & Copple, C. (1997). Preface, In: S. Bredekamp & C. Coople (Eds), *Developmentally appropriate practice in early childhood programs* (Rev. ed., pp. v–vii). Washington, DC: National Association for the Education of Young Children.

Clark, K., & Holquist, M. (1984). *Mikhail Bakhtin*. Cambridge, MA: Harvard University Press.

Cochran-Smith, M. (2004). *Walking the road: Race, diversity, and social justice in teacher education*. New York: Teachers College Press.

Cochran-Smith, M., & Lytle, S. (1993). *Inside/outside: Teacher research and knowledge*. New York: Teachers College Press.

Compton-Lilly, C. (2002). *Reading families: The literate lives of urban children and their families*. New York: Teachers College Press.

Dahlberg, G., Moss, P., & Pence, A. (1999). *Beyond quality in early childhood education and care: Postmodern perspectives*. London: Falmer.

Darling-Hammond, L. (1996). The right to learn and the advancement of teaching: Research, policy, and practice for democratic education. *Educational Researcher*, 25(6), 5–17.

Davies, B. (2000). *A body of writing 1990–1999*. Walnut Creek, CA: AltaMira Press.

Ellsworth, E. (1997). *Teaching positions: Difference, pedagogy, and the power of address*. New York: Teachers College Press.

Foucault, M. (1977). *Discipline and punish: The birth of the prison*. London: Penguin.

Foucault, M. (1980). *Power–knowledge: Selected interviews and other writings, 1972–1977*. Brighton, UK: Harvester Press.

Freire, P. (1986). *Pedagogy of the oppressed*. New York: The Continuum Publishing Co.

Gallas, K. (1995). *Talking their way into science: Hearing children's questions and theories, responding with curricula*. New York: Teachers College Press.

Garrison, J. (2000). Emerson's "The American Scholar" and the current status of philosophy of education. *Taboo*, 4(1), 101–107.

Gee, J. (1992). What is literacy? In: P. Shannon (Ed.), *Becoming political: Readings and writings in the politics of literacy* (pp. 21–28). Portsmouth, NH: Heinemann.

Giroux, H. A. (1988). *Teachers as transformative intellectuals: Towards a critical pedagogy of learning*. Granby, MA: Bergin & Garvey.

Gore, J. M., & Morrison, K. (2001). The perpetuation of a (semi-) profession: Challenges in the governance of teacher education. *Teaching and Teacher Education*, 71, 567–582.

Harré, R., & van Langenhove, L. (Eds) (1999). *Positioning theory: Moral contexts of intentional action*. Oxford, England: Blackwell Publishers.

Heshusius, L. (1994). Freeing ourselves from objectivity: Managing subjectivity or turning toward a participatory mode of consciousness? *Educational Researcher*, 23, 15–22.

Hicks, D. (1996). Discourse learning, and teaching. In: M. Apple (Ed.), *Review of research in education*, (Vol. 21, pp. 49–95). Washington, DC: American Educational Research Association.

Karier, C. J. (1973). Business values and the educational state. In: C. J. Karier, P. Violas & J. Spring (Eds), *Roots of crisis: American education in the twentieth century* (pp. 6–29). Chicago: Rand McNally.

Lewis, A. C. (2002). School reform and professional development. *Phi Delta Kappan, 83*(7), 389–488.

Lubeck, S. (1996). Deconstructing "child development knowledge" and "teacher preparation". *Early Childhood Research Quarterly, 11*, 147–167.

Lubeck, S. (1998). Is developmentally appropriate practice for everyone? *Childhood Education, 74*, 299–301.

Lubeck, S., & Post, J. (2000). Creating a Head Start community of practice. In: L. Diaz Soto (Ed.), *The politics of early childhood education* (pp. 33–58). New York: Peter Lang Publishing.

Lubeck, S., Jessup, P., deVries, M., & Post, J. (2001). The role of culture in program improvement. *Early Childhood Research Quarterly, 16*, 499–523.

McGhan, B. (2002). A fundamental education reform: Teacher-led schools. *Phi Delta Kappan, 83*(7), 538–540.

McWilliam, E., & Taylor, P. G. (1998). Teacher im/material: Challenging the new pedagogies of instructional design. *Educational Researcher, 27*(8), 29–35.

Mills, C. W. (1956). *The power elite*. New York: Oxford University Press.

Miller, R. (1997). *What are schools for? Holistic education in American culture (3rd Rev. ed.)*. Brandon, VT: Holistic Education Press.

National Association for the Education of Young Children. (1996). *Guidelines for preparation of early childhood professionals*. Washington, DC: National Association for the Education of Young Children.

Novinger, S., & O Brien, L. M. (2003). Beyond "boring, meaningless shit" in the academy: Early childhood teacher educators under the regulatory gaze. *Contemporary Issues in Early Childhood, 4*(1), 3–31.

Pacini-Ketchabaw, V., & Schecter, S. (2002). Engaging the discourse of diversity: Educators' frameworks for working with linguistic and cultural difference. *Contemporary Issues in Early Childhood, 3*(3), 400–414.

Palmer, P. J. (1998). *The courage to teach: Exploring the inner landscape of a teacher's life*. San Francisco: Jossey-Bass Publishers.

Regenspan, B. (2002). *Parallel practices: Social justice-focused teacher education and the elementary school classroom*. New York: Peter Lang.

Ryan, J. (1999). *Race and ethnicity in multi-ethnic schools: A critical case study*. Toronto: Multilingual Matters.

Soja, E. (1996). *Thirdspace: Journeys to Los Angeles and other real-and-imagined places*. Cambridge, MA: Harvard University Press.

Ware, L. (2001). Writing identity and the other: Dare we do disability studies? *Journal of Teacher Education, 52*(2), 107–123.

IMPROVISATION: POSTMODERN PLAY FOR EARLY CHILDHOOD TEACHERS

Carrie Lobman

ABSTRACT

This chapter briefly discusses the postmodern critique of developmental psychology and then presents a Vygotskian-influenced alternative understanding of development as a non-linear, relational, improvised activity engaged in by groupings of people. This reconstruction of development was the basis of a professional development project in which early childhood teachers participated in a 6-week improv workshop. The goal of the project was to reconnect the teachers with their ability to improvise or to participate in process-oriented, meaning-making activity. The project was based on the hypothesis that developing teachers' ability to improvise would give them an alternative to relating to children as being on, or off, a developmental trajectory.

I am an early childhood educator, a postmodernist and an improv comedian (like you see on TV or in a comedy club). Learning to improvise has changed how I see children and teaching, and how I relate to what I see. When you improvise, you have no script. You create with whatever people are saying and doing in the moment. You cannot step back and assess, evaluate or draw on what you think you know about who people are. I have come to see improv as a postmodern activity because it draws attention to the relationality of human life – the success or failure of an improvised scene is not located within any individual, it is created collectively. Improv, I believe, has much to offer to the field of early childhood education. It gives us a way to create collectively with the children and families with whom we work without making judgments based on external standards of normal and abnormal development.

In order to show what I mean by seeing things differently, let us examine a typical scene from a preschool classroom through various lenses, including the lens of improvisation. The following interaction took place during a meeting time in a class of 4-year-olds. As with many preschool classrooms, the class meeting included a sharing time when children were invited to tell a story or show an item from home. On this particular day Angela, the teacher, prompted Matthew to share his bird's nest with the class.

ANGELA	Matthew, what did you bring today that you wanted to share? Did you bring a nest?
Matthew	I brought a nest and it had an egg in it, and now the egg is broken.
ANGELA	Someone touched it and it broke.
Matthew	It's very delicate.
Robbie	I know what was inside the egg – a bird!
ANGELA	Was there a bird inside this egg, Matthew?
Matthew	How did Robbie know that?
ANGELA	When someone broke the egg, *there was a bird?*
Robbie	I just know that when you have a nest – that's what birds live in.
ANGELA	When you brought *this* nest in and there was an egg, was there a bird inside *THAT* egg?
Matthew	Yeah.
ANGELA	(Shaking her head) When it was whole – there was a bird inside it?
Matthew	Yeah.
ANGELA	*Really?*
Robbie	Who cracked it?
Bobby	I guess the bird did.
Robbie	Yeah, when the bird poked its beak and broke the egg open.

Improvisation: Postmodern Play for Early Childhood Teachers 245

ANGELA	But *this* egg got broken by a *person's* finger.
ANGELA	Did the bird come out when the person touched it and it broke?
Matthew	I don't know, I didn't see it when the bird broke the shell and flew away.
ANGELA	Did anyone see it?
Robbie	I think it's playing hide and seek right now and doesn't know we're in meeting.
Jennifer	Where could it be hiding?
Robbie	Birds like to play games.
Jennifer	I think they're playing dress up.
ANGELA	It could be, does someone want to peek in the dress up corner and see if the baby bird is there?
Matthew	Carrie, can you check the dress up corner?

If we look at this exchange through the lens of developmentally appropriate practice (Bredekamp, 1986; Bredekamp & Copple, 1997), we are likely to notice several things. First, we might identify as positive the opportunity children are given to share their own ideas in a forum that is structured and supported by the teacher. Second, we might notice that the children's fantasy about the bird breaking through the egg is developmentally appropriate. Third, "knowing" that children at this developmental stage have trouble distinguishing between fantasy and reality, we might also see a missed opportunity for the teacher to demonstrate the difference between the two, and be concerned that the teacher did not find a way to correct the children's misconceptions about the bird's nest and the nonexistent bird.

If we look at this same exchange through some of the postmodern and critical lenses that have been applied to early childhood education, what might we see differently? For one thing, we might expose the shifting power relationships that are being constructed between the children and the teacher (Dahlberg, Moss, & Pence, 1999; Morss, 1996; Walkerdine, 1984). In the first half of the dialogue, the teacher is attempting to assert her authority over the children by trying to get them to admit there was never a bird in the egg. She used the indirect language of child-centered pedagogy; she doesn't "correct" the children, but she clearly has a "right" answer for which she is looking.

From a feminist perspective we can deconstruct the gender relationships at play between the dialogue participants (Walkerdine, 1984). All but one of the children who spoke was a boy, and the teacher was a woman. If we look line by line, we can see how the boys ignored the teacher's attempts to enter the conversation and silenced her until she participated to their liking.

What might we see when we look at the dialogue through the lens of improvisation (Sawyer, 1997; Lobman, 2001, 2003)? Overall, I think we might better see the creative process at work. The conversation began as a traditional "show and tell" presentation, but the children quickly took it in a different direction. They began creating what in improv terms is called a "yes and" story. They used each "offer" that was made to tell a story collectively. They did this by completely accepting what the person before them said and by adding the next piece of the story. In the beginning, the teacher was not accepting the children's offers, in improv terms she was negating, but her participation transformed midway and her talk began to contribute to the story. The lens of improvisation can help us see that meaning is made together. Further, it suggests that when improvisation is practiced self-consciously it creates opportunities for teachers and children to be creative together.

Early childhood teachers' interactions with children are often limited to short, somewhat scripted interactions that involve providing materials and making suggestions that help children get started and keep playing (Kontos, 1999; de Kruif, McWilliam, & Ridley, 2000). It is less common for teachers to engage in conversation or play with children in a way that enhances or expands the activity. Even when teachers do join children's activities during free play the interactions are short and there is a lack of rich conversation or deep involvement (Kontos, 1999). Teachers often respond in ways that stop the play or divert children's attention to more product-oriented tasks. Often choosing predictable responses or roles, they are not likely to create new roles that relate directly to what children are actually doing (Enz & Christie, 1994). In other words, teachers are reluctant to improvise with the children with whom they are working. In a previous research study (Lobman, 2001, 2003), I examined four early childhood teachers' interactions with children's play through the lens of improvisation. I looked for whether the teachers picked up and built with children's offers and I found that while there were moments when teachers did creatively improvise with children, they often did not.

This chapter describes a project in which teachers were taught directly how to do improv. Seven early childhood teachers participated in a 6-week improv workshop. The goal of the professional development project was to reconnect the teachers with their ability to improvise – meaning to reconnect them to their ability to participate in process-oriented, meaning-making activity – to create collectively with other people without knowing what was going to happen next. The project was based on the hypothesis that developing teachers' ability to improvise might give them an alternative to relating to children as being on, or off, a developmental trajectory.

DEVELOPMENT: REVOLUTIONARY ACTIVITY

For over a decade, postmodernists in early childhood education have focused on deconstructing child development and critiquing the effect its dominance has had on early childhood curriculum and practice. Postmodernists have generally viewed child development as a conception that embodies the problems of modernism. For many, the conception (and the field of developmental psychology) has done little more than solidify the myth of the normal child – and, by comparison, the abnormal or atypically developing child (Bloch, 1992; Burman, 1994; Cannella, 1997; Morss, 1990). We have learned much from this critique and my own work as an early childhood educator has been informed and enriched by it. However, in my practice I have tried to go beyond critique and to deconstruct development only as part of the process of reconstructing it from a postmodern perspective. Throughout this chapter I use the term *development* rather than *child development* in an attempt to move away from the structural notion that development is a linear progression beginning in infancy and ending with adulthood. In sharing my current understanding of development I hope to stimulate dialogue about early childhood education that includes a voice yet to be studied seriously by many postmodern colleagues – Lev Vygotsky.

As part of the critique of developmental psychology, many postmodernists have rejected or ignored the work of Vygotsky because they see him as "refining the notion of developmental change – but not challenging it" (Morss, 1996, p. 20). While Vygotsky was not a postmodernist, I believe that he has much to offer those of us interested in moving beyond deconstruction, and towards a postmodern, creative practice in early childhood education. Vygotsky's work is inconsistent; much of his most well-known writings focus on learning theory, educational practice, and evaluation in ways that fall solidly in the modernist camp (Vygotsky, 1978, 1987). Vygotskian theory has been used by traditional forces in the field of early childhood education to import "culture" into the theoretical canon that informs practice (Bredekamp & Copple, 1997), but this inclusion has not presented a serious challenge to traditional understandings of child development as a natural progression through a series of stages.

However, Vygotsky's work as a dialectical methodologist, his writings on practical-critical activity and his understanding of play and performance, when fused with a postmodern conception of human life as being socially, culturally, and politically constructed, can offer a way forward from the dualistic, explanatory bind of modernism and toward a creative, collective, emancipatory practice of early childhood education.

Outside early childhood, there are a few examples of Vygotskian understandings of learning and development being used to develop innovative educational programs and creative teaching practices (Cole, 1996; Holzman, 1997; Hume & Wells, 1998; Moll, 2000). There are also postmodernists in disciplines outside of education who have used Vygotskian-inspired methodology to create practices that are dialectical and improvisational (Feldman & Silverman, 2004; Gildin, 2003; Holzman, 2000; Massad, 2003; Salit, 2003) and in the process have discovered that Vygotsky's activity theory can be used to make postmodernism "more radical and more rigorous – and thereby, less vulnerable to critiques from the left and the right" (Holzman, in press).

Newman and Holzman (1993, 1997) are postmodernists who have built on Vygotsky's theories to create a new understanding and practice of human development. While their work has been deeply influenced and shaped by Vygotsky's (1978, 1987) writings on thought and language, play and performance, they have worked to improvise and create with Vygotsky rather than explain him. To put it another way, they relate to a historical Vygotsky, one that is not limited to the societal moment within which he lived, but who is part of the continuous human activity of creating history. In doing so, they have created an understanding of development that is not determined by stages, products or normalcy. As Morss (1996) puts it, "This revolutionary Vygotsky is committed to the kind of practical-critical activity that changes the world and makes history" (p. 81). In the following sections I lay out the elements of this postmodern Vygotsky that have influenced and shaped my improvisation project with early childhood teachers.

What is Activity?

According to Holzman (2000), Vygotsky (1978) proposed that the unit of study should not be the isolated individual but the individual-in-society and that the object of study is practical-critical activity:

> Activity, in the sense of revolutionary practical-critical activity, is human practice that is fully self-reflexive, dialectical, transformative of the totality, and continuously emergent.

It is human practice that abolishes the present state of things by the continuous transformation of mundane and specific life practices into new forms of life (p. 81).

In simpler language, while we as human beings may be "determined" by "the present state of things," we have the capacity, through our everyday practice, to transform the way things are into something new, which then becomes "the present state of things" (a new totality). What is important to human development in general and early childhood in particular is the characterization of people as changers and creators of new circumstances.

If we see development as an ongoing social activity then we go beyond a critique of the grand narrative of universal development to argue that people are not reducible to descriptions at all, whether they are universal or culturally specific. The difference between the activity of developing and theories of development is like the difference between an improvisation and a scripted play.

The relational activity of infants and their caregivers is a wonderful example of transformative activity. When a baby is born she is immediately included in the social/cultural life of her family. She does not evolve into a family member, nor does she first learn the cultural and social rules of her community and then participate as a member. She learns the cultural and social rules by participating as a member. Her arrival also immediately transforms the family. Actually, as any parent knows, it is almost ridiculous to talk about it as being the same family. The baby, together with her family, actively participates (albeit not self-consciously) in the creation of an environment where the family reshapes itself, and in the process the baby learns all sorts of things (i.e., how to speak a particular language, eat with a fork or chopsticks, demand or not demand attention). The baby is not "in" an environment created by the family, nor is the family creating an environment where the infant can develop. The activity of the infant and the family collectively creating a new performance is what produces the environment for the family (and the baby as a member of the family) to develop.

One can look at the activity described above and focus on the baby as an individuated learner who is learning particular societal skills. In the process of a family collectively creating itself, they do create the conditions whereby babies and children become socialized to a particular society and a particular role in that society. The baby learns to speak English, or Hindi, or Greek. The baby develops object permanence and later the ability to think abstractly. The baby learns the racist attitudes of her family. From this perspective it is tempting to see development as happening inside the baby and to equate the activity of development with those products.

However, to do so is to ignore the social creative process. The relationship between developmental activity and the learning of societal roles and rules is dialectical. The process of engaging in practical-critical activity (which is not determined by an end product) creates the possibility for learning particular societal performances, which can be (but often is not) used to create continued practical-critical activity. When we focus solely on the fact that we are able to adapt (as individuals) to society, we miss or distort the creative process by which those activities emerge (in history). If we shift the focus slightly toward the process, and see the ensemble activity of the family, then we are able to see how people of all ages can and do participate in the creation of collective environments where development can emerge.

While this capacity is human and ordinary, it is not usually self-consciously practiced. In the language of theatrical performance, it is as if we often feel compelled to act out an already written play (how to be a good parent, teacher, etc.). People often describe this as being stuck in a particular role. However, it is possible for people to create environments where we can improvise our activity, rather than act out roles. We can create environments where practical-critical activity can occur.

How Do We Create Development? The Zone of Proximal Development

How does this happen? How do we create environments where development is possible, or more accurately, how is the creating of environments for development developmental? Again, Vygotsky is of use here. Vygotsky's conception of the zone of proximal development (ZPD) can break us out of the individualistic bind in which modernist psychology puts us. He argued that development does not happen inside the child, but that it comes into existence socially:

> Every function in the child's cultural development appears twice: first on the social level and later on the individual level; first between people (interpsychological), and then inside the child (intrapsychological). This applies equally to all voluntary attention, to logical memory, and to the formation of concepts. All the higher mental functions originate as actual relations between people (1978, p. 57).

There have been many interpretations of the ZPD and how it can be of use to educators. Many modernist Vygotskians have been working with a conception of the ZPD as a place/environment/context within which learning occurs. From this perspective the ZPD is a *social* mechanism by which *individuals* develop and what has interested psychologists and educators is how the individual child or several children learn while in social interaction with more skilled peers or adults. In general they have looked for the ways in which the novice learns, while the more skilled partner creates the ZPD within which learning can take place (Bodrova & Leong, 1996; Rogoff, 1984; Wood, Bruner, & Ross, 1976).

In contrast, in Newman and Holzman's (1993) reading of Vygotsky, the creation of the ZPD is not a tool for the development of the individual – it is collective activity and what develops is the collective. The "more developed" partner does not create the ZPD so that the "less developed" child can learn – the ZPD is created by the improvised, collective activity of the participants.

Let us return to the environment created by infants and their caregivers as an example of the collective creation of the ZPD. Infants and their caregivers create an environment collectively where the infant is able to play at being a speaker and in doing so becomes one. When an infant babbles, "ba, ba, goo, ba, dah" the caregiver might pick her up and say, "Oh you're getting tired are you? Well let's hurry home so you can take a nap." As I discussed previously, the infant is not "in" an environment created by the caregiver, nor is the caregiver individually creating an environment where the infant can learn to speak. The activity of the infant and the caregiver playing with language is what creates the environment for the infant to go beyond herself and become a speaker.

This view of the ZPD shifts the focus away from the learning that is occurring *in* the ZPD and toward the active creation *of* the ZPD. From this perspective, the ZPD is not an instrumental tool for learning particular things, but is more a "tool and result" activity (Newman & Holzman, 1993, pp. 86–89). The activity of creating the ZPD, of creating the environment for development is inseparable from the development that occurs.

One way to understand the activity of creating the ZPD is that people are who they are and who they are not simultaneously; they are in the process of becoming. In his conception of the ZPD, Vygotsky provided a way of shifting the focus from the modernist obsession with products, labels, and stages and toward the process of people creating environments where it is possible for them to be who they are and who they are not.

Once again it is important to make a distinction between developmental psychology's focus on the products of development – including *becoming* a socially well-adapted adult and the dialectical activity of "being and becoming." In developmental psychology and the educational approaches it has informed, the relationship between being and becoming is not dialectical but dualistic. Depending on the particular theoretical framework, the focus is either on creating a classroom environment that is appropriate for the developmental stage of the children – for who they are; or preparing children for the future – who they will become. From this perspective "being" is about finding out and relating to who someone is and "becoming" involves progressing to a new, predetermined, stage of development. When I use the term "being and becoming" or "being who you are and who you are not," I am talking dialectically. From a dialectical perspective there are no end points to development. Children are continuously in the process of becoming, even as they are who they are. While we can label them with descriptors as if they are fixed in time and space, who they are becoming is continuously emergent and improvisational.

IMPROV AND TEACHER DEVELOPMENT

Creating environments for being and becoming does not come easily or naturally. In general, as we get older we are in environments that support the acting out of societally acceptable roles and activities. Environments where children can keep being who they are and who they are not place a new demand on teachers. Teachers have to be willing to go on a creative journey with children without knowing exactly what is going to happen. Creating environments where children can be who they are and who they are not requires that teachers get better at improvising.

In my experience as a teacher educator, prospective teachers are often afraid to engage in improvised relational activity. They have been through years of schooling that all too often trains them, in a behaviorist way, to stop relating to others in playful ways. Not surprisingly, by the time people enter teacher education programs they have lost some of the skills associated with playfulness; willingness to look silly or foolish, to not know what is going to happen next, to do what one does not know how to do.

Early childhood teacher education programs teach prospective teachers about the importance of play for children's development but rarely do they teach the importance of cocreating playful environments with children. Improv is an adult activity that closely resembles the play of early childhood (Johnstone, 1981; Nachmanovitch, 1991; Newman, 1996). It can help prepare teachers to go on a creative journey with children, to relate to children as both who they are and who they are becoming. When I was a preschool teacher I took an improv comedy class with a professional comedian and it quickly transformed my teaching. I began to relate to the children in my class as ensemble members, as cocreators of the learning environment with me. I stopped focusing on individual children with fixed identities, and

I began to see the class as a group with whom I was producing an improvised performance. In the class ensemble individuals developed their performances and took on new roles.

I was working with children aged 4 and they were playing/making meaning all the time; they were constantly creating short improvised scenes. Improvisation taught me how to participate in that activity with them without taking over or distorting it for my own purposes. From inside play I could challenge some of the children's assumptions about the way things are; I could be a mommy who hated to cook, or a superhero who cried, not as an imposition or a lesson, but as a creative choice that challenged *them* to keep making creative choices. I showed them that we could continuously play with, and create with, the meanings we see in the world.

I also became more creative. Learning to improvise expanded significantly my repertoire of responses to what children were doing and saying. In improv classes I got practice in using everything to create the performance. I reconnected with my ability to say and do the unexpected. I no longer felt as constrained by my position as expert in the classroom and I began listening more carefully to what children were doing, playing, and offering. As I did this, I began to use more of what they were offering, even the things that did not fit with what I expected young children to do or say. For example, a group of children aged 4 who often used to curse ended up doing a survey of what words were considered "bad" by the other children and staff. We were able to create a "polling performance" from what I would otherwise have considered a behavior problem.

In a previous research study (Lobman, 2001, 2003), I examined the interactions among teachers and children through the lens of improvisation. The teachers in that study had not been taught to improvise – improv was a lens that I was using to examine their interactions. The findings from that study suggested that when teachers interacted with children in ways that were consistent with the rules of improvisation, they were able to create a rich, playful meaning-making environment. It is the teacher education implications of this that excited me. Seeing what is happening between children and teachers as improvisational opens the possibility of teaching adults new ways of relating to the children in their class.

In order to find whether learning and practicing improvisation skills in a workshop could carry over into the early childhood classroom, I designed and implemented a pilot program for seven early childhood teachers. I was curious to see whether learning to see their work with children through the lens of improvisation, and developing their improvisational skills, would have an impact on their practice. Would being more self-conscious about their ability to improvise allow teachers to be more creative in their work in the classroom? Would they become more open to going on a creative journey with children? If so, what would that experience look like and what would the teachers say about it?

THE IMPROVISATION WORKSHOPS

It is 2:15 p.m. on a Friday afternoon at The Randolph Childcare Center. Ten people are moving around a large, empty room. They move very, very slowly. As they pass they greet each other without speaking – with a slow motion nod, an excruciatingly deliberate handshake or just a stare. Every once in a while someone giggles. When the group starts to move faster, Cathy, the improv instructor, says, "Don't speed up... If you laugh, laugh slowly, if you have an itch, scratch slowly." The teachers move even more deliberately and they begin to move additional parts of their bodies – a hand here, a shoulder or a hip. Cathy says, "Good, take the time to look around the room, at each other. Often in life we don't realize how fast we are moving until we slow down. Listen to the sounds in the room. Listen to the sounds outside of the room. Notice each other." After a few more minutes Cathy adds, "OK, now when you make eye contact with someone, make a funny face. Slowly." There is a pause in the group, and then someone sticks their tongue out at someone else and that person crosses their eyes and distorts their face. Someone starts laughing and cannot stop. Cathy reiterates, "Its alright to laugh, just make sure you laugh in slow motion, make it part of the performance." After a while, Cathy adds another element, "Start talking to each other... in gibberish." She turns to the person next to her and says, "Gob deeee fiddle junipo?" The teacher laughs nervously and then says, "Junip nascento julepskee."

Setting and Participants

This was the initial warm-up exercise of the 6-week improvisation workshop for teachers at the Randolph Childcare Center in New York City [The name of the childcare center and all participants have been changed]. The center serves approximately 150 children from 3 months to 5 years of age in 10 classrooms. A head teacher and two assistants staff each classroom. The center is part of a large, urban research university and provides childcare to the children of faculty and students from around the world. The philosophy of the center is based on the principles of developmentally appropriate practices (Bredekamp & Copple, 1997) and the children and teachers spend most of their day in free play activities. The infant and toddler rooms are on a flexible schedule that is based on the children's daily needs. The preschool classrooms have a more standardized schedule, but each room has at least 4 h of free playtime a day.

Seven of the 30 teachers on staff at the center participated voluntarily in the improvisation workshops. A month before the beginning of the project I did a presentation at a staff meeting where I told them about my belief that learning to improvise could be helpful to them as early childhood teachers, gave a brief talk about improvisation and development, and played a 5-min storytelling game with the group. Fourteen of the 30 staff members expressed an interest in participating in the workshops. Due to classroom staffing issues only one teacher from each classroom could participate. I selected the seven participants to represent a range of teaching experience and education.

Six women and one man participated in the workshops. Three of the teachers were head teachers and four were assistant teachers. They ranged in experience from second year teachers to veterans of 25 years. The group was multiracial. One woman was Japanese, two of the women were Latina-American, the man and two women were Anglo-American, and one woman was African-American. All three of the head teachers had Masters' degrees in either early childhood or elementary education. Of the four assistants, three of them had Bachelor's degrees, but not in education, and one of them had an Associate's degree in elementary education. Only Matthew, the male teacher, had any previous experience as a performer. He had worked as an actor and had taken some improv classes as part of his theatrical training. Despite the fact that all seven teachers worked at the same childcare center, many of them did not know each other well before the workshops began. Due to the physical layout of the center, as well as programmatic divisions, many of the teachers rarely spent time together.

Two professional improvisers led the workshops. Cathy is the president of a consulting firm that specializes in teaching performance skills as a means of business development. She has been a professional improviser for over ten years and has been teaching improvisation for the last seven years. I hired her because of her commitment to the value of improvisation for ordinary people in everyday life, not just for professional performers. Hillary, who is a professional clown, improviser and theatre teacher, assisted her.

Data Collection

Data sources included participant observations of the improv workshops, three semi-structured interviews, and a focus group. I interviewed the teachers prior to the workshops regarding their beliefs and practices about play and their perceptions and opinions of their role in the classroom during free playtime, and their reasons for participating in the improv workshops. The improv workshops took place for 1.5 h a week for 6 weeks, and were located at the early childhood center. The workshops were led by two professional improvisers, and I attended the sessions as a participant observer. The sessions were all videotaped. I conducted a second interview with each teacher after the third class. After the completion of the project I interviewed all of the teachers regarding their experience of the workshop and the effect on their teaching. Three weeks after the final improv workshop I also conducted a focus group of all the participants.

Workshop Design

The improv workshops introduced the teachers to the basic skills of improvisational theatre including creating the ensemble, the giving and receiving of offers, and "yes and." The workshops were designed to give the participants the experience of themselves as performers and players and to help them see the ways in which this could help them develop their work in the classroom and with children, colleagues, and families. This was accomplished by creating a challenging, non-competitive environment where the teachers were working as an ensemble. Throughout the 6 weeks Cathy, the primary trainer, encouraged the group to talk about the experience and to make connections to their work with children.

Creating the Ensemble

One of the keys to going on a creative journey, whether in an improv group or in the classroom, is to see yourself as part of an ensemble. In improv it is by giving oneself over to what is being created collectively that people are able to do and say things they would not dare to do as an individual. The teachers, although used to working with groups of children, were not necessarily used to working collectively. The first part of every improv workshop involved transitioning into the ensemble.

The improvisation workshops were organized as a series of exercises, games, and scene work. Each week began with 20 min or more of warm-up activities that focused on slowing down and transitioning into an improvisational mode. The slow motion activity that was described at the beginning of this section is an example of one of the warm-up exercises. These exercises provided a shift in the pace, mode, and speed with which the teachers moved. For improvisation to be successful people have to be willing to do weird things and the warm-up activities helped the group segue into being weird – together.

These transition exercises also provided the teachers with an opportunity to break out of their "teacher" identities and to be playful. For example, the experience of being unnaturally slow gave them a taste of what it is like to not just do what you normally do, and to reconnect with their ability to "be who they are not." It also introduced them to their new playmates. These activities always involved the entire group working together, and because they involved *everyone* being weird they helped to create an environment where people could take risks.

The teachers experienced the warm-up period as one of the most challenging aspects of the improv workshops, but they also said that it was critical in making the switch from their individual classrooms to being part of an ensemble. As Jessica said, "If you slow down then you can see other people, but if I'm just thinking about it in my head then I can't see anyone else."

When I spoke to the teachers prior to the first workshop several of them talked about feeling uncomfortable being silly or looking foolish, and during the first couple of weeks there was quite a bit of nervous laughter during the warm-up activities. As time went on the teachers were less distracted. During a conversation after the final workshop Louise brought up this change.

> Louise: ... it seemed like [in the beginning] after every time we said or did something we would also say something to break the mood and somebody would laugh. There would always be an undercurrent of other things...ha, ha, ha... . And it would distract from things... . Not only did I notice that it was distracting from the concentration of it, but also from the listening in terms of concentration. In the beginning we were like all la,la,la and talking about things and embarrassed and distracted and then we started getting more serious and listening in a different way. I think we started listening and watching each other instead of being embarrassed.

As the weeks went on the teachers were able to make the transition into the ensemble more rapidly and were able to work together to do complex and focused work. Much of the change that occurred could be seen visually rather than verbally. During the warm-up activities the teachers' movements came to resemble a dance troupe. This does not mean that the people who were clumsy or awkward became graceful – what changed was the group's ability to be aware of everyone's movements and to incorporate them into the overall activity. In 6 weeks the teachers went from being a self-conscious and somewhat ambivalent group of individuals who were concerned with looking foolish, to an ensemble that was able to move and work in rhythm with each other.

Learning to Say "Yes and ..."

In order to go on a creative journey with children teachers need to be able to see what is available to be created with, and they need to be able to create with what is available. Improvisation provides a structure within which it is not only possible to do these things; it is necessary for the activity. A primary purpose of the workshops at the Randolph School was to introduce the teachers to the basic building block of improvisation, "yes and," and to develop their ability to play "yes and" in the workshops and in life.

"Yes and" is both an exercise, and a philosophical tenet of improvisation. Professional improvisers on TV or at a club are basically doing "yes and." The exercise "yes and" is a collective storytelling activity. The group makes up a story as if they are one person – they tell it in one voice. Each person has a sentence and each sentence begins with the words "yes and." The 'yes' signifies that the person has heard and accepts everything that came before. Not only what the person right before them said, but everything that has been said so far. The "yes" requires that each person be very attentive and focused and uses everything that is offered for the ongoing creation of the story. The 'and' directs each person to add a little something to it.

While "yes and" appears to be about telling a story it is actually a listening game. In order for the story to be successful the participants have to hear what someone else is saying and then simply say what happens next. Great ideas, brilliant funny thoughts, do not help the story develop. The type of listening that is needed for a successful "yes and" story challenges what most people think of as listening. Listening in "yes and" is integral to responding; it involves being able to accept and use all of what your fellow performers are saying and doing. It is not enough to just sit quietly and look as if you are paying attention to what is being said, and then saying whatever you feel like. The activity of listening taught in these workshops required that the teachers be so attentive to what was being said that they were able to respond directly to everything that came before. This type of listening needed to be learned, and as they learned to play "yes and," participants were able to develop new skills.

The First Story: The Coldest Day
The teachers played "yes and" in the first workshop. Once Cathy had described the activity the group sat on the floor and began a story. Each participant, except the first one, began their sentence with "yes and" and then added a new sentence to the story. The story proceeded clockwise around the circle.

Cathy   It was 6am on Wednesday morning and Sally got up out of bed.
Louise   Yes and she put on her pajamas.
Jessica   Yes and she also put on a pair of snow boots.
Evelyn   Yes and she tripped over her laces.
Carrie   Yes and fell flat on her face.
Sonia   Yes and she got up and went into the kitchen.
Jenny   Yes and took the frozen peas out of the freezer.
Hillary   Yes and she put them in the sink to thaw.
Matthew   Yes and took out the butter for melting them.

At this point Cathy stopped the activity in order to teach another critical improvisation skill – the "acceptance of offers." Offers are the material with which improvised scenes and stories are created. The rules of improvisation require that all offers be accepted and are used to build. If two performers are on stage and one says, "It sure is hot here on the moon," the other one must accept that they are on the moon and add the next piece of the story: "Let's hike over to the dark side and see if we can find some shade." The giving and receiving of offers makes improvisation an excellent place to practice our human ability to create with other people.

Cathy used the story that had just been told to point out some of the ways in which the participants were not listening to each other, and showed that there were several "offers" that had been made in the story that were not used as the story continued.

> Cathy: Good. I'm going to stop us for a second. I just want to note that there were a couple of offers that I think we didn't pick up on, as a matter of fact many offers ... . People were picking up on offers here with the frozen peas and taking them out to thaw and taking out the butter. So we had a connected thing over here. But we had the

unusual circumstance over here, if I recall correctly, which is that she woke up and got into her pajamas.

At this point the group laughed at what she said and spent several moments joking about people putting on their pajamas after they got out of bed. Cathy participated in the joke, and then brought the conversation back around to the question of "accepting offers."

Cathy   So that was sort of an unusual thing. That was an offer and nobody ... What was your line? (Pointing to Jessica)
Jessica   Put on her snow boots.
Cathy   So we had some strange things happening, we've got the pajamas and the snow boots, so we've got some things happening. And then what was yours? (Pointing to Evelyn)
Evelyn   She tripped over her laces.
Cathy   So she tripped, fell flat on her face which was building off of that and then we lost it. Literally when we got here we lost all of that. And I thought perhaps that we were going to pick up on it with the frozen peas and she would use it on the injury on her face. I mean that wouldn't have been the only thing to do, it just would have... . It was an offer and literally we didn't build with it. We were just putting in information to tell our part of the story, but didn't get connected until we got here. Do people know what I'm talking about, do you notice that?
Group   Uh huh. Yeah...

Several teachers said that they had a tendency to think about what they were going to say before it was actually their turn to talk, and that doing this led to a disconnect between what they were thinking was happening and what was actually being said.

> Jessica: ...even though you [Cathy] said don't think about what you are going to say, you're kind of thinking about it so then after Evelyn said what she said, I was like, "Uh..." because I had to change what I, you know, was going to say. And I think it got a little easier as we went on to just like...be more open to the input whatever it was... And then there was a shorter pause between the time I heard it and the time I spoke. Because before I would be like, "Yeah and..."

While Jessica was talking about planning in her head, Matthew described listening to the 'yes and' story as it went around the circle and thinking about how he would respond if he were next.

Matthew: I was thinking when hearing some of the other ones, "Oh I wish I could respond to that." But then I thought you know I'm going to hear something and it's going to be just as much fun to respond to and then it would be my turn and I wouldn't be sure what to say because I would have been thinking all this time instead of listening ...

The improv exercise "yes and" helped the teachers to become more aware of what prevented them from connecting and creating with each other. They came to realize that if you are thinking about what you are going to say or are wishing you could respond to something other than what is being said, then you cannot possibly be relating fully to the person or people who are involved.

"Yes and" is one of the improv exercises that draws attention to the relationality of human activity. While we have the experience of being alone with our thoughts even when we are with other people, we are actually with other people. In "yes and," the teachers were able to see the direct impact of being "in your head" rather than in the relational activity. Continued practice with "yes and" stories also gave them the experience of what happens when you stop planning so much and respond directly to each other.

"Too Much Formaldehyde Spoils the Body"
In the following activity the teachers were working in pairs to create quick three-four line scenes. The first performer began the scene by doing a physical activity (pantomiming something rather than speaking). The second performer came onto the stage and said something in character that identified what the activity was. Within a few lines they had to identify together what their relationship was (i.e., husband and wife, teacher and student) and where they were (i.e., on the moon, in a restaurant, at the copy machine). The key to the success of the scene was for each of the performers to contribute new information that built on what came before. In the following example, Sonia and Jessica begin by negating each other, but, with direction from Hillary and Cathy, they were able to say "yes and" and create an interesting exchange:

Sonia   (Begins the scene by pantomiming putting something over her head and then begins moving her hands around in a circle in front of her. From my vantage point it looks like she has put on an apron and is now mixing something in a bowl.
Jessica   (Comes onto the stage and starts to ask a question). What are you doing, getting ready to prepare the...Woops? (She stepped back).

Hillary   Great catch, good for you Jessica. You tell her what she is doing. She made the first offer, the physical movement is the first offer, and you build with that offer. You say, yes and.

Hillary pointed out that if Jessica asked a question at this point she will be ignoring the fact that Sonia has already made an offer – by making the physical movement. It is now Jessica's turn to "build with that offer." Just like in the "yes and" stories, the job of each of the participants is to accept all offers and then add something new. Asking a question does not contribute to the creation of the scene and it puts all the responsibility onto Sonia.

Sonia   (keeps moving her arms around in a circle).
Jessica   (starts to step back onto the stage; she stops and says to Hillary) Now she went too far into her thing…
Hillary   You saw what she did and we saw what she did, we're with you.
Jessica   But I was on a different thing…
Cathy   Not anymore.

Jessica was able to see that what she was going to say did not build with what Sonia was doing and would therefore have been a negation of Sonia's offer. In improvisation when a player does not accept an offer it is called negating, and it usually serves to stop the scene from developing. Negation leaves the other performers out on a limb and it stops the activity of the scene. Improvisers are taught to make their fellow performers look good, not stupid. Improvisers never want to work at cross-purposes to their fellow performers: the basic rule is "Don't negate." Jessica nodded her head and then stepped back onto the stage again:

Jessica   You know you can't mix up formaldehyde that much if you are going to prepare a body. Too much formaldehyde spoils the body.
Sonia   (Stared at her for a moment and then stopped what she was doing and said): Gee you really screwed that up Jessica. (Jessica laughed).

In this part of the scene it is Sonia who has negated Jessica. She remained committed to her version of what the scene should look like and when

Jessica put a different name to the activity, she balked. However, Hillary and Cathy used this as a moment to identify the importance of working as a team and trusting your partner to justify and use your offers.

Hillary	(stepped in). That's great that that happened. Who knew what you were putting in the bowl. You thought it was eggs, but then you hear, 'you can't mix the formaldehyde that much if you are preparing a body.' So now you know that it is formaldehyde and you have to build with that.
Sonia	So I have to go with what she's saying, not what I'm thinking?
Hillary	Yes, yes.
Cathy	Exactly, just like your physical activity was an offer, her words are another offer. You build with that offer. It is formaldehyde!
Hillary	But what is so great about this is that you as a team are going to make this work, no matter what. It's a great opportunity to now justify what Jessica has said.

The job of everyone in a scene is to accept and build with offers. In this case, Sonia and Jessica are working as a team – and as a team there are no wrong or right offers. This experience, if embraced, can be freeing because it is not anyone's individual responsibility to make the scene work, it is the team's responsibility.

Sonia	(Turned back to Jessica and said in character) I have to put this much formaldehyde in to prepare the dead body of your father.
Jessica	Mother, I know he would have been pleased that you are carrying on his work here at the funeral home.
Cathy	Great! (The 'audience' claps).

At the end of this exchange Sonia and Jessica have created a scene together by accepting each other's offers and saying "yes and." Neither of them had total control of the scene, what was created was built collectively. This is a good example!

The group created dozens of exchanges such as this, over the 6 weeks and each was an opportunity for the teachers to experience what it is like to go on a creative journey with other people without knowing where it is going to end. They had the experience that young children have when they play; there was no blueprint for the activity and it was therefore up to the participants to use what was available at any given moment to go somewhere together.

"Accept the Duck"
During a discussion at the end of the fourth workshop, Cathy gave an example of how difficult she finds it to accept offers she does not like when she is working with her professional improv troupe.

> Cathy: I have a lot of scene work where I am in a scene with someone and I don't like what they are doing. When they are in the scene I am constantly thinking I just can't believe you are doing this now – this does not work in this scene. So I spoke to my colleague and he said, 'But they are in the scene with you and to whatever extent you are trying to change what is going on or ignore the person and their offers, the audience sees it.'
>
> And that is so true, the audience is seeing what is happening and for example, they see that there is a woman to my right who appears to be quacking like a duck and I don't seem to be paying any attention to it. There *is* a duck in the scene and when I deal with the fact that there is a duck in the scene, even though I didn't want the duck to be in the scene, then we can make something happen and then the scene has a shot. And from a personal experience, when I do that, instead of feeling miserable I feel like, "Woah! I could do something with that." And we surprise ourselves that somehow we could make this work with a duck in the scene. And I can't help but think this is relevant to teaching.

Cathy described the experience of trying to create a scene when your fellow performers are saying and doing things (making offers) that you do not like. She pointed out that wishing they would just stop or go away does not build the scene. The only way to build the scene is by accepting the offers.

The teachers were very responsive to Cathy's story. Everyone nodded and several people said that they often dealt with children or events that they felt did not belong in the classroom and that they wished were not happening. The image of a quacking duck as representative of offers you do not like seemed to resonate with the teachers and they used it over and over again in the rest of the conversation, and in future discussions and scenes.

The teachers talked about their experience of working with children that they felt were difficult and they began to play with what it would mean to take a more improvisational stance in the classroom. Sonia responded by saying that she feels like there are "quacking ducks" in her classroom "several hundred times a day" and that sometimes she just "can't stand it one more minute."

> Sonia: What I hate is when you have the duck over and over and over again and you just don't want to work with the duck or you feel like it would be better for the duck if he stopped being a duck.

Sonia brought up the point that the "offers" that children make are not only annoying to her, but are sometimes not helpful to the child.

After Sonia spoke Cathy opened her mouth to respond, but Louise interrupted her and made the connection between the frustration that Sonia was expressing and the improvisation workshops.

> Louise: One thing I've learned from this class is to accept that the duck or the child is in the scene with you – which is not the same as letting the child do whatever they want. You may not let the child do whatever they want, but you accept them as being in the scene with you and then you have to figure out what to do with what they are offering you.

The statement Louise made is a powerful one. She said that it is not a choice between letting children do whatever they want and wishing they would stop. She pointed out that in teaching, as in improv, you have to figure out what to do with the offers that are given to you. You do not get to choose what offers you get. Jessica responded by giving an example from her own classroom.

> Jessica: That's the whole thing about accepting the Duck! I think I haven't been accepting the duck! I just realized it. I have a new child in my room and here we are it's December and the class is finally gelling and we know what we are doing and I was so disappointed when he came into the class and began "ruining" it. He wasn't doing what we were doing. He was ruining our class and I was so disappointed. And now I am thinking I have to "accept the duck." He is our duck and he is in our scene, the class's scene. We are doing a different scene now because he is in it. How can I make the classroom big enough to accept him?

In this conversation the teachers began to make a connection between what they had been learning in the improv workshops and their performances as teachers. Sonia pointed out that what is difficult in improvised scenes is also difficult in the classroom, with the added dilemma of feeling responsible for helping children to make good choices. Louise and Jessica saw the possibility that using their newfound improv skills could change how they worked with children.

Improv and Teaching

Several weeks after the final improv workshop I conducted a more formal assessment of the teachers' experience through a series of interviews and a focus group. The teachers were universally vocal about how much they enjoyed the workshops and in particular that they saw them as valuable because they were a "fun, creative, stress-relieving activity." When it came to discussing the effect of the workshops on them as teachers, several themes emerged. Some of these themes were particular to individuals and others seemed to be valid for the whole group.

"It's a Philosophical Thing"

Jenny was the youngest and newest of the teachers. She was also the most vocal about the ways the improvisation classes had impacted on her as a teacher, and in other areas of her life. In my preliminary interview with Jenny I asked her why she had chosen to participate in the improvisation workshops.

> Jenny: Because I feel like I am always speechless. (Laugh). I feel I always, especially here [at Randolph] there is such an emphasis to use certain words and to specifically not use other words and to say things a certain way. And to say it the right way. And I feel so often I just get so tongue-tied. I don't end up saying anything, or I take so long to say it that the child has moved on to something else. I worry all the time about saying and doing the right thing and I guess I think improv could help with that.

Jenny identified what many new early childhood teachers feel. Childcare centers and schools often have a language all their own and teachers are expected to use certain words and not others. This language does not always come naturally to teachers and it can leave people feeling speechless.

In the first two improvisation workshops Jenny was in several situations where she had to speak before she was "ready." In these interactions she clearly appeared flustered, but she followed Cathy's direction to "just speak, something will come out." After the third workshop I had another conversation with her about how she was feeling about the workshops.

> Jenny: It's changed my life. I mean it. It has. It's opened up a new door and new coping skills. I'm sure I will see it in the classroom. The basic things of letting a project go not just where you plan it, but where they take it. I have this vision of how something is supposed to happen and then I'm not offered that and to give that up...and it's the same thing in the classroom. You have this vision of what the day is going to be like and when things don't exactly turn out that way. So I feel like it's more of a philosophy I have to embrace. That it has philosophical implications. It's a philosophical thing. I feel like it's a good life lesson...

I asked her to say more about what she saw the philosophy of improv as being and how it was different from how she had been thinking, living, and teaching.

> Jenny: I know that I personally am kind of; at least I feel that I am kind of rigid and strict and the whole idea of offers. That whole thing is the premise of improv, I feel like that helps me in life to let go of what my image of what this was going to be and go with what I have. Which is such a great philosophy. So, I feel like its been good that way.

In this conversation Jenny stressed the ways in which the workshops had changed how she was approaching her life outside the classroom. She gave an example of being able to relax more with her friends and family because she is less concerned with what was supposed to happen and more focused on what is happening.

At the conclusion of the workshops Jenny was able to identify specific ways that learning to improvise had changed her relationships with the children.

> Jenny: I am talking to the children in a more candid way. As well as, being silly I guess, v. not being silly. I think both ways... I experience more comfort and more ease with not being able to say the right thing. With saying to children, "Wow, I don't know what to say about that, what do you think?" And stuff like that...

Over the course of the 6 weeks Jenny went from focusing on the "correct language" to telling children when she was at a loss. She had previously expressed a concern with not feeling like a "real teacher," and it seemed as if she believed that she could only speak to children when she had expertise or knew what to say. By the end of the workshops it appeared that she was less determined by having something to say, and more willing to create the conversation with the children.

Re-thinking Play

One of the strongest statements about the workshops came from Louise. Louise was the teacher who everyone identified as the most surprising member of the ensemble. After the third workshop I asked each of the teachers if they had been startled by anybody's participation, and they all said Louise. Louise herself said that she was surprised by how much she was enjoying the workshops because she is not "that kind of person" and she is usually "afraid of letting go."

At the very end of the focus group interview I asked the teachers if there was anything else they wanted to say and Louise immediately spoke. She talked about how the improvisation workshops had changed her, and in particular how they had changed her relationship to play.

> Louise: The other thing I was thinking of was the thing about play. Was that when we met on Fridays it seemed like we were playing. As a person I don't play, like I won't go into details of my thing, but I don't like playing... I like to watch playing, but I don't like to participate in it, if someone asks me to be a cow, "I'm like, forget about it... yeah go ask somebody else, whatever..." But I think that it helped me think about and play a little bit more and I kind of feel a little bit sad because I don't play enough. I think about what that's all about and... then in terms of teaching even in terms of what you are talking about too, is that to have teachers reconnect with play. To become people who

play. That it's not just something that *they* [the children] do, but it's something that you could do with them and not just as an observation, but also as a participant. To learn more and to also be empathetic about in what ways play is important to them... .

Louise's statement points to a critical aspect of learning to do improv. It can reconnect teachers with what it means to play and help them to see children's play in a new way. Louise was talking about beginning to be able to see the value in "being a cow" or to put it another way, the value in being able to be "who you are not." Play is critical for continuous development because it is in play that we are able to go beyond our identities and roles and create new possibilities. Louise's comments were a small indication that, for her at least, the workshops had changed how she saw play and possibly how she would relate to play in the future.

Going on a Creative Journey

One of my hopes in providing the teachers with these workshops was that they would become better improvisers and would be more able and willing to go on a creative journey with the children with whom they work. During the final interview several of the teachers said that they had begun to change how they interacted with children. They had begun to listen to children improvisationally – from the vantage point of building with them.

During the initial "yes and" exercise Suki had said that she tended to listen to the person next to her until she had the gist of what the person was saying. During the final interview she said that she now listened to children "all the way through" before responding.

> Suki: I listen to kids better now. I was trying to think why...because of the directions that Cathy and Hillary gave us, I think maybe that's why. The yes and game made me listen to the kids more. In the yes and game you have to listen to how the person finishes his story and the sentence. Now I don't stop kids, I let them finish their sentence and then I respond.

Jessica also said that she has started to create space for the children in her class to say what they have to say, rather than going directly to her own agenda.

> Jessica: I find the same with me especially with one particular student. He's my youngest. Say we have to take off our shoes because we are going to movement. And he's doing something completely different. So then I'll go over and I'll be like, "Marc let me help you." And I'll just do his shoes. And he's like kicking and screaming. And in the past I would go into this whole, "Marc we're going to movement, I don't want you to miss movement." But now, I'm like, "Marc, what do you want to tell me?" And he's like... "da, da, da da." And I've realized he just wants to tell me something, it doesn't matter

what it is and then he can take off his shoes and go to movement. That whole tantrum thing is just gone.

All seven of the teachers identified ways in which they now listened more to children. In improvisational terms they talked about how they now said, "yes" much more often. Interestingly, they were not able to identify ways in which they were now able to say, "yes *and*" to the children. There was no mention in the interview of taking what the children were saying and adding on to it.

Near the end of the focus group interview I asked the teachers whether they thought these workshops would be helpful for other groups of teachers and if so how. In response to this question the teachers spontaneously broke into a "yes and" story.

Matthew	Doing these exercises as they progressed and you begin to feel more and more creative doing them and you kind of feel good about yourself and especially if you're a new teacher and unsure, it can help you go into the classroom and you know how to deal with the unexpected.
Jenny	Yes and it teaches teachers to listen to kids more and its important because you don't know what's going to come out from them until you listen.
Suki	Yes and if you listen to them, really listen, then you get to go with them wherever they're going.
Louise	Yes and you don't know what's going to come out of you either.
Jessica	Yes and some of what is so fun about this is that you don't know what's going to happen next, but it's going to be okay.

I felt as gratified by the format of their answer as I did by the content.

CONCLUSION

A modernist understanding of child development positions teachers as experts in children's development, separating them from the children with whom they are working and placing them in the role of helping to facilitate experiences that will foster what is essentially viewed as a teleological process. In the alternative, postmodern Vygotskian perspective outlined in the first half of this chapter, development is understood as a non-linear activity, specifically, the continuous changing organization between being and becoming. To the extent that teachers relate to teaching as if they are playing out a scripted play – one in which each child is on a developmental trajectory and the teacher is orchestrating that development, they are not supporting and fostering developmental activity. Creating environments where children can be who they are and who they are becoming requires teachers to step out of their role as experts and create collectively with the children. This does not come easily to teachers because traditional understandings of development are such a prevalent part of early childhood teacher preparation. The improv workshops described in this chapter were designed to help teachers engage in a more postmodern, relational activity by helping them to be a more creative, emergent part of children's lives in the classroom.

Through these workshops the teachers learned some of the skills required for collective creativity. They began to listen in new ways – not for what they expected to hear, but for what was being offered. They began to make offers that were premised on the collective doing something together rather than worrying about "getting it right" as individuals. The improv workshops gave the teachers practice in being more creatively responsive to each other, and by their own account this began to impact on how they responded to children in the classroom. They said that they had begun listening to what children were actually saying, rather than assuming they knew what was being said.

The teachers did not find learning to improvise easy. They were thrown off guard when someone did something unexpected or that did not fit with their idea of what was supposed to happen. As in the classroom, where the teachers said they had trouble "accepting the duck," the improv workshops challenged the teachers' sense of order and control. The exercises gave them practice in creating with these unexpected, and sometimes uncomfortable, moments. They learned to say "yes and" and stay in the moment rather than critiquing or controlling what was happening.

Critiques of developmental psychology that find its linear bias and normalizing impact problematic can be aided by casting a postmodern eye on Vygotsky's work. What we find is an activity-theoretic conception of development – not development in the modernist sense of following a fixed trajectory or adapting to a societal role, but development as non-linear, relational, improvised activity engaged in by groupings of people. This open and fluid understanding of development opens the door to more creative practices in early childhood education, particularly ones that can give teachers an alternative to relating to children as being on, or off, a developmental trajectory. The improv workshops, described in this chapter, gave the teachers the experience of going on a journey together without knowing where they were going to end up. In my opinion being able and willing to go on this kind of creative journey is what is needed for teachers to support children developing – a life improvisation.

REFERENCES

Bloch, M. (1992). Critical perspectives on the historical relationship between child development and early childhood education and research. In: S. Kessler & B. Swadener (Eds), *Reconceptualizing the early childhood curriculum: Beginning the dialogue* (pp. 3–21). New York: Teachers College Press.

Bodrova, E., & Leong, D. (1996). *Tools of the mind: The Vygotskian approach to early childhood education*. Columbus, OH: Merrill.

Bredekamp, S. (1986). *Developmentally appropriate practice in early childhood programs*. Washington, DC: National Association for the Education of Young Children.

Bredekamp, S., & Copple, C. (1997). *Developmentally appropriate practice in early childhood programs* (Rev. ed.). Washington, DC: National Association for the Education of Young Children.

Burman, E. (1994). *Deconstructing developmental psychology*. London: Routledge.

Cannella, G. (1997). *Deconstructing early childhood education: Social justice and revolution*. New York: Peter Lang.

Cole, M. (1996). From Moscow to the fifth dimension: An exploration in romantic science. In: M. Cole & J. V. Wertsch (Eds), *Contemporary implications of Vygotsky and Luria C 1995 Heinz Werner Lecture Series*, (Vol. XXI, pp. 1–37). Worcester, MA: Clark University Press.

Dahlberg, G., Moss, P., & Pence, A. (1999). *Beyond quality in early childhood education and care*. London: Falmer Press.

de Kruif, R., McWilliam, R., & Ridley, S. (2000). Classification of teachers' interaction behavior in early childhood classrooms. *Early Childhood Research Quarterly, 15*(2), 247–268.

Enz, B. & Christie, J. (1994, April). Teacher play interaction style and their impact on children's oral language and literacy play. Paper presented at the annual meeting of the American Educational Research Association, New Orleans, LA.

Feldman, N., & Silverman, B. (2004). The "Let's Talk About It" model: Engaging young people as partners in creating their own mental health program. In: K. E. Richardson (Ed.), *Advances in school-based mental health: Best practices and program models* (pp. 12:1–12:24). Kingston, NJ: Civic Research Institute.

Gildin, B. L. (2003). All stars talent show network: Grassroots funding, community building and participatory evaluation. *Youth participatory evaluation: A field in the making, Special issue of New Directions for Evaluation, 98*, 77–85.

Holzman, L. (1997). *Schools for growth: Radical alternatives to current educational models*. London: Lawrence Erlbaum Associates.

Holzman, L. (2000). Performance, criticism and postmodern psychology. In: L. Holzman & J. Morss (Eds), *Postmodern psychologies, societal practice, and political life* (pp. 79–90). London: Routledge.

Holzman, L. (in press). Activating postmodernism. [Special Issue]. *Theory & Psychology*.
Hume, K., Wells, G. (1998). *Making lives meaningful: Extending perspectives through role play*. Retrieved January 4, 2005, from University of Toronto, Ontario Institute for Studies in Education Website: http://tortoise.oise.utoronto.ca/~gwells/Drama.html.
Johnstone, K. (1981). *Impro: Improvisation and the theater*. New York: Routledge.
Kontos, S. (1999). Preschool teachers talk, roles, and activity settings during free play. *Early Childhood Research Quarterly, 14*(3), 363–382.
Lobman, C. (2001). *The creation of a playful environment in the early childhood classroom: A case study of a toddler and a preschool classroom*. Unpublished doctoral dissertation, Teachers College, Columbia University.
Lobman, C. (2003). What should we create today? Improvisational teaching in play-based classrooms. *Early Years: International Journal of Research and Development, 23*(2), 131–141.
Massad, S. (2003). Performance of doctoring: A philosophical/methodological approach to medical conversation. *Mind/Body Medicine, 19*(1), 6–13.
Moll, L. (2000). Inspired by Vygotsky: Ethnographic experiments in education. In: C. Lee & P. Smagorinsky (Eds), *Vygotskian perspectives on literacy education: Constructing meaning through collaborative inquiry* (pp. 256–268). Cambridge, England: Cambridge University Press.
Morss, J. (1990). *The bioligising of childhood: Developmental psychology and the Darwinian myth*. New Jersey: Erlbaum.
Morss, J. (1996). *Growing critical: Alternatives to developmental psychology*. London: Routledge.
Nachmanovitch, S. (1991). *Free play: Improvisation in life and art*. New York: Penguin/Putnum.
Newman, F. (1996). *Performance of a lifetime*. New York: Castillo International Press.
Newman, F., & Holzman, L. (1993). *Lev vygotsky: Revolutionary scientist*. London: Routledge.
Newman, F., & Holzman, L. (1997). *The end of knowing: A new developmental way of learning*. London: Routledge.
Rogoff, B. (1984). Adult guidance of cognitive development. In: B. Rogoff & J. Lave (Eds), *Everyday cognition: Development in social context* (pp. 95–117). Boston: Harvard University Press.
Salit, C. R. (2003). The coach as theater director. *Journal of Excellence, 8*, 20–41.
Sawyer, K. (1997). *Pretend play as improvisation: Conversation in the preschool classroom*. New York: Lawrence Erlbaum Associates.
Vygotsky, L. (1978). *Mind in society*. Cambridge, MA: Harvard University Press.
Vygotsky, L. (1987). In: R. W. Rieber & A. S. Carton (Eds), *The collected works of Lev Vygotsky*. New York: Plenum Press (Original works published in 1934, 1960).
Walkerdine, V. (1984). Developmental psychology and the child-centered pedagogy. In: J. Henriques, W. Holloway, C. Urwin, C. Venn & V. Walkerdine (Eds), *Changing the subject: Psychology, Social Regulation and Subjectivity* (pp. 153–202). London: Methuen.
Wood, D., Bruner, J., & Ross, G. (1976). The role of tutoring in problem solving. *Journal of Child Psychology and Psychiatry, 17*, 89–100.

SET UP A CONTINUATION ORDER TODAY!

Did you know that you can set up a continuation order on all Elsevier-JAI series and have each new volume sent directly to you upon publication? For details on how to set up a **continuation order**, contact your nearest regional sales office listed below.

To view related Educational Research series, please visit:

www.elsevier.com/education

The Americas
Customer Service Department
11830 Westline Industrial Drive
St. Louis, MO 63146
USA
US customers:
Tel: +1 800 545 2522 (Toll-free number)
Fax: +1 800 535 9325
For Customers outside US:
Tel: +1 800 460 3110 (Toll-free number).
Fax: +1 314 453 7095
usbkinfo@elsevier.com

Europe, Middle East & Africa
Customer Service Department
Linacre House
Jordan Hill
Oxford OX2 8DP
UK
Tel: +44 (0) 1865 474140
Fax: +44 (0) 1865 474141
eurobkinfo@elsevier.com

Japan
Customer Service Department
2F Higashi Azabu, 1 Chome Bldg
1-9-15 Higashi Azabu, Minato-ku
Tokyo 106-0044
Japan
Tel: +81 3 3589 6370
Fax: +81 3 3589 6371
books@elsevierjapan.com

APAC
Customer Service Department
3 Killiney Road #08-01
Winsland House I
Singapore 239519
Tel: +65 6349 0222
Fax: +65 6733 1510
asiainfo@elsevier.com

Australia & New Zealand
Customer Service Department
30-52 Smidmore Street
Marrickville, New South Wales 2204
Australia
Tel: +61 (02) 9517 8999
Fax: +61 (02) 9517 2249
service@elsevier.com.au

30% Discount for Authors on All Books!

A 30% discount is available to Elsevier book and journal contributors on all books *(except multi-volume reference works)*.

To claim your discount, full payment is required with your order, which must be sent directly to the publisher at the nearest regional sales office above.